The Prelude to Pentecost

The Prelude to Pentecost
A Theology of the Holy Spirit

Bishop R. L. Speaks

Wipf & Stock
PUBLISHERS
Eugene, Oregon

Wipf and Stock Publishers
199 W 8th Ave, Suite 3
Eugene, OR 97401

The Prelude to Pentecost
A Theology of the Holy Spirit
By Speaks, R. L.
Copyright©1985 A. M. E. Zion Publishing House
ISBN 13: 978-1-55635-340-6
ISBN 10: 1-55635-340-5
Publication date: 2/21/2007
Previously published by A. M. E. Zion Publishing House, 1985

Reproduced by permission of A. M. E. Zion Publishing House

Contents

	Preface	vii
	Acknowledgements	ix
	Introduction	xi
I	The Call to Pentecost	1
II	The Prelude to Pentecost	12
III	The Experience of Pentecost	23
IV	The Holy Spirit in Historical Perspective	33
V	The Concept of the Divine Spirit in African Religions	47
VI	The Nature of the Holy Spirit	57
VII	The Doctrine of the Trinity	67
VIII	Channels of Spiritual Power	86
IX	The Five Plateaus Leading to the Summit of Spiritual Power	115
X	The Holy Spirit in Human Life	121
XI	The Guidance of the Holy Spirit	140
XII	The Holy Spirit Will Give You Health	146
XIII	The Role of the Holy Spirit in Missions	151
XIV	The Wesleyan Concept of Spiritual Holiness	154
	Notes	171

Preface

The greatest need in today's world is a church that possesses a powerful witness in these troubled times. The church today must offer more than pep pills of personal piety, laxatives of racial tolerance and the surgery of social revolution.

If the church is to fulfill the expectation of Christ, its Founder and Head, it must possess the power to transform human nature. This can only be done through our Christian witness. Power to witness is more than a human achievement. It is a gift of Divine Grace. "Ye shall receive power, after that the Holy Ghost is come upon you; And ye shall be witnesses unto me both in Jerusalem, and in all Judea and in Samaria, and unto the uttermost part of the earth" (Acts 1:8).

The power to witness effectively is what makes the difference between a Christian and a church member. Every church member is not a Christian. A Christian is a church member whose life counts, tells, and makes a difference for Jesus seven days in the week.

It is the plan of Christ that the world should be won through our Christian witness. We make such a witness through the life we live. This witness is made possible by the power of the Holy Spirit working within human life.

Powerless Christians are the church's greatest curse and Christ's greatest shame. How to receive the power to witness is the Christian's first consideration. The Holy Spirit is the Christian's source of power. Without this power there can be no effective Christian witness.

If the church is to become truly the body of Christ and the extension of the Divine Incarnation, it must dare to change the world by redeeming mankind. Before the church can change the world it must first be changed by the power of the Holy Spirit.

If the church is to become an effective witness it must be dynamic and relevant. It must be courageous and daring. It must dare to lead Christian believers into a genuine spiritual revival.

It must dare to build temples of love upon the dung hills of hate; it must dare to build a new community of brotherhood upon the shifting sands of racism; it must dare to build a new society of peace upon the wastelands of human strife.

The church must dare to stem the tide of crime, drug addiction, immorality and secularistic materialism. This takes power; Holy Ghost power. The church today needs this power. This power is still available. There are two obstacles that must be overcome if the church is to receive this power. They are sin and unbelief.

Jesus died on the cross to make freedom from sin possible. The Holy Spirit dwells within me to make freedom from sin actual. The Holy Spirit does in me what Jesus Christ did for me. Each believer must trust Jesus Christ for his soul's salvation and receive the power of the Holy Spirit to work out that salvation in his personal life and in human society.

This book is written in the hope that the Christian Church will return to Pentecost.

If the church of today will obey the command of the risen Christ, it will experience a new power that will transform humanity. "And being assembled together with them commanded them that they should not depart from Jerusalem, but wait for the promise of the Father which saith He, 'Ye have heard of me.' For John truly baptized with water, but ye shall be baptized with the Holy Ghost not many days hence" (Acts 1:4-5).

Acknowledgements

No person is self-sufficient. Every achievement is a cooperative enterprise. The writing of this book is no exception.

This book would not have been possible without the help of my beloved wife, Janie A. Griffin Speaks who is indeed a source of inspiration and a paragon of cooperation.

I wish to thank Miss Gwendolyn Harris and Mrs. Mabel Miller Jones for typing, proofreading, and preparing the manuscript.

I am indebted to the Reverend Frank S. Walker, Sr., of Austin, Texas, a schoolmate at Drew University, a friend of many years, and minister in the United Methodist Church, and to Dr. Roy Valencourt, Professor of New Testament Studies, Hood Theological Seminary, Salisbury, N.C. for their helpful criticism. Their insights and suggestions contributed greatly to the finished product.

The illustrated cover design was created by the Reverend Bobby Simmons, A.M.E. Zion minister and Art Instructor, North Carolina Public Schools.

Introduction

The call to Pentecost is the most urgent demand of our age. There are only two alternatives for our civilization—Pentecost or Armageddon; Spiritual Renewal or World Revolution.

Our civilization is standing on the precipice of destruction. Only the power of the Holy Spirit can rescue us from the threat of a hydrogen holocaust. Our world is experiencing violent revolutions. The vicissitudes of fortune, which spare neither man nor the proudest of His works, but bury empires and cities in a common grave, have brought us to a critical juncture in human history.

There is an ever-rising crescendo of frustration, political disenchantment, injustice, and racial hatred that is moving relentlessly toward a modern Armageddon. Unless something is done to defuse the time bombs of racism, economic injustice, political corruption, and religious meaninglessness, our civilization is going to explode into an atomic inferno.

Our world is faced with two alternatives: the transforming power of the Holy Spirit, or the catastrophic power of hydrogen destruction.

Humanity is experiencing a crisis of faith. We have lost our spiritual reason for being. Scientific discovery, automation, computerization, and dehumanization are robbing us of our self-identity and self-esteem. We no longer know who we are, why we are, or where we are going. We want to build a new world, but we do not know what kind of world we want to build.

We are asking the wrong questions; therefore, we are getting the wrong answers. What is the answer to the question of war and peace, freedom and tyranny, hunger in the midst of plenty, shrinking natural resources and rapidly increasing world population?

The only answer is the power of the Holy Spirit working within the human soul and in human society. It is the divine "Spirit of God transforming the world by the love of God." Jesus said, "Ye shall receive power, after that the Holy Ghost is come upon you; And ye shall be witnesses unto me both in Jerusalem and in all Judea, and in Samaria, and unto the uttermost part of the earth . . . and when the day of Pentecost was fully come they were all of one accord in one place and suddenly there came a sound from heaven as of a rushing mighty wind and filled the house where they were sitting."[1]

If ever there were a time in human history when human society needed to be transformed by the power of the Holy Spirit, it is now. If ever the

Christian church needed to be empowered by the presence of the Holy Spirit, it is now. If ever the souls of men needed to be cleansed and purified by the fires of the Divine Spirit, it is now.

The world needs a return, a renewal, a repeat of the Pentecostal experience. Pentecost does not occur in a vacuum. There must always be a prelude to Pentecost.

> God inaugurated His Kingdom in Christ. The coming of this Kingdom involves the transformation of the human community now marred by sin with its resultant oppression and poverty into a community of justice, love, and peace.
>
> The Holy Spirit, applying the finished work of Christ, wills to accomplish this social and polticial transformation in and through people, especially in and through those who acknowledge the risen Christ as the Lord of history. And therefore, we are to pray for, work toward, and hope for the attainment of this goal.
>
> The present work of the Holy Spirit is the first fruits of His transformation (Romans 8:23). Though we have no grounds for thinking that this transformation will be complete in this world, we nevertheless believe that all Christians must strive for it in order to bear witness to God's promise to complete this transformation in the world to come.[2]

The Holy Spirit is the key to a renewed person, a renewed church, and a revitalized society. It is He who creates the beloved community.

> Life in the Spirit is human life lived out . . . to its utmost in consonance with God's gracious purpose.[3]

The church is at its best when it becomes an instrument of the Holy Spirit. The Holy Spirit is the presence and power of Christ taking the initiative within the human heart, the church and the Spiritual community.

He stimulates, guides, and empowers the church in its effort to transform society into the Kingdom of God. The Holy Spirit works within the human spirit making one aware of God's self-disclosure in Jesus Christ. He creates the church. He also creates within us that awareness that both the world and human history lie within God's care and divine providence.

> For we wrestle not against flesh and blood, but against principalities, against powers, against the rulers of darkness of this world, against spiritual wickedness in high places.[4]

It is the Holy Spirit who enables us to discern the signs of the time, and who leads us into new avenues of service in these changing times. He also leads us into a deeper understanding of the liberating presence of Christ within the human being and within the community.

Finally, only the Holy Spirit can teach us how to transform human institutions into effective instruments of constructive change.

Introduction

> O that the world might know
> The all atoning Lamb
> Spirit of faith, descend, and show
> The virtue of His Name
> The grace which all may find
> The saving power, impart
> And testify to all mankind
> And speak in every heart.[5]

> Teach us to utter living words of truth
> Which all may hear
> The language all men understand
> When love speaks loud, and clear
> Till every age, and race, and clime
> Shall blend their creeds in one
> And earth shall form one brotherhood
> By whom Thy will is done.[6]

In this book, we shall attempt to do four things: to demonstrate what the Holy Spirit is; to show how one can receive Him; to describe how you can know that you have received Him; and to point out what must be done to keep Him within you.

The Prelude to Pentecost

CHAPTER I

The Call to Pentecost

And when the day of Pentecost was fully come they were all with one accord in one place and suddenly there came a sound from heaven as of a rushing mighty wind and it filled the house where they were sitting.[1]

When the Holy Spirit works within the human spirit
Pentecost is born from within,
All outward signs of material grandeur
Whatever power they fain possess.
Comes from the innermost center of the soul
Here God abides in Majestic fullness
Although surrounded by barrier upon barriers of
    sin and self He refuses to be eternally hemmed and stifled
In Christ, that clear perception which is truth
Clears away these perverting walls of carnal affection
He bursts forth upon the scintillating darkness
And lights the way to love, joy, and peace.[2]

INTRODUCTION

The Call is a summons, an invitation. It is an effort to get one to make a new beginning. It is that which goes before to prepare the way. Nothing is spontaneous. For every effect there is a cause. Jesus understood the law of cause and effect as no man ever has. Nothing happens in a vacuum. The Way has to be prepared. Although He had promised to send the Comforter, He realized that the hearts of the disciples had to be prepared to receive Him. The disciples knew this. Therefore:

> When they were come in, they went up into an upper room. . . . There all continued with one accord in prayer and supplication with the women

and Mary, the mother of Jesus, and with His brethren. . . . And when the day of Pentecost was fully come, they were all with one accord in one place.[3]

The Interpreter's Bible puts this event in proper perspective when it states:

> The conviction, that shortly after the resurrection the Christian community received the Holy Spirit is a constant factor in New Testament writings. But there appeared to have been more than one tradition concerning the times and circumstances of the gift. In the fourth Gospel the spirit is bestowed by Jesus Himself on the day of resurrection: "He breathed on them and said to them, 'Receive the Holy Spirit.' "[4]
>
> According to Acts, the Spirit descended on the day of Pentecost, fifty days after the resurrection. But both traditions bear witness to the fact that, as a result of the resurrection, the disciples became conscious of a new inward power which completely transformed their whole outlook; and this they attributed to the possession by the Spirit of God. It is indeed this new sense of power that is the significant factor in the experience of Pentecost. For Pentecost can hardly have been the first occasion when the little community felt the presence of the Holy Spirit. But now they became conscious of the spiritual power.[5]

Before Penetcost, the disciples had felt the presence of the Holy Spirit. But it was at Pentecost that the disciples felt possessed by the Holy Spirit. The Holy Spirit was not a power that they possessed and controlled, but they were possessed and controlled by the power of the Holy Spirit. This made the difference. From the day of Pentecost onward, they were a people possessed.

The question here is how can one become possessed by the Holy Spirit?

The Holy Spirit is a gift of grace. It is received as an act of saving faith. It is Christ himself who bestows upon the believer the Power of the Holy Spirit. It was the Power of the risen Christ that empowered the Church on Pentecost.

It was the Holy Spirit that created the beloved community. He taught the people to respect leadership. They were inspired to learn from the apostles. The early church was a Koinonia, a fellowship of love. They were concerned about one another. There was creative goodwill among them. The spirit of sacrifice pervaded the new community.

It is the Holy Spirit that gives the local congregation power to bring Christian morality to bear upon the outside world. The Holy Spirit makes possible a twofold movement of Christian growth within the body of Christ. He enables it to develop both in width and depth. The church is given power to grow numerically, intellectually, and morally.

The church of Christ was not born at Pentecost but it was empowered at Pentecost. It was endowed with power from on high in order to carry

The Call to Pentecost

out its worldwide mission. This spirit appeared as a mysterious wonder-working power which enabled the disciples to witness effectively. The church was founded by Jesus during his earthly ministry. The Holy Spirit gave it power.

The Holy Spirit who descended at Pentecost was not new to the life of the church. This same Holy Spirit rested upon Christ at his Baptism and gave him power to set at liberty those who are bound.

> It is noteworthy that in Luke's narrative as it stands, in spite of his own conception of the Spirit as an intermittent supernatural power given at special moments, the Spirit is democratized. The Spirit is poured out upon all flesh—on sons and daughters, on manservants and maidservants alike in fulfillment of a prophetic utterance and therefore in accordance with the revealed will of God. . . . The Spirit is, therefore, for all who are in need. It is a continuation of the power of the kingdom delegated to this same Jesus on earth, who in the power of the Spirit, came to heal the broken hearted, to open the eyes of the blind, and to deliver the captives.[6]

The Pentecostal experience was not only for the early church; it is both a need and a possibility of the church in every age. We need it today. We can experience it. In order to experience it, we must seek it, for the same purpose that the early disciples sought it. We must seek it in the same way. If it is slow in coming, we must wait for it. It is the purpose of the Spirit to create the beloved community, first in the church, and then throughout the world.

This is accomplished by the Holy Spirit working within the human heart. It is the Holy Spirit that frees us from the law by fulfilling the demands of the law. The Holy Spirit inspires saving faith through which we receive God's saving Grace; therefore, fully satisfying the righteous demands of the law.

> Those who live as their human nature tells them to have their minds controlled by what human nature wants. Those who live as the spirit tells them to have their minds controlled by what the spirit wants. To have your mind controlled by human nature is death. To have your mind controlled by the spirit results in life and peace . . . but if Christ lives in you, although your bodies are going to die because of sin, yet the spirit is life for you because you have been put right with God.[7]

> If the Spirit of God, who raised Jesus from death lives in you, then he who raised Christ from death will also give life to your mortal bodies by the same presence of His Spirit in you.[8]

In the above passage, Paul is describing the purpose and inner workings of the Holy Spirit. He comes to grips with sin in the human heart and lays the foundation for the spiritual community. Paul Tillich describes it as follows:

> Under the impact of the spiritual presence, two things happen in which the injustice within communal justice is conquered. The churches in so far as they represent the spiritual community are transformed from religious communities with demonic exclusiveness, without losing their identity.[9]

It is the purpose of the Holy Spirit to use the church as the instrument by which He will transform the kingdom of this world into the kingdom of our God and His Christ. The church is the instrument used by God to bring His kingdom into the world. The Holy Spirit gives the church the power.

THE HOLY SPIRIT

I. *His Works*

The Holy Spirit leads the soul to Christ. He delivers the soul from the body of death by leading the soul into a new relationship with God. The Holy Spirit transforms the words of the kingdom into the Living Word. He makes Christ both living and real within the soul. The world is still asking,

> Who will deliver me from this body of death.[10]

The Holy Spirit answers, "Through Jesus Christ our Lord." The Holy Spirit transforms our view of God from one of angry wrath to a God of gracious love. He transforms our life from one of empty meaninglessness to divine meaning and Holy purpose.

> The Holy Spirit is a present and active power within us throughout the entire experience of conversion which begins with an awareness of God's goodness and experience of shame and guilt, proceeds to sorrow and repentance and ends in gratitude for possession of new life given us through God's mercy in Jesus Christ.[11]

It is the Holy Spirit that makes possible both prevenient and saving grace. He begins with justification, continues in regeneration and santification, and proceeds to Christian Perfection.

The Holy Spirit works in the soul to bring us to the full stature of a mature Christian faith.

> The Council of Trent teaches that the beginning of justification in adults takes place by means of the Lord's prevenient grace which moves us to conversion enabling us freely to choose to follow the inspiration God gives us when he touches our hearts with the light of the Holy Spirit. When the Scripture says, "Turn to me and I will turn to you," we are reminded of our freedom. "When we answer, turn us Lord to you and we shall be turned,"

> we confess that we are prevented (moved first) by grace. In justification God, through the atoning work of Christ, restores a sinner to a right relationship with Himself. In such a restoration, the initiative, the agent, and the consumation are the ministry of the Holy Spirit as He brings Christ to us and leads us to Him. When a sinner is led to Christ and receives Him, he is reborn and is given the power to turn away from a life curved back upon itself toward a new life, opened up to the love of God and neighbors.[12]

The Holy Spirit leads us to Christ and continues to work in us His perfect work.

II. He Performs the Work of Salvation

It is the Holy Spirit that performs the work of salvation in us. He pours the love of God into our hearts. God is in Christ and the Holy Spirit is in Christ reconciling us to God by grace through faith. All of this is done by the divine initiative of the Father through his Holy Spirit.

> The Spirit Himself bears witness to my spirit that I am a child of God.[13]

At Pentecost, Jesus keeps his promise to give his Holy Spirit to his disciples. This Holy Spirit brings about the forgiveness of sins, because it is His role to teach us all things necessary for our salvation. Not only does the Holy Spirit call to our memory all that Jesus said, but also interprets the meaning of Christ in our situations. The Holy Spirit makes Christ the Lord of our life. It is the Holy Spirit that brings about the new birth; it is a birth in the spirit.

The Holy Spirit sanctifies the newborn Christian. Sanctification leads to perfect love, purifies the desires of our hearts, enlightens the conscience, clarifies the subconscious, and rectifies the human spirit.

> Life in the spirit is human life lived out in faith, hope and love to the utmost in accordance with God's gracious purpose in and for His children. As Wesley puts it, the end of human existence is the recovery and the supplanting of the perfection in which that existence was justly conceived and created.[14]

John Wesley gives immortal expression to the consummation of the work of the Holy Spirit when he writes:

> Hence (in the end of creation) will arise an unmixed state of holiness and happiness far superior to that which Adam enjoyed in paradise . . . and to crown all. There will be a deep and intimate and uninterrupted union with God—a constant communion with the Father and His son Jesus Christ through the Holy Spirit. A continual enjoyment of the three-one God of all the creatures in him.[15]

It is the Holy Spirit that creates the Christian experience. The Holy Spirit leads the human spirit from faith to faith in an ever-rising crescendo of godly awareness of the work of the Holy Spirit in the world. The Holy Spirit creates an interpersonal relationship among God, man, and society. This relationship is guided by divine providence. God reveals himself in many ways, but He reveals himself finally and completely in Jesus Christ. The Holy Spirit makes Christ real in the human heart, thereby making God's self-revelation complete and final. In the first creation, it was the Holy Spirit that moved upon the face of the deep, thereby working with God the Father in His first work of creation. In the new creation it was the Holy Spirit that overshadowed the Virgin Mary, thereby making possible the new creation through the incarnation. Creation and salvation are closely linked through the work of the Holy Spirit. Here we see that God's work of creation and salvation are closely linked to God's word, God's breath of life, and God's spirit.

The spirit of God and the Word of God through both the Old Testament and the New Testament never cease to express God's will for His world. The consummation of God's work in the gift of His spirit even now brings to pass God's plan of salvation.

> Therefore, brethren, we are debtors, not to the flesh, to live after the flesh. For if ye live after the flesh, ye shall die; but if ye through the Spirit do mortify the deeds of the body, ye shall live. For as many as are led by the Spirit of God, they are the sons of God.[16]

The Holy Spirit prepares the soul to enter the Kingdom of God. The Kingdom of God is spiritual, therefore, each soul must be spiritually prepared.

> The Kingdom of God is not meat and drink, but righteousness and peace and joy in the Holy Spirit.[17]

Before the church can perform its task, it must be spiritually prepared.

The Kingdom of God is an inward experience that is divinely bestowed and spiritually discerned. The Holy Spirit plants the seed of righteousness and peace in the human soul. This peace is a spiritual sensation. It is a foretaste of Heaven. It fills the human heart with love and joy. It is this blessing of love, happiness, and holiness that Christ refers to as "Blessedness."

> Blessed are the pure in heart for they shall see God.[18]

This state of blessedness is referred to by Jesus as the Kingdom of God or the Kingdom of Heaven. It is the immediate fruit of God's work in the soul. Without saving faith, we are sinners before God. We are corrupt in every part of our being and in every faculty of our souls. We have strayed completely from the path of righteousness. We are estranged from the ground of our being. Man is sick unto death. He cannot heal himself. Christ is the only balm in Gilead that can heal the sin-sick soul. It is the Holy Spirit that makes man aware of his need of the atoning blood of Christ. It is the Holy Spirit that leads the soul to the foot of the cross, seeking forgiveness and power.

III. *The Holy Spirit Is the Guide, the Guardian, and the Comforter of the Church*

The Holy Spirit is the lifeblood of the church. The church is the Body of Christ. He cleanses, energizes, purifies, and recreates the Body of Christ. Each member of the church is an ear, eye, foot, hand, or some organ of the Body of Christ. Each has its peculiar function. Each function is essential to the well-being of the body.

It was the Holy Spirit working through the human spirit that gave to the church the Holy Scriptures. The Holy Spirit works through natural channels. He inspires the writer and guides the copiers, enabling them to perform their sacred task. Even today it is the Holy Spirit that inspires and guides the modern scholar from serious error in Biblical interpretations. The Bible is one of the greatest miracles of all times. It is not just another ordinary piece of literature. It is the work of the Holy Spirit that makes it holy. Not only is the Holy Spirit the chief author of the scriptures, it is the Holy Spirit that convinces the believer that the Bible is the Word of God for him. It was John Calvin who said:

> They who have been inwardly taught by the Spirit feel an entire acquaintance in the scripture. It is self authenticating, carrying with it its own evidence and ought not be made the subject of demonstration and arguments from reason, but it obtains the credit which it deserves with us by the testimony of the Spirit, for through it our conciliator.[19]

In the words of the second Vatican Council:

> The church is the people of God on a Pilgrimage at the service of the world.[20]

The church essentially is not of this world. Jesus said:

> They are not of the world, even as I am not of the world. . . . As thou hast sent me into the world, even so I also sent them into the world.[21]

The church is a called out, sanctified people. It is a colony of heaven. It is preserved and empowered by the Holy Spirit. The pneumatic dimensions of the church must be integrated into every aspect of its life. The work of the Holy Spirit is revealed in many ways. He manifests Himself in and through the whole of the Christian life. Spirit is revealed not just in speaking in tongues. It is revealed in preaching, teaching, healing, and striving for freedom and justice. The Holy Spirit empowers the church to strive for human liberation. Cardinal Suenens says:

> More and more people agree that the great problem which the modern church must solve is precisely that of finding the necessary bond between institution and liberty. But we do not have to invent this bond. It is not of human making nor does it result from an agreement we negotiated among ourselves. This bond has a personal name, "The Holy Spirit." He, by nature, is the bond of unity, the Creator of communion.[22]

Judicial decisions of the church are determined by its sacramental nature. All of its institutional and judicial elements are made sacred by the Holy Spirit working in and through the church. The legal aspects of the church must always be dominated by the Holy Spirit. It is the Holy Spirit that gives to the church its charismatic powers. These powers are gifts fully bestowed by divine grace upon men for the benefit of the entire church.

> The church without charisma would not be a church at all: Its very essence would be affected.[23]

The Holy Spirit is the presence of Christ giving life and unity to His church.

IV. *The Role of the Holy Spirit in Society*

The Holy Spirit serves as the vital link connecting the church to two worlds, the temporal and the spiritual.

The Holy Spirit is the love of God flowing into the human heart. He enables us to love God as we ought to love Him. As the Holy Spirit flows into us He purifies us, and through us He flows out into others to bless and cheer a loveless world.

> Holy Spirit, Love Divine
> O'er life's path thy radiance shine
> Purify my every thought
> Help me love thee as I ought.[24]

The New Testament refers to the Holy Spirit as a Dove. The Dove is the lovebird of the Bible. He is the bird without gall, full of peace. Therefore, he is a fitting symbol of the loving nature of the Holy Spirit. Solomon speaks of the Spirit of God as having "the eyes of doves by the rivers of water." Charles Wesley gives the Role of the Holy Spirit poetic expression when he writes:

> Heavenly all-alluring Dove
> Shed thy overshadowing love
> Love, the sealing grace impart
> Dwell within a single heart.[25]

The Holy Spirit comforts, strengthens, consoles, and anoints us with heavenly love and celestial fire. That which is gross in us, He etherealizes; that which is carnal in us, He spiritualizes; that which is earthly in us, He celestializes; that which is weak, He energizes; that which is in darkness, He illuminates; that which is in bondage, He emancipates. The Holy Spirit is He who makes the Holy Trinity one.

The function of the Holy Spirit is the creation of the spiritual community.

> The spiritual community is not a group existing beside other groups, but rather a power and a structure inherent and effective in such groups, that is in religious communities.[26]

This spiritual community includes all religions that express an ultimate concern or a faith in God.

> For as many as are led by the Spirit of God, they are the sons of God. For ye have not received the Spirit of bondage again to fear; but ye have received the Spirit of adoption, whereby we cry, Abba, Father. The Spirit itself beareth witness with our spirit, that we are the children of God: and if children, then heirs; heirs of God, and joint-heirs with Christ; if so be that we suffer with Him, that we may be also glorified together. For I reckon that the sufferings of this present time are not worthy to be compared with the glory which shall be revealed in us, for the earnest expectation of the creature waiteth for the manifestation of the sons of God. For the creature was made subject to vanity, not willingly, but by reason of Him who hath subjected the same in hope, because the creature itself also shall be delivered from the bondage of corruption into the glorious liberty of the children of God. For we know that the whole creation groaneth and travaileth in pain together until now. And not only they, but ourselves also, which have the first fruits of the Spirit, even we ourselves, waiting for the adoption, to wit, the redemption of our body.[27]

The New Testament Church is the "Ecclesia," the assembly of those who have been called out of all nations by the "Apostoloi," the Messengers of Christ, to the congregations—"Ellectheroi," those who have become free citizens of the Kingdom of Heaven. The Christian Church is the Koinonia—a fellowship of loving concern and creative goodwill—composed of those who believe in Jesus as the Christ. The church is both local and universal.

> But there is also the over-all unity of these local assemblies in the church universal.[28]

The church is both a spiritual reality and a social group. The church both determines existence and is being resisted by existence. It is through the church that the Holy Spirit uses the word and the sacraments as instruments in His creative work. The Holy Spirit is the power of faith creating faith. It is the power of love in the world. The church is the new creation into which the individual and local church is taken and used to create the beloved community. He is its invisible and essential spirituality. The role of the Holy Spirit is to lift up Christ, extol His love and sacrifice, quicken the conscience of the sinner, lead to Christ, impart faith, and give the assurance of salvation. The human intellect is at its best when it is touched and inspired by the Holy Spirit.

> The Spiritual community is the inner Telos of the churches and that as such it is the source of everything which makes the churches.[29]

It is the Holy Spirit working in the church that gives to the believer a foretaste of eternity within time. It frees the imprisoned Christ from our intellectual formulae, abstract dogmas, and dehumanizing institutions. It makes the Bible a living history of the life of God within His world. The Holy Spirit must never be separated from the Bible, which is the Word of God. It is the Holy Spirit that infuses the church's institutional autonomy with wisdom, power, and life. He makes it a divine organism instead of a dead organization. Yet, when the church attempts to isolate the spirit from the Word, it leads to false illuminism, degrading emotionalism, and destructive antinomianism. When the Spirit is separated from the Word, it leads to all kinds of deviations, which give rise to movements that are all emotion and no content. The Word of God gives permanence to the Spirit, and the Spirit gives reality to the Word. But when the Spirit is separated from the Word, the kind of orthodoxy that embraces the Word degenerates into spiritual anarchy.

The church is called upon to live in two opposing worlds. Tillich describes them as the world of Essence and the world of Existence. The church is possessed with two natures—being and nonbeing. Only the Holy Spirit can hold these two together in the state of creative tension. Only the Holy Spirit can create the spiritual community within the church. Each Christian's prayer should be:

> Spirit Divine, attend our prayer and make our hearts thy home. Descend with all thy gracious power, come Holy Spirit, come. Come as the wind with rushing sound, with Pentecostal grace and make thy great salvation known, wide as the human race.[30]

The church itself is not the spiritual community. It possesses the spiritual community. The spiritual community is theological, while the local church is both theological and sociological. It is always possible for a particular local church to become the church spiritual. The goal of each local church should be to become the spiritual community. The church has two parallel histories—one secular, the other sacred. This makes the church paradoxical in character. The paradoxical character of the church is the source of much confusion and criticism. How can the church be at the same time sacred and secular? How can it be the body of Christ and at the same time be plagued with demonic tendencies?

> The holiness of the church and of individual Christians is not a matter of empirical judgement, but rather a faith in the working of the new being within them. One could say that a church is holy because it is a community of those who are justified through faith by grace. . . . They are holy because they stand under the negative and positive judgement of the Cross.[31]

The spiritual community must always precede the institutional church.

> The decision of the individuals to form a covenant is the act which creates a church. The presupposition of course is that such a decision is determined by the spiritual presence, which implies that the individuals who form a covenant do it as members of the spiritual community.[32]

The spiritual community is made possible by the power of God working in the hearts of men. This power is at work long before it coms into consciousness. Christian conversion is never momentary or sudden. Although it may appear to be instantaneous, a closer examination will reveal that it is a gradual process. This is what some theologians mean by natural grace. No one can tell exactly when the Divine Spirit begins His work in the human heart. The Holy Spirit precedes the church into the world. He went before the Apostles and prepared the hearts of the hearers to receive the Gospel. It is also the work of the Divine Spirit that brings the soul to the point of conversion.

> But conversion is not necessarily a momentary event; it is in most cases a long process which begins unconcsciously long before it breaks into consciousness, giving the impression of sudden, unprecedented and overwhelming crisis.[33]

The work of salvation is performed by the Holy Spirit. At best we are only channels and instruments through which He works. The purpose of the Holy Spirit is to use human instrumentality to create the spiritual community.

CHAPTER II

The Prelude to Pentecost

Prelude means that which introduces a performance. It is an attempt to introduce the characters in a play. It is an announcement that something original is in the offing and is about to happen. It is that part of an act which introduces the original play or the original event. By its nature, a prelude itself is not the act; it serves only to introduce an act. It is a preparation for the actual event. This being so, it becomes necessary for all the elements in the prelude to be so set up in preparation that it can effectively serve the purpose of introducing the act or performance. Since one cannot have a play without a prelude, we see at the very onset the importance of prelude. It likewise becomes urgent that a thorough preparation take place to ensure that the prelude will be effective in achieving its purpose; to introduce the performance.

Since the prelude is vital to a comprehensive understanding of that which follows, it behooves the playwright to use all his faculties of imagination and creativity in producing a lasting effect on the minds of the hearers, or the minds of the audience, and to convey the totality of the purpose for which the program is being introduced. The prelude as preparation is not limited to that which serves as an announcement of a play, an act, or an event; it also serves as an introduction to the various transitions and periods in history. In our own historical becoming, it prepares us for a new stage in life. It can be the attempt to prepare oneself for a new job. It can be an attempt on the part of a young couple to prepare themselves for marriage. The preparation itself is not the marriage, but as they begin to prepare for the preparation for the marriage, consciously or unconsciously they attract the eyes of observers. They draw attention to the fact that something is about to happen in the lives of the would-be couple. We see at once that a prelude is as vital to the total program of the play as the play itself, because it is in the very character of the prelude to introduce and help to bring into focus the intentionality of the play. In other words, if the prelude is badly performed or presented, the intentions of the play that follows are totally and completely lost forever. Because the prelude serves as an attention-getter and as a channel of communication, it attempts to communicate to the audience that something very vital, something very significant, something very important, something which focuses on life is about to happen; something good for you, either for your entertainment, or your moral uplifting, or for the soothing of the sorrows of the spirit is about to take place—so be in a position to listen. If the prelude is not properly done or properly presented, the effect of the follow-up program is lost forever. The audience is lost, and the beneficial aspect of the play is also lost. All the preparations, the nightmares, and the heartaches that went into producing the play, including the imagination and the creativity, are made forever futile.

CHANNEL OF COMMUNICATION

So we see again that the prelude serves as a channel for communication. It tries to communicate the message inherent in the play. To achieve an understanding of the play, therefore, the prelude that serves to introduce the introduction to the play or act must be properly executed. This means that all the elements that make the prelude a prelude should be given a thorough handling.

From what we have said so far of the importance of the prelude, we can conclude that a prelude is a very vital factor in growth, in understanding and in life's vocation. Because this is so, anything that serves as a prelude should be handled with extreme caution and care. Every part of the prelude should serve as a stage to help introduce the act that follows. The prelude is a necessary and effective means of introducing the play. Its purpose is not to call attention to itself, but to help in calling attention to that which follows. If all the characters, therefore, and all the elements are given the most detailed handling, it brings salvific values and therapeutic salvaging. *The Living Webster Encyclopedic Dictionary of The English Language* defines prelude as: something preparatory or leading up to what follows; an introductory happening or performance; a short introductory strain preceding the principal movement; a separate, relatively short, instrumental piece; a piece of music introducing an opera, shorter than a formal overture; music played at the beginning of a church service as a verb, prelude is defined as: to introduce with a prelude, to serve as a prelude, to give or play a prelude.

PENTECOST THE LAW AND THE HOLY SPIRIT

Pentecost originally was a Jewish agricultural festival. It was celebrated fifty days after the event of the Passover. Every male Israelite was bidden to take part in the festival. In pre-Judaism, there was *cessation* of labor of any kind so that the male-born Israelite might devote a continuous period of time exclusively to the celebration of the feast. It was the celebration of a new beginning. It marked the beginning of springtime, the renewal of life, and the hope that the earth would be continuously productive.

Later on in Judaism, Pentecost changed in character from an agricultural festival to a commemoration of the giving of the Law in Sinai. It marked the period of the reception of the Law of God by Moses and the people of Israel. During each Pentecost festival, the Jews gathered to celebrate the giving of the Law. Why the giving of the Law became a permanent festival is an interesting question in Jewish history. One of these days, someone, somewhere, will research it for the benefit of mankind. Suffice to say in our present context, that the Law to the Jew or the Israelite meant the totality of God's revelation to His people.

The giving of the Law was the revelation of the will of God to the Israelites. It showed His purpose, His intentionality, and His plan for the survival and the maintenance of the Jewish nation. Possessing the Law, therefore, meant the possession of the Will of God. There can be no knowledge of God without the knowledge of the Law. The Law therefore became the vehicle through which and by which one could get to know Yahweh. To have the Law was in essence to possess the knowledge of God. We may even assume in this historical context that without the revelation of the Law, the revelation of God to the Israelites would have become a blurred vision. The Law became the extension and continuation of the renewal of the Covenant enacted between God and Abraham. In other words, to the Israelites, the Law was the apex or the culmination of that which was initiated between God and Abraham, when Abraham was called from the Ur of Chaldees to the promised Land. To break the Law, therefore, was not only to break the cordial relationship between individual Israelites, but also to place in jeopardy the totality of the Abrahamic Covenant. That is, if one broke the Law, he jeopardized the very foundation of Israelite existence. One cannot, therefore, fully understand the Pharisees' aversion to the breaking of the Law until and unless he sees it in the light of the peculiar and unique position of the Law in relationship to the Covenant between Yahweh and the Israelites.

The Law served as the guiding principle of the Israelites' mode of existence. It gave them a direction and a thrust. It helped, as it were, to lead them to the center of life. The Law helped them to bring into proper perspective and directional focus the tripartite nature of the Covenant, that is, the relationship between man and man, man and himself, and man and God. The Law told the Israelites that they could never adequately fulfill their vertical mission to Yahweh without their horizontal relation to their neighbors.

Not to have the Law is to be outside of the Abrahamic Covenant. To have the Law was to be in a situation where one could do the will of God. To have and keep the Law, therefore, was to have and keep God and to be in a uniquely and peculiarly privileged position in the sight of God. And this is clearly brought out in:

> How shall a young man steer an honest course? By holding to thy word. With all my heart I strive to find thee, let me not stray from thy commandments. I treasure thy promise in my heart, for fear that I might sin against thee. Blessed art thou, O Lord; teach me thy statues. I say them over one by one, Have found more joy along the path of thy will. I will meditate on thy precepts and keep thy paths ever before my eyes. In thy statutes I find continual delight; I will not forget thy word.[1]

So we see that the possession of the Law was synonymous to the possession of the Knowledge of Yahweh. It leads to the possession of righteousness, that is, right living, to loving justice, and to living the fuller life of the child of the Covenant. Since there can be no knowledge of the Law without the knowledge of God, the possession of the Law therefore called for a celebration because the Law revealed God to the people of the Covenant. The whole life of the future of the Israelites, their destiny, their eschatological hope, their anticipatory expectation for a bright future with God, was inherent in the fact of possession of the Law. In this light, therefore, we do a lot of injustice to the concept of the Law by viewing it solely from its legalistic aspect; by not attempting to look at it from the spirit inherent. The spirit of the Law was to lead the children of the Abrahamic Covenant to the realization of the fuller intentionality of the calling of Abraham by God in the first place. The Law reveals to the Israelites that they have been called for special mission and, as such, have been placed in a peculiarly privileged position; that is, of being the vehicle through which God was to communicate and reveal Himself to the whole of His creation. The end of creation and for that matter of creaturely existence is to have the knowledge of God. To have the knowledge of God is to know God intimately. To know God is to know the purpose for which man was created. It is to know that one was not created to serve the self. To have the Law is to be brought into a right perspective of God, making it possible for the child of the Covenant not to worship the modern trinitarian God of Me, Myself, and I.

The Law, therefore, was the guide in the darkness leading into light. The knowledge and the possession of the Law set the Israelites apart from other nations. It made them a peculiar possession of Yahweh. It told them unequivocally that they belonged to God, and this is brought out forcefully in the preamble to the decalogue:

> God spoke and these were His words; I am the Lord your God who brought you out of Egypt, out of the land of slavery. You shall have no other god to set against me.[2]

So you see from this preamble that the Israelites became a peculiar possession of God, and this is surmised by the possession of the Law, so that the

Israelite henceforth kept the Law because he was in a peculiar relationship with God. It was the Law that revealed to us the standing of the Israelite in the sight of God, and, parenthetically, revealed the knowledge of God. I want to maintain and reiterate that without the Law, Israel would never have existed as a community, because the Law is the revelation of God. And without the revelation and possession of the knowledge of God, the bases and the foundation of Israel's existence would have been supplanted and undermined.

It should now be clear why the reception of the Law was observed as a "historical salvific happening with pomp and pageantry." Pentecost, which was originally an agricultural festival bringing into constant focus the reality of renewal and the beginning of life, was replaced contexturally with the giving of the Law—commemoration of the giving of the Law in Sinai—because: (1) the law brought a new realization of the content of life; (2) it revealed the purpose of God for the Israelites; (3) it demanded that the Israelites strive to know the Will of God; (4) it made them aware that they were not to love for the self, but that they were a peculiar possession of God; (5) it gave meaning to their existence; (6) it made it possible for them to realize that they stood in a unique position in the sight of God; (7) it assured them that they were created for and belonged to God; (8) it showed them that the meaning of their existence was found only in their relation to God; (9) it showed that they existed because they belonged to God for a specific mission, that of bringing others to have the knowledge of God; (10) it revealed that the end of their existence and their anticipatory expectation for the future was grounded in the very being of God.

These were therefore the reasons why the Israelites, both at home and in the diaspora, would gather together to celebrate the feast of Pentecost, fifty days after the great event of the Passover, fifty days and seven Sabbaths after Passover. And whenever they gathered for the celebration, it was one of joy and of eager expectation that the blessings accruing from the possession and the keeping of the Law would be their inherited portion. They inherited the blessing of standing in a unique and privileged position in the sight of God, as they were called chosen and elected by God for a specific purpose and mission, that is, being an instrument through which God would reveal Himself to humankind. This is why the failure to keep the law to the letter was marked with frustration and the sense of guilt and remorse by the Israelites. This is reflected in the saying of Paul, in one of his epistles:

> the good that I should do I'm not able to do it, but the evil that I'm not supposed to do is what I do; Oh wretched man that I am, who will deliver me from the bond of sin.[3]

It was to one such celebration of the Pentecost in Jerusalem, where the Jews from the diaspora had come to join with their brothers in Jerusalem

The Prelude to Pentecost

to commemorate the giving of the Law in Sinai, that the Holy Spirit descended upon the disciples of the resurrected and ascended Jesus Christ.

To the Christian church, therefore, Pentecost was no longer the commemoration of the giving of the Law in Sinai. It marked the historical event of the outpouring of the gift of the Holy Spirit. The revelation of God's presence with, in, and among His people and the church. Pentecost marked a new stage of life in the lives of the early followers of Jesus Christ. It was on the day of Penetcost that they all experienced anew the privilege of few selected men and women called out for a specific mission of God.

The day of Pentecost became the historical point of departure from the age-long myopic conception and hitherto philosophical interpretation of the possession of the Holy Spirit or the Spirit of God as the privilege of the few wellborn. The day of Pentecost confirmed the universality of the Holy Spirit and its reception by all men of faith, regardless of race, creed, color, or social, economic or political background and previous social standing as understood by Joel.

> And it shall come to pass afterward, that I will pour out my Spirit upon all flesh, and your sons, and your daughters shall prophesy, your old men shall dream dreams, your young men shall see visions: And also upon the servants and upon the handmaids in those days will I pour out my Spirit.[4]

In Galatians, Paul, a Jew who lived all of his formative life under the law until his encounter with Jesus on the Damascus road, had this to say:

> But when the fulness of the time was come, God sent forth his Son, made of woman, made under the Law, to redeem them that were under the Law, that we might receive the adoption of sons. And because ye are sons, God hath sent forth the Spirit of His Son into your hearts, crying, Abba, Father. Wherefore thou art no more a servant, but a Son, then an heir of God through Christ.[5]

The writer of the Epistle to the Hebrews echoed Paul:

> God, who at sundry times and in divers manners spake in time past unto the fathers by the prophets, has in these last days spoken unto us by His Son, whom He has appointed heir of all things, by whom also He made the world. Who being the brightness of His glory, and the express image of His person, and upholding all things by the word of His power, when he had by Himself purged our sins, sat down on the right hand of the Majesty on High; Being made so much better than the angels, as He hath by inheritance obtained a more excellent name than they.[6]

Jesus said he did not come to abrogate the Law, He came to fulfill it. It is significant to note that Matthew places the entirety of Jesus' Ministry in the setting and the context of the Sermon on the Mount. Jesus is the New Moses. The Sermon on the Mount has five divisions. The Pentateuch of Moses has five divisions—five books: Genesis, Exodus, Leviticus, Numbers, and Deuteronomy. Jesus Himself was the New Moses. Jesus was the fulfillment of the Prophet prophesied by Moses in:

> The Lord thy God will raise up unto thee a Prophet from the midst of you, of thy brethren, like unto me, unto him ye shall hearken according to all that thou desiredst of the Lord thy God in Horeb in the day of the assembly saying, Let me not hear again the voice of the Lord my God. Neither let me not see this great fire anymore, that I die not. And the Lord said unto me, they have well spoken that which they have spoken. I will raise them up a prophet from among their brethren, like unto thee, and will put my words in his mouth; and he shall speak unto them all that I shall command him. And it shall come to pass, that whosoever will not hearken unto my words which he shall speak in my name, I will require it of him.[7]

Jesus as the New Moses expanded Moses. He gave a new meaning, a new understanding, a new dimension, a new intentionality to the Law. He revealed the humanity and the life-giving aspect of the spirit of the Law. The basis of the new Law is Love.

> It has been said of them of old, an eye for an eye, and tooth for a tooth, but I say if you are smitten of the left cheek turn the other also.[8]

Moses gave the Law, but the power to keep the Law was made possible by the incarnation and the person of Jesus Christ. Jesus gave the power to overcome the schizophrenia—the split personality and the attendant frustration brought about by the inability to keep the Law. Jesus Christ through the power of the Holy Spirit actualizes this possibility. Paul underwent frustration and psychological trauma in his futile attempt to keep the Law. It was the power of Jesus Christ which enabled him to overcome the human ambiguity of the self.

> The good that I desire to do, I do not do, but the evil I ought not to do, I do. Oh wretched man that I am, who shall deliver me from the bond of sin. But thanks be to God who gives us the victory through Jesus Christ. That which the law was unable to do in that I was weak, Jesus Christ accomplished. The life therefore, which I live is no longer I, but Jesus Christ crucified, yea resurrected, who lives in me?[9]

The end of the Law is to lead to the knowledge of God. The end of revelation of the Son of God, Jesus Christ, is to reveal the fulness of the God head. John said:

> God so loved the world that He gave His only begotten Son that whosoever believeth in Him should not perish but have everlasting life.[10]

The Prelude to Pentecost

Jesus Christ through the power of the Holy Spirit comes to relate us to God. He helps us to know God intimately, making it possible for us to keep the Law of God. John further says that the law was given by Moses, but Grace and Truth came by Jesus Christ. Paul's psychological imbalance, resulting from his inability to keep the Law, was overcome by the Holy Spirit, creating both the conclusive atmosphere and the healthy climate in which he could keep the Law of Grace, blending his will with the will of God.

It is significant to note that Jesus Himself did not baptize His followers with water, even though He might have suffered His disciples to do so. The baptism performed by Jesus was the Baptism of the Holy Spirit.

> And John bare record, saying, I saw the Spirit descending from Heaven, like a dove, and it abode upon him. And I knew him not; but he that hath sent me to baptise with water, the same said unto me, upon whom thou shalt see the Spirit descending, and remaining on him, the same is He which Baptizeth of the Holy Ghost.[11]

Jesus' baptism was beyond the baptism of repentance. (It was the second state.) He baptizes with the Holy Ghost and fire, purifying all the impurities in the human soul and giving man the endowment to surrender the will of his volition to God. Placing his life at the disposal of God's usage. To be used by God is to be obedient to God. To be obedient to God is to keep His Commandments—His laws. Jesus said, "If ye love me ye will keep my Commandments."

Pentecost, to the early disciple, meant renewal and revitalization of life. It was the day when the fulness of God's presence was showered on the disciples, it was the empowerment of the Christian church. So, to the early disciples, Pentecost was no longer an agricultural festival turned into the commemoration of the giving of the Law of Sinai, but, more importantly, it became the historical occasion when the Holy Spirit of God descended upon them.

That day was a unique day in their lives. Something extraordinary, something strange, something possessing salvific value took hold of their lives. It impinged on their earthbound, circumscribed, temporal existence, lifting them up to a new sphere of existence. Why do we say that the experience that took hold of the disciples brought with it a new beginning, a new possibility? We say so, because it was on this particular day, the day of Pentecost, that the promised comforter, the third person in the Godhead, visited the disciples. It brought a new freshness of hope which hitherto was unknown to the disciples. It lifted them to the presence of God significantly. It made them experience God in a unique way unknown to them before; God's presence was not only within them, it was with them, by them, and for them. They realized for the first time in their lives that God was with them, not only with them, but in them and going with them. They witnessed a tremendous change in their lives as their attitudes, their prejudices, their lack of faith, their lack of commitment, were being healed. They witnessed a renewal, a rehabilitation, a redirection, and a being brought back into the centre of Being; that is, a being brought back of God Himself.

They discovered that this tremendous upsurging of the Divine Spirit the Divine Power, the Divine presence was making them into new people, the people of God, the chosen ones, the new Israel, people with destiny, a commission, a vocation, and a purpose. The intentionality of that purpose was to live for God by the way of obedience to His Commandments. They realized that they were being enabled from within with the unleashing of a tremendous power, making it possible for them, for the first time in their lives, to be more willing to obey God than to obey the self, the world, and the powers that be.

Their whole outlook was changed to the extent that people watching the dynamics taking place doubted whether the disciples were beside themselves. What the disciples went through and witnessed on the day of Pentecost was so overwhelming that their whole nature, the totality of their personality, the totality of their being, was completely and totally overhauled, thus making them a new people.

Their newness lay in the fact of their being ready to respond to and obey the call of God. The calling which they hitherto forsook at the crucifixion of the Lord Jesus Christ, they were eager, without any external pressure whatsoever, to gladly obey.

This is what the experience of Pentecost does to the follower of Jesus Christ who stands in a position to listen to the voice of God. On that historic day of Pentecost, when they were all endued, embued, empowered, and visited by the Spirit of God, they became new people, courageous people, daring people, people who were prepared to lay down their lives in the cause of service to God and to fellow man. They experienced a boldness which was not characteristic of this world. It was a boldness inspired by, initiated, and authored by God Himself. If this was not so, how can we, that is, those of us living in the twentieth century, understand the extraordinary courage of Peter, who on the eve of the crucifixion, denied his Lord in the very presence of his Lord, before a poor maid in the court. Yet we are told that on the day of Pentecost, this Peter, who for fifty days was sweating, perspiring, and groveling before a maid, was able on the day of Pentecost, when visited and overshadowed and overpowered and empowered, was able to stand this time not before a maid, but, before the full session of the Sanhedrian. In doing so, he accused them of being the stumbling block in the way of the universal revelation of God to His world.

The Peter whom we met during and after the resurrection has now been turned into a complete person, instead of being indecisive, a rehabilitated person, who stands, head up and shoulders high, proclaiming the name of God. In the very presence of the people who thought they had destroyed the Jesus of Nazareth by crucifying Him, he declared that "the Jesus of

Nazareth whom they killed was Yaweh's anointed Messiah; that eternal life and the realization of the true valuable life is attainable only in Jesus.'' For all to become authentic persons, fulfilling their destiny and personhood, they have to come to God by way of Jesus Christ.

As we read the book of Acts (where we have the history of the Acts of the Holy Spirit in and through the apostles), we do not fail to see the finger of God at work in the disciples, whether witnessing, whether doing the work of the steward, or whether being called upon to give the ultimate sacrifice; that is, exposing the self to death. We see the power of God experienced anew in a unique way operational in the life of the disciples.

Peter was so much imbued with the Holy Spirit, that his shadow falling on sick people restored them to life.

Pentecost brought a new perspective into the lives of the disciples. It was the fulfillment of all their hopes, their dreams, and their aspirations. They saw in Pentecost that the event that took place on the day of Pentecost was the arrival of God Himself. The event was no longer described as salvation history, but rather it become salvation in history. So when the disciples referred to Pentecost, they recalled the day, the moment, the occasion, the time when God Himself came to be inside His people and to be with them. This historical awareness elevated Pentecost from being an agricultural feast and the commemoration of the reception of the Law to the historical moment when the Church of Jesus Christ was inaugurated, empowered, and brought into the fulness of being.

When talking of Pentecost as Christians, we refer to:

(1)   The historical moment when God through Jesus Christ went forth as the Holy Spirit to be a living witness among His people. Pentecost in Christian terminology brought a new awareness of the divine presence to the people of God. No longer was belonging to the people of God defined in terms of being of the stock of Abraham physically, but it was the calling out of men and women, boy and girls. People of all shades and different backgrounds came together, united by the blood of Jesus Christ. They were prepared to die by their confession in Jesus Christ and live by their profession of faith that Jesus Christ is the Lord's anointed, the Messiah, and the only way by which and through which we can come to possess the new life, realizable only in God.

(2)   Pentecost meant that God was now accessible to the individual Christian, that no one dare call himself a Christian who has not come under the influence of the Holy Spirit of God. it must be emphasized that the Holy Spirit is not an entity floating somewhere in space, but that it is God Himself descending. it is God revealing His own presence in the life of His new creation; that is, the people belonging to the church.

One cannot be, therefore, a follower of Christ, unless one is expected to take up his or her cross and follow Jesus, to meet the demands of Christian Discipleship in his or her immediate existential and contemporary situation, and to be able to bear authentic witness of the presence of the Holy Spirit in his or her life. Because, you see, the task of the Holy Spirit is to bear witness of Christ, to bear witness to the truth of the Christ event. The Holy Spirit in the life of the believer reveals the fulness of the Godhead. The believer bears witness that Jesus Christ is the only begotten of the Father and that one cannot go to God without first knowing Jesus Christ. Jesus Christ is the revelation of God's presence, God's power, God's majesty. All the attributes of God inheres in Him. Pentecost, therefore, became the focal point of the meeting ground of God and the Christian. The Holy Spirit given on the day of Pentecost is the gift of God Himself to the church. It is the fulfillment of the promise of God Himself to the church. It is the fulfillment of the promise of God that He was going to live in and among His own people.

CHAPTER III

The Experience of Pentecost

One of the greatest problems of Western Civilization is the church's loss of power. Religion is the hinge of history. Religious faith is the cement of society. Religious ethics are the foundation of national government.

When religion loses its power, culture collapses, civilization crumbles, and national governments become an enemy of the people. Only the Holy Spirit can restore the vitality of religion and the power of the church.

Who is the Holy Spirit? The Holy Spirit is God. He is fully and perfectly divine, just as are the Father and the Son, possessing, as they do, all the divine attributes. He is all wise; knows everything, is everywhere, present at the same time, and is all powerful, and eternal. There never was a time when He was not, and there will never be a time when He will cease to be. The Holy Spirit is that mystical union between God and His people.

> And when the day of Pentecost was fully come they were all with one accord in one place and suddenly there came a sound from heaven as of a rushing mighty wind and it filled the house where they were sitting.[1]

The Holy Spirit is the most misunderstood and the most neglected gift that God has given to man. Anything that we fail to use, we will lose. Because we have failed to use this gift, we have lost its power. There is nothing in the world more powerful than a Christian who is filled with the power of the Holy Spirit. The great achievements in life are not accomplished by might or by power, but by the Spirit of God. The average Christian has only a slight understanding of how the Holy Spirit works in his life. If I should ask you, "Have you ever received the Holy Spirit into your life," what would you say? If you are honest, many of you would answer, "I don't know." There are many church people who do not know what the Holy Spirit is.

The Holy Spirit is God within the human heart. He is the Christ restoring the divine image within man. He is Christ making the believer into a new creature.

Imagine someone without artistic genius or training sitting down before Raphael's famous picture of the Transfiguration and attempting to reproduce this masterpiece. You can imagine how crude it would be. But if it were possible that the spirit of Raphael could enter into the man and completely transform his very being, it would be entirely understandable that he could reproduce that masterpiece. For it would be simply Raphael reproducing Raphael. The Holy Spirit is God reproducing Himself in us. This power of the Holy Spirit enters the heart of every true believer in Jesus Christ. The Holy Spirit is eternal life living in the heart of the believer. This is what Paul meant when he wrote:

> It is not I that liveth, but Jesus Christ that liveth in me.[2]

The Holy Spirit is divine love expressing itself through you. He is the fullness of God in you. He is the light of truth shedding heavenly peace upon the human soul. The spirit of man is the candle of the Lord. Only the Holy Spirit can kindle the human spirit. It was Albert Schweitzer who said:

> Because I have confidence in the power of truth and of the Spirit, I believe in the future of mankind.[3]

There is a story told about the great musician Mendelssohn. Once he visited a Cathedral containing one of the most priceless organs in Europe. He listened to the organist, then asked permission to play. "I don't know you," was the reply, "and we don't allow any chance stranger to play upon the organ." At last the great musician persuaded the organist to let him play. As Mendelssohn played, the great Cathedral was filled with such music as the organist had never heard. With tears in his eyes he laid his hand upon Mendelssohn's shoulders. "Who are you?" he asked. "Mendelssohn", came the reply. The old organist was dumbfounded. "To think that an old fool like me nearly forbade Mendelssohn to play upon my organ."

If we only knew what wonderful harmonies the Holy Spirit can draw out of our lives, we would not be content until He had complete posssession, and was working in us, and through us to do His will. The Holy Spirit will not force His way into our lives. He takes control only when we surrender to Him in faith. This surrender is a process that starts within the hour we believe and continues as long as life lasts. This is what is meant by growing in grace. The Holy Spirit grows in us as it unfolds through us. The more we permit the Spirit to unfold through us, the stronger in Spirit we become. The Holy Spirit within us is made possible by faith in Chist. The more faith we possess, the more power we have. "I can do all things through Christ who strengthens me."

The Experience of Pentecost

The greatest favor that anyone can do for himself is to move self out of the way and allow the Holy Spirit to play upon the heart strings of his soul. There are some things that the self cannot do for itself. The self is man's greatest enemy. Only the Holy Spirit can liberate the self from itself. The power of the Holy Spirit enables the self to fulfill itself by transcending itself. When the Holy Spirit takes control of one's life, He brings with Him the power of self-transcendence.

Many families are torn apart. Many marriages are breaking up. Many individuals are living empty and meaningless lives because they refuse to move over and allow the Holy Spirit to play upon the heart strings of their souls.

We as a society need to allow the Holy Spirit to work among us. He has the power to bring about peaceful change.

In Wakefield, Mass., an organized band of infidels was influencing many young people to join its ranks. The Christians of the community came together to discuss what they could do. They decided to meet each night in prayer. They were joined by many others who learned of their effort. One day the infidel leader was brought under powerful conviction. He sought out a Christian and was saved. It was not long before the whole band of infidels was converted. The whole community acknowledged that it was the work of the Holy Spirit.

In many of our churches today, we need to move over and let the Holy Spirit take control.

A group of clergymen were discussing whether or not they ought to invite Dwight L. Moody to their city. The success of the famed Evangelist was brought to the attention of the men. One unimpressed minister commented, "Does Mr. Moody have a monopoly on the Holy Ghost?" Another man replied quietly, "No, but the Holy Ghost seems to have a monopoly on Mr. Moody." The church needs Christians over whom the Holy Spirit has a monopoly. There is nothing in the world more powerful than a Christian who is filled with the Holy Spirit.

The Holy Spirit is a divine monopoly. When He comes in there is no room for sin or self. He fills every waking moment and every sleeping hour. He purges us of all unrighteousness and makes us right in the sight of God. He gives us power to do God's work. He gives us power to overcome the enemy, to win the victory for right.

WHO IS THE HOLY SPIRIT?

He is the creative power of God working in human life. This power is not something new; it existed before the world was! We are told in the first chapter of the Book of Genesis that, "The earth was without form, and void, and darkness was upon the face of the deep. And the Spirit of God moved upon the face of the waters." The Holy Spirit was at work in creation. He is the divine power performing the creative acts of the divine will. The Holy

Spirit is God manifesting Himself through His creation. He is not some New God or some different divinity. He is God the Father manifesting Himself through the Spirit of His Son. He is the Holy Spirit assuming different roles, meeting different needs, and performing different tasks. He is empowering believers according to His riches in Glory. The Holy Spirit is as real as He is invisible. You cannot see Him with the natural eye. Neither can you hear Him with your natural ear. Nevertheless, because He is invisible does not mean that He is not real. The most real things in life are the things that are unseen. You cannot see love, you cannot see faith, you cannot see electricity, you cannot see atomic energy. Yet all of these things are real. So it is with the Holy Spirit. Though you cannt see Him, He is real. The Holy Spirit is subtle, invisibly hidden from the physical senses, yet He is the most real, as well as the most powerful, reality in life. The Holy Spirit is like the fragrance of a flower, pervasive, but elusive, definite though imperceptible, irrefutable though intangible. No one has ever seen the fragrance of a flower, or handled it, or, however acute the senses, heard it make a sound. Yet that fragrance is real. It has its influence upon human life. So it is with the Holy Spirit. Although you cannot see Him, when He comes, you will know He is there, because you can feel the effects thereof.

It was the Holy Spirit who was at work in the Old Testament. In the Book of Hebrews, we find the honor roll of men and women who were filled with the Holy Spirit. Abraham, Isaac, Jacob, Joseph, Moses, Joshua, Elijah, David, and a host of others who were leaders in their age, and accomplished great things in their generation; not by might, nor force of arms, nor physical or political influence, but by the Spirit of God. They subdued kingdoms, wrought righteousness, obtained promises, stopped the mouths of lions, quenched the violence of fire, escaped the edge of the sword, were made strong out of weakness, waxed valiant in the fight, and turned to flight the armies of the enemy. The Holy Spirit was at work in the life of Jesus Christ. He was the purest, most sublime, and the only perfect example of a man completely possessed by the Spirit of God. It was the Holy Spirit who came upon Mary, and she conceived and brought forth one whose name is Emanuel, meaning God with us. It was the Holy Spirit who led Jesus into the wilderness to be tempted of the Devil. It was the Holy Spirit who gave him the power to turn water into wine, to cast out devils, heal the sick, give sight to the blind, preach the gospel to the poor, and raise the dead. When on the cross, His work was ended. He committed His Spirit to the Spirit of His Father. It was the Holy Spirit who enabled Him to descend into Hell and rise from the dead on the third day.

The Holy Spirit gives us freedom to do God's will. The Holy Spirit is the power of the risen Christ flooding the lives of those who will believe in Him. When the Holy Spirit comes into your life, it connects the human soul with the spiritual powerhouse. If this light bulb is to give light, it must first be connected with the electrical powerhouse. It might be a perfectly good

The Experience of Pentecost

bulb, but unless it is connected, it will not give light. Likewise, unless you are connected with the divine source of spiritual power, you cannot do the will of God.

When the Holy Spirit takes control of your life, you will experience a new kind of power. He will bring you a strange new feeling of joy, love, and freedom. The Holy Spirit will transform your life. He will give you the power to do what God wants you to do.

WHAT HAPPENED AT PENTECOST

What happened at Pentecost was not the work of a new power. The Spirit that filled the disciples on the day of Pentecost was the same Spirit that led Christ into the wilderness to be tempted by the Devil. It was the same Spirit that Prophet Ezekiel spoke about when he said:

> A new heart also will I give you, and a new spirit will I put within you.[4]

At Pentecost this same Holy Spirit provided new power to meet a new need. God had already promised this when he said, "As thy days so shall thy strength be." The time had come when the Christian Church must be established with power. Christ had promised Peter that he would build his church.

> And I say unto thee, thou art Peter, and upon this rock I will build my church; and the gates of Hell shall not prevail against it.[5]

Christ is now keeping His promise by sending His Spirit with power upon the disciples.

On the day of Pentecost, the Holy Spirit came into the Christian church and enabled the followers of Christ to perform mighty works of preaching, healing, witnessing, and winning others to Christ. When the Holy Spirit came into their lives, He made them courageous and bold. They stood up and said what they wanted to say, even though they knew that their words might mean death. It was the Holy Spirit that made their witness effectual. People listened to what they had to say. People were moved to accept the Christian faith. They were drawn into the Christian community. And they were filled with the Holy Spirit and began to speak in other languages, as the Spirit gave them utterance. Their cup of joy was filled to overflowing. Their enthusiasm was high, their emotions were stirred, and their lives were changed.

The story is told of a poor half-witted fellow whose companion, working beside him, dropped. He was found trying to hold up the dead man and trying to make him stand and sit upright. Finding his efforts without avail, he was heard saying to himself, "He needs something inside him."[6]

This is the trouble with so many of our churches today. We need the

Holy Spirit on the inside. Only the power of the Holy Spirit can change the church into the likeness of God. Only then can the church change the world.

WHAT IS THE MEANING OF PENTECOST?

The greatest need of the church today is a Pentecostal experience. Has the Holy Spirit ever come into your life? Have you had a Pentecostal experience? Much of deadness, confusion, strife, and indifference in the church are due to the absence of the Pentecostal experience. There are some things in the church which only the Holy Spirit can do. No amount of persuading, no amount of teaching, and no amount of ogranization can do it. The Pentecostal experience delivers the church from internal strife. This is one of the major obstacles to spiritual progress. It is nothing new. It has been with the church down through the years. There was strife among the widows in the early church over the distribution of material help. Strife separated Paul and Barnabas. It was the Holy Spirit that enabled the church to overcome its internal strife. That is why each of us needs the Pentecostal experience.

Louis H. Evans expresses the true meaning of Pentecost when he writes:

> The church had to wait for that day, for that coniousness of being led by the Spirit. It must always be so. Whatever the church has done in any age, it has done in the power of the Spirit, and through this Spirit today and tomorrow, it will always bring about its really vital accomplishments.[7]

The presence of the Spirit of Christ in the church is a vital necessity for the church in all ages. We must strive to be instruments of the Spirit. Only when we have yielded to the power of the Holy Spirit can we find the power to change the hearts of men. Just as the automobile cannot perform without gas, so no church can achieve its purpose without the Holy Spirit. When the gasoline flows, the automobile moves. When the Holy Spirit moves, the church has power. Anything done without the Spirit is marking time. A spiritless church is an empty church. In fact, it is no church at all. It is just another social organization occupying a church building. The church is only a church when it refuses to live on the surface of its faith, but dares to launch out into the depth of the Spirit. Only when the Holy Spirit comes with all His quickening power can the church turn this upside down world right side up. Only the Holy Spirit can open our closed minds and enable us to think honestly and clearly. So often the church refuses to think, but spends its time rearranging its prejudices. The Holy Spirit brings happiness through involvement, security, enlistment, joy through Christian concern, and fulfillment; not by running away, but by standing up to life.

It delivers the church from weakness. When Jesus came down from the Mount of Transfiguration, He found His disciples wrestling with devils which they could not cast out. Jesus became disgusted and disappointed with the

The Experience of Pentecost

weakness of His disciples. He said to them, "These can only be cast out by prayer and fasting." The church today is weak. There are devils within that have not been cast out. We lift our helpless hands to Jesus saying, "Master why can we not cast them out?" And Jesus answers, "These can be cast out only through prayer and fasting." I challenge you to fast and pray for the Holy Spirit. For it alone can deliver the church from weakness.

The Pentecostal experience will enable the church to bless the world. Our world today is tottering on the brink of a nuclear holocaust. We are all walking the narrow ledge of hydrogen destruction. We are playing Russian roulette with social time bombs of racial strife, economic exploitation, and moral degradation. The world needs a church that offers more than the pep-pills of false piety, or the laxative of political change, or the surgery of world revolution. Only a church endowed with the power of the Holy Spirit will be able to cut away the malignant growth of sin and cure the cancerous infection of hate, bitterness, and strife. Each of us needs to pray the prayer of the poet:

> Holy Spirit, Truth Divine,
> Dawn upon this soul of mine.
> Word of God, and inward light,
> Wake my Spirit, clear my sight.

The Holy Spirit is a gift from God. He cannot be bought. He cannot be counterfeited. If you have Him, you will know it. If you have Him, others will know it. If you are not certain about whether you have Him, then it might be a sign that you haven't received Him.

What really happened at Pentecost? We do not fully know all that happened there. For Pentecost is one of those eternal mysteries which enshrouds the mystical union between Christ and His Church. But this we do know: that the disciples had an experience of the power of the Spirit flooding their lives, their very beings, such as never had happened before. It was on this day that the Holy Spirit came into the church in a special way. The Holy Spirit became the guide of the church. He infused it with a strange power. He brought with Him a dedication to duty, the power of progress, and a peace that passed understanding. The leaders of the church became men of the Spirit. Peter and the rest of the Apostles were no longer interested in becoming ecclesiastical potentates. They became inflamed with a passion to witness to the risen Christ. Peter's courage and eloquence before the Sanhedrin were the results of the activity of the Holy Spirit. I can see Peter now, as he stands in the midst of the Sanhedrin. I can hear him say:

> Ye rulers of the people and elders of Israel, be it known unto you all and to all the people of Israel, that by the name of Jesus Christ of Nazareth who, ye crucified, whom God raised from the dead, even by Him doth this

man stand here before you whole. This is the stone which was set at nought of you builders which is become the head of the corner; neither is there salvation in any other, for there is none other name under heaven given among men whereby we must be saved.[8]

That kind of talk took courage—Holy Ghost courage. When Paul and Barnabas were on their first missionary journey, they came to Paphos and preached the word with great success. It was here that one Barjesus tried to hinder the work of the church. Then Paul, filled with the Holy Ghost, set his eyes on him and said:

> O full of all subtility and all mischief thou child of the Devil, thou enemy of all righteousness, wilt thou not cease to pervert the right ways of the Lord? And now behold the hand of the Lord is upon thee and thou shalt be blind for a season. And immediately, there fell on him a mist and a darkness, and he went about seeking someone to lead him by the hand.[9]

It was the Pentecostal experience that gave the leaders their power to conquer the enemy. Even the deacons, stewards, and trustees of the early church were men filled with the Spirit. Stephen, Barnabas, and Phillip were all Spirit-filled men. The only way to be a good leader in the church is to have a Pentecostal experience. John Wesley was not a success until after his Aldersgate Street experience. The church today needs Pentecostal power.

THE WAY BACK TO PENTECOST

The way back to Pentecost is a return to a vital faith in the risen Christ. It is a prayerful waiting upon His Divine Spirit.

After the disciples had been convinced that Jesus was the risen Christ, they came to him and said:

> "Lord, wilt thou at this time restore again the kingdom of Israel?" He said unto them, "It is not for you to know the time or season which the Father hath put in his own power. But ye shall receive power, after that the Holy Ghost is come upon you; and ye shall witness unto me both in Jerusalem, and in all Judea, and in Sameria, and unto the uttermost part of the earth."[10]

In their hearts the disciples desired something better. They were not satisfied with the same old society. They wanted Jesus to turn the clock of time back to the days of David. Instead of giving them what they wanted, Jesus presented to them a greater challenge than they had ever dreamed. They asked for a kingdom, but Jesus offered them the world.

The first prerequisite of Pentecost is to desire something better. So many of us in the church today are satisfied to live in the twilight zone of religious reality. There is too much complacency in the church. We are at ease in Zion.

The Experience of Pentecost

The Bible tells us, "Woe unto those who are at ease in Zion." The requirement of Pentecost is to want something better. We must refuse to be satisfied with things as they are. Jesus is not satisfied with things as they are. He is expecting us to grow in grace. But first we must desire it. Like the disciples of old, we must go to Christ and say, "Lord, when will thou restore the church?" Jesus is not only ready to restore His church, He is waiting to give us the world through the power of the Holy Spirit.

The second requirement is to seek the Holy Spirit. The disciples obeyed their master.

> And when they were come in, they went up to the upper room. These all continued with one accord in prayer and supplication.[11]

These early disciples sought divine guidance. They all prayed the same prayer, sang the same songs and sought the same things. They sought the power of the Holy Spirit. God is waiting to give us that power, but we must desire it and we must seek it in prayer. The church must pray for it. We must unite in a prayerful search for the better tomorrow.

> And when the day of Pentecost was fully come they were all with one accord in one place. They were together both in mind and body.[12]

If we want the power of the Holy Spirit we must come together. The church must be united in faith and in expectation. The church must expect to receive Him. They expected something good to happen. They believed that God would keep his promise. They waited in that upper room. They expected Christ to come. He came, no doubt, in a way unexpected and strange to those who looked on. Their hopes were realized. Their faith was validated. They became a source of Divine Power that reshaped the world, changed human relations, and transformed society. God has not withdrawn his promise. The church can experience a New Pentecost. The church must meet the Pentecostal requirements. If we are to transform our society, we must find the way back to Pentecost.

> O Spirit of the living God
> Thou light and fire Divine
> Descend upon the church once more,
> And make it truly thine.
>
> Teach me my Lord and King
> In all things Thee to see
> That what I do in anything
> To do it as for Thee

If you can pray that prayer from the depths of your heart, then you have taken the final step toward Pentecost.

The way to Pentecost is through prayer. If you want the power of the Holy Spirit, ask God for it. The Bible tells us that:

> These all ontinued with one accord in prayer and supplication.[13]

Prayer is the key to heaven. It can unlock the storehouse of divine power. The gift of the Holy Spirit was given in answer to prayer. Prayer is more than just saying words. It is the sincere desire of the heart. The early church was a praying church; therefore, it was a powerful church. If you want Spiritual Power you must learn to pray.

If you truly pray and the Holy Spirit does not come at once, wait on Him. The scripture teaches us that:

> And being assembled together with them, commanded them that they should not depart from Jerusalem, but wait for the promise of the Father, which saith He, "Ye have heard of Me."[14]

Very often we go to church, we study the Bible, we say many prayers, and sometimes when we are under great pressures we truly pray. Many of us however, do not know how to reach the source of Spiritual Power. Because of this failure, many well-meaning Christians think that there is nothing more to religion than a profession, either ceremonial or ritualistic. They think that the power of the Holy Spirit is for a few of the peculiar Christians or for the early church. My friend, this Pentecostal power is for you. You need it. You can have it. In order to have it you must meet the divine condition of self-surrender, humility, prayer, patience, and faith.

CHAPTER IV

The Holy Spirit in Historical Perspective

From the earliest of time, man has been aware that all physical phenomena pointed to something beyond the physical—that beyond the realm of the senses, lay a vast world of the spiritual. Although this spiritual world is invisible, it controls the physical world. This elemental natural and vital force was called by the Greeks, "pneuma." This pneuma filled all things. It even resided within the human personality. Biblical scholars described it as follows: Holy Spirit,

> The mysterious power of God, conceived in the first place as the mode of God's activity, manifested especially in supernatural revelation to selected individuals and in their being possessed by a force which gave them marvelous strength, courage, and wisdom, and the knowledge of God's will and His dealings with men, later identified with the personal presence of God, and regarded as the distinctive endowment of His People; and in the New Testament understood as the mode of God's operation in the church, made possible through the work of Christ and mediating the glorified Christ to His People and the Church to its exalted head.[1]

It is difficult to do justice to the root meaning of the Holy Spirit by limiting its etymology only to the Greek and Hebrew derivatives of the terminology, since in every society, the idea of God's Spirit has been expounded, even if sometimes in a crude form. Therefore, we shall not confine the term solely to what is found in the Greek and Hebrew. It does not give us the richness of concept necessary for a clear understanding of thought, other than the traditional one. Therefore, we will not confine ourselves to the Judeo-Greco development of the concept of the Holy Spirit. For the purpose of our Christian and classical understandings of the term, we shall introduce other concepts. Because of the impact of the Black Church upon American life, we have also included a section on the concept of the Divine Spirit in African religion.

The verbal noun *Pneuma* means the elemental, natural, and vital force within the human personality.

> It acts as a stream of air in the blowing of the wind and the inhaling and exhaling of breath. It transfers its power as the breath of the spirit. The divine spirit may be either attached, detached or both, outwardly and inwardly, filling with inspiration and gripping with enthusiasm.[2]

The root word itself suggests a residual potency of power or energy. The cosmological effect of *Pneuma* may be the "storm" which blows powerfully, the fair wind which rises quickly and unexpectedly and which may be favorable or unfavorable, the breeze—the light breath of wind (from heaven) which is divinely soft and which quietly invigorates. At the very beginning of human awareness man conceived of a divine intelligence, a supernatural power at work in the world.

> For some, *Pneuma* as the agent of natural meteorolgical processes influences climate, health, and even human character. Always however, there is force in *Pneuma*. Power flows from it, is mediated by it, and disappears with it.[3]

This power is life giving. The withdrawal of this power results in death or a diminished existence.

> True in the microcosm of organic life, and especially in men and animals, *Pneuma* is physiologically the "breath" which again both process and matter is either inhaled or exhaled in breathing.[4]

This power is always present in the function of organic life.

In all the varied functional nature of *Pneuma* in Greek thought, the one undergirding principle is that *Pneuma* is the "Force Vitae" which is also the animation of the life principle operative within the physiological context of organic cosmos.

While *Pneuma* was always associated with organic functions, it was not thought to be absent from the inorganic sphere. Matter itself was considered the work of *Pneuma*. *Pneuma* is the essence of the cosmos. It is the power that created the substance out of which the cosmos is made. While *Pneuma* is usually associated with the wind, it is not limited to any one basic element of the cosmos, but is that divine power which creates and sustains these elements. This is implied in Aristotle's concept of the prime mover which is itself unmoved. Aristotle is right when he designates a prime mover that moves all things. He is in error when he insists that the prime mover remains unmoved.

If the Greek *Pneuma* is to be the prime mover, it must move all things and in turn be moved by all things. It is the ability to move all things and be moved by all things that make the Holy Spirit divine. No God is truly divine who is not at the same time absolutely transcendent and eternally imminent. This is the paradox that makes the Holy Spirit divine. This is the mystery that unites God and His people.

In the early development of the *Pneuma* concept, a clear-cut distinction is not made between the spirit of man given by God and the charismatic spirit given for particular and specific function. The relation between the human and the divine spirit is a mystery that defies rational explanation. It is not irrational, but super-rational. It demands a Wholistic response of Being.

> In the transferred employment of *Pneuma* for mental and spiritual realities classical Greek firmly maintains the basic etymological idea of powerful material, moving breath with its many functions in man and the cosmos.[5]

In Aristotle's *Metaphysics*, (XI, 7, p. 1072 b 21.) the characteristic feature of the Greek concept of spirit, as represented by *Pneuma*, is that of something which is elementally dynamic, which fills vitally, which snatches away in enthusiasm. To the Greek, the chief characteristic of *Pneuma* is power. For the Christian, the chief attribute of the Holy Spirit is love. Love is the fulfillment of the law of life. Later in Manticism and in poetry, *Pneuma* took on the meaning of a

> breath which inspires, stirs, enthuses and fills. . . . It is experienced by the select souls of poets, priests and prophets especially the Pythia at Delphi, in specific physical and spiritual operations.[6]

For the Greek, the power is given intermittently. For the Christian, the power of the Holy Spirit is indwelling and abiding.

In the Greek, it is also assumed that the oratorical erudition of the rhetorician is generated in *Pneuma*. In the light of its inundating nature, it was conceived as something divine. In other spheres, it was sometimes predicated as the Spirit of the gods.

It is evident from the above that secular Greek made no reference to *Pneuma* as the "Holy Spirit." The closest it came to it was its reference to the spirit of the gods. As one studies the Greek conception of the *Pneuma*, he sees how in many ways Greek thought prepares the way for Christian theology, yet awaits the fulfillment of Christian theology. In this sense, Christ is not only the fulfillment of Hebrew prophecy, but also of Greek philosophy.

> There is as yet no instance of the concept of a *Pneuma hagion* in secular Greek. Here Biblical Greek has coined a new and distinctive expression for

> character and content which *Pneuma* has in Judaism and Christianity. . . . The usage of the New Testament was felt to be equally distinctive in Latin. Here *Pneuma hagion* was not translated by the current and in part, stoically loaded terms *sacer* or divine spiritus (divine spirit) or afflatus which were equivalents for the Greek Theion, heron *Pneuma* in the religious and philosophical tradition, but the special and no less original expression spiritus sanctus.[7]

At several points, stoicism comes quite close to Christian thought. One can readily see how this concept prepares one for the next step, that of identifying the Holy Spirit as God Himself.

> In the religious philosophy of Stoicism *Pneuma* is used linguistically for the being and manifestation of deity itself.[8]

From the time of the Wisdom Literature and Philo, under Jewish and Christian influence, the *Pneuma* is personified and identified as an independent agent of God or God ipse. We may refer to this as the unGreek development of the meaning of *Pneuma*.

In mythology and religion, we find *Pneuma* occupying a high place. In early Greek cosmogony, the wind was regarded as originative life. Bringing dead matter into life and aliveness, the wind was inherently and potentially life-reviving. Egyptian mythology and cosmogony gave the highest form of the idea of the wind as life-giving force. The first development of the idea of the wind as generator of life is found in Egypt. In the cosmogony of Hermopolis, the breath of wind is linked with the God Amun. . . . "Interpretatic Graeca" equated the god of the moving air in his life-creating omnipotence with Zeus and *Pneuma*. In Egypt, we first encounter the idea of a God begetting a Divine Son in a mortal woman by breath. Hebrew theology is the child of Egyptian theology. Here we see a close similarity between the two.

Pneuma and Inspiration—Inspiration, while it is generated by *Pneuma*, is not *Pneuma* itself.

> It is the pneuma which imparts of its essence to man and nature, sometimes via inspiration. The four cultural spheres of Greek life: Manticism, mysticism, poetry, and eroticism, these are linked, according to Plato, by the fact that all are dependent on the work of the divine pneuma.[9]

In poetry, *Pneuma* inspires speech.

> Theologically significant is the idea that *pneuma* is the cause and source of ecstatic speech in which the priestess becomes so directly the "divine voice" that the Delphic *pneuma* can be called the voice which blows forth from Stomomion mouth.[10]

Thus, in Manticism we see the spirit associated with voice. The Greek word phone is also translated as sound; for example, the sound of a wind instrument. It is very significant to note that even in Manticism, we have reference to *Pneuma* being the source of prophecy.

> . . . from the standpoint of religious phenomenology the New Testament bears witness to the same original combination when it constantly links pneuma and *Propheteuein* (Luke 1:67; 2 Peter 1:21; etc.), when it refers to speaking with tongues as a gift of the spirit (a reflection of Pythian prophesying in Corinth 1 (Corinthians 12-14), or when it speaks of the crying out either of the unclean spirit which departs from a man or the Holy Spirit which fills him.[11]

> Plato in his analysis of the functional nature of *Pneuma* as inspiration did not contest with the idea as expressed in Manticism. He also believed that *Pneuma* once it converged on a person entered into every faculty of the human body, took possession of him and almost emptied him of his self-awareness, rendering him a ready vehicle for use by the gods. Since the possessed uttered prophetic utterances Plato suggested the need for a judge who validated the truth of the uttered speech. Within this context we find a parallel in Plato and Paul. The only difference being that Paul advanced the view that the speaker of tongues himself be made responsible in interpreting what he utters.[12]

Plato's idea about the divine inspiration issuing forth in prophecy is followed unflinchingly by Philo, Plutarch, and the early Christian Apologists. A critical look at Plato's view reveals that prophetic utterance was limited to a special "class of people," the philosophers. Paul came close to a similar view when he replaced Plato's philosophy with the spiritual man. Delphic inspiration-Manticism is for Plato the formal element and prototype by which he explains the musical inspiration of the poet and by which he also fashions the aspect of enthusiasm or eros in his own philosophy in discussions of rhetoric, poetry, and politics.

> An idea which is originally cultic and religious, then systematized and apprehended critically, became in this way general intellectual phenomenon which is not limited to Manticism, but appears also in other spheres of actuality.[13]

Here is a basic theme that extends beyond the question of Manticism to the whole of Plato's philosophy. In the face of all human products, discoveries, and achievements, there must be someone who can test a right and finally judge that which is physically born, technically produced, or spiritually conceived and inspired by others in the light of its true reality and worth. Mathematicians, geometricians, and astronomers must also submit their findings to the dialectician, who alone can assess and apply them correctly.

As concerns the famous Delphic oracle imported to Socrates by Chairephon, Socrates himself became its critic and thus made it true. It is in accordance with this Platonic principle that Celsus, the opponent of Christianity, deals with the religious doctrine advanced by barbarians.

Plutarch adopted Plato's view on the nature of the spirit's endowment. Lamblichus, in his theory and phenomenology of Manticism, deduces that the Spirit of God descends as a pure gift, untainted by or influenced by any cosmic, spiritual, or corporal factors.

Pneuma in natural science and philosophy—Although we do not encounter the early use of *Pneuma* in Anaximenes and Diogenes of Apolonia, we discover that later Greek thought assigned the energizing force sustaining the cosmos to the influence of the *Pneuma*. In the school of Pythagoras as well as Empedocles,

> . . . the bond which unites men not only among themselves and upwards to the gods, but also downwards to the animals is the spirit which works through the world. In the field of medicine from Hippocrates on *Pneuma* occupied a very unique place in Greek medical vocabulary. *Pneuma* was the vital and decisive element, health depended on the measure of its circulation in the body. "As a meteorological phenomenon the spirit influenced both the physical constitution and the character.[14]

Working of the Spirit as advanced by Aristotle later influenced Stoic philosophy. His pneumatology was capitalized upon in Stoa. His pneumatology offers an explanation of the whole world, both organic and inorganic, its constitution and unity, its tension and vitality, its being as a whole, and the individual qualitative nature of each individual creature within it. It assimilates both nature, science, and the popular belief in the divine, life-giving power of breath. The doctrine of *Pneuma*, as found here in philosophy, is a most consistent and historically most influential systematic development.

> Along with the elementary physical aspect, the Stoic concept of *Pneuma* has a psychological-anthropological, cosmological, and metaphysical-theological aspect. Only rarely equated with air as one of the four elements, *Pneuma* is mostly regarded as a substance of its own which unites fire and air in itself. As the source and divine principle of the four elements, it surpasses and permeates those by its greater rarity, activity and vitality. . . . Invisibly fine corporeality, air-like form, the bearing of warmth or fire, spontaneous movement and tension make *Pneuma* the mighty substance which permeates, moves, vivifies, and gives soul to all reality in all its forms. . . . In ascending degree of purity, strength and tension *Pneuma* gives individual unity to lifeless things like stone or wood in the inorganic world . . . as the spirit operating in nature it gives growth to plants, and as physical spirit it gives soul to animals: in man this consists of a specially light and fine spirit which is native to a man, which carries warmth and which glows with fire. From its seat in the

heart, the centre of the soul's life, it circulates in special channels through the organism, making possible not only the vital functions but also those of mind and soul especially the activity of the five senses, also conceiving, speaking, and thinking.[15]

One finds in the foregoing quotations an indication that the Spirit-pneuma was not personified in Greek philosophical and religious thought. It was only operative because it was the agent of the gods. By contrast, in the New Testament we are confronted with the dynamic personal Holy Spirit a distinct personality operating within the God-head in its confrontation with the community of believers. (There is, however, a paradox in the church doctrine of the Holy Spirit.)

HOLY SPIRIT IN THE OLD TESTAMENT

In the Old Testament, it is the Spirit of God that gives meaning and order to the universe.

> The earth was without form and void and darkness was upon the face of the deep, and the Spirit of God was moving over the face of the waters.[16]

The Hebrew writers were familiar with the Egyptian, Babylonian, and Indian mythologies, but they transcended these mythologies to project a more sublime concept of the work of the Divine Spirit. To them:

> The high and lofty One that inhabits eternity alone is God. Over whatever is waste and void His spirit moves, moves broodingly and creatively according to a holy purpose which nothing can be strong enough to turn aside. That is good to remember when life seems empty within, or whenever in the life of the world around us darkness seems to descend.[17]

The Old Testament writers believed that this Divine Spirit still broods over the universe. He is still creating, He is still carrying out the Divine Will. The Holy Spirit is not immoral, neither is it non-moral. It is Holy, which means that it has moral dimensions. Therefore, the Ten Commandments are the highest manifestation of the Holy Spirit.

In Hebrew, Ruach (nephesh), or in Arabic, Ratra means to blow, breath, or wind. Ruach is found 264 times in the *Septugagint*. Spirit, known in the Old Testament as Ruach, has different shades of connotation. The etymology of Ruach in Hebrew and Raha in Arabic means spirit, to smell, to blow (nephesh means living soul). Ruach is sometimes referred to as breath, wind, etc. Ruach in man is the principle which gives life to the body. The entry of Ruach gives life; its absence means death. It is the seat of the emotion, the intellectual functions, and the attitudes of will. It is the spirit of life. God is the vital force behind the Ruach. The Ruach of God is effective, divine power. God's Ruach is the force behind the cherubim. It gives unusual bodily power and sets the prophet on his feet. The Ruach of God induces ecstasy; it is responsible for prophetic or ecstatic speech. God gives the prophetic message by the Ruach. It gives the charisma of leadership. It is the opposite of the demonic in man.

RUACH AS GOD'S CREATIVE POWER

It is the divine power which creates physical life. God is this power. He injects it into His people. It is the Divine Power which gives mental abilities, insight, artistic sense, skill, enlightenment, perspicacity and wisdom. It is that which gives charismatic powers to the prophet as a man inspired of God. It equips earthly potentates with wisdom, understanding, constancy, and piety.

The Ruach makes good morality in man possible.

> It is God's judging and saving power. God confronts his people in judgement through the Ruach, the Spirit brings paradisial fulness, material fortune, social peace. His Ruach brings his people rest.[18]

Ruach, as it relates to God Himself, denotes God's incorruptibility and sustaining power—His unfathmable power and wisdom as Creator, etc.

THE SPIRIT AS GOD HIMSELF

It is significant to note that in the Old Testament, God Himself is the bearer of the Spirit. He endows men with the Spirit at His own free will. God's Spirit, not man's, is responsible for bringing into existence a new community of people. It turns the jungles of human hopelessness into an oasis of creative hopefulness. It is the source of the prophetic message.

> In principle then, it is plain, especially in classical prophecy, that the spirit of (Yahweh) Ruach of Yahweh is power, morally defined power. This power is effective i.e. it is the working out of God's personal will, directed to religious and moral end. It is also a historical reality, a power working within Israel. . . . Ruach Yahweh though experienced as the work of God's will is inscrutable . . . through the dynamics of the Ruach Yahweh may be detected, the logic defies analysis.[19]

We discover in the Old Testament that the writers are careful to emphasize the fact that the Spirit finds its source in God, and by so doing, the Cosmos is stripped of an immanent spirit, which leads to pantheism.

The Old Testament writers dared to use the spirit of man to interpret the working of the Divine Spirit in man and society. The spirit of man is that function in the life of man that unites the power of Being with the meaning of Being.

> Man in experiencing himself as man, is conscious of being determined in his nature by the spirit as a dimension of life, this immediate experience makes it possible to speak symbolically of God as Spirit and of the Divine Spirit.[20]

The Hebrews believed that the Divine Spirit dwells within the human spirit. It is this Divine Spirit within that makes man unique among all other creatures.

> Then God said, "Let us make man in our image, after our likeness, and let them have dominion over the fish of the sea, and over the birds of the air, and over the cattle and over all the earth, and over every creeping thing that creeps upon the earth." So God created man in His own image.[21]

It is this Divine Spirit that invades the human spirit and drives it beyond itself. Paul Tillich describes this experience.

> Although the ecstatic character of the experience of Spiritual presence does not destroy the rational structure of the human spirit it does something the human spirit could not do by itself. When it grasps man it creates unambiguous, life.[22]

SPIRIT IN JUDAISM

The development of the concept of the Spirit in Judaism follows closely that of the Old Testament. The only difference is the additional new dimension in the understanding of the spirit as an eschatological gift.

> The eschatological spirit will come down from on high as a possession of the community and life personified power and stand in the midst of the renewed community. The elect servant will be a bearer of the pneuma and the spirit will rest on the prophet.[23]

In Qohelth, *Pneuma* is always an anthropological-psychological expression. In Wisdom, *Pneuma*, as the principle of life in man, originates from God who inbreathes it or loans it. It is the incorruptible God giving Himself to the individual entity. *Pneuma* as life principle is differentiated from *Pneuma* as sophia (Wisdom). This *Pneuma* (sophia) given us by God is special and for particular and specific functions.

In Philo's thinking, *Pneuma* belonged to God. He (God), however, allows men to participate in its activities. It is the *Pneuma* which differentiates men from beasts. A distinction is made between *Pneuma* as divine impression and *Pneuma* as divine spirit. *Pneuma* for Philo is a heavenly breath, and even something better than a heavenly breath.

> ... the pneuma which represents the rational soul is an impress of the divine power but the pneuma which man receives as a morally striving rational being is also an emanation of the divine.[24]

Prophecy is for Philo the highest form of knowledge. Prophecy is initiated by *Pneuma*.

RUACH IN PALESTINIAN JUDAISM

Ruach in Palestinian Judaism deals more with angelology, evil spirits, the soul, etc. Ruach etymologically is wind, one quarter of the basic elements of the world. In rabbinic anthropology, man is dichotomised into body and spirit. The body is earthly and spirit heavenly.

> The Spirit of God in the true sense is an entity which stands outside man, and which comes to him from God in special situations and under special circumstances.[25]

THE SPIRIT AS ADVOCATE

> The concept of the spirit as advocate is only weakly referred to in Judaism. This is undoubtedly connected with the fact that the spirit is not a special heavenly being. That Michael and other angels are advocates for Israel and for individuals before God is a common notion in Judaism.[26]

THE AUTONOMY OF THE SPIRIT

The Spirit is projected in Judaism as autonomous yet,

> ... for all the autonomy of the Spirit it is perceived that the Spirit finally proceeds from God Himself.... The Spirit is not regarded as substitute for God's presence. The divine presence in man can be expressed by saying that the Holy Spirit rests on him or that the Skekinah rests on him.... The Holy Spirit is not identical with the Shekinah. While the Shekinah is simply God in His presence, the Holy Spirit is a special divine entity which is sent by God and which acts, independently within the limits set by the Divine Will.[27]

THE HOLY SPIRIT IN THE NEW TESTAMENT

It is gratifying to note that the New Testament does not go to the trouble to develop a concept of the Holy Spirit. The New Testament takes the presence, the person, and the source of the Holy Spirit for granted. Consequently, one finds a highly developed concept of the Holy Spirit with overtones of the Greek, Hebrew, Judaistic, Hellenistic, and Gnostic backgrounds. The Holy Spirit is already here when Jesus begins his earthly ministry. In Matthew and Luke, the Holy Spirit inspired the prophets. For a period of time in the New Testament, the ever-abiding presence of the Holy Spirit makes possible the creation of the Jesus community—the New Israel—the new people of God gathered from among all nations.

> In Lukan writings there is considerably more emphasis on the operation of the Spirit than in the other Synoptics. Luke sees the Spirit as active in a great renewal of prophecy before the birth of John, and John's own mission; the spirit rests on Jesus and in its power He carries out His mighty works; after the death, resurrection, and ascension of Jesus. The same spirit which rested upon Him is bestowed upon the community of His followers, so that the work of the spirit links together, and binds into a single operation of God, the whole series of events which began in the Jerusalem Temple at the annunciation to Zechariah had reached a climax in the free proclamation of the Kingdom of God in the capital city of the Gentile world by the leading apostle.[28]

THE PLACE OF THE SPIRIT IN PAULINE THEOLOGY

> More important in the thought of Paul, is his conception of the Spirit as the mode of Christ's presence in and among His people. The spirit in the Lukan writings is the link between the ascended Christ in heaven and His people on earth.[29]

For Paul, the Holy Spirit is not an unknown force working outside of man and separate or independent of Christ. For him, the Holy Spirit is the mode of Christ's presence in and among His people. This differs somewhat from the Lukan conception. In Luke, the Holy Spirit is the link between the ascended Christ in heaven and His people on earth. In Paul, the ascended Christ within becomes the Hope of Glory. Therefore, Paul could declare:

> It is no longer I that lives, but Christ that liveth in me. Because Christ, through the Holy Spirit, liveth within me; nothing can separate me from the love of Christ. For I am persuaded, that neither death nor life, nor angels, nor principalities, nor powers, nor things present, nor things to come, nor height, nor depth, nor other creature, shall be able to separate us from the love of God which is in Christ Jesus our Lord.[30]

It is through the Spirit that the resurrected Christ lives in us. It endows us with a new uplifting. This is what the poet had in mind when he wrote:

> I know I have been changed for the angels in heaven done changed my name.

It is the Holy Spirit within that transforms the inner man and renews the outer man. Again, the poet dramatizes the reality within this spiritual transformation when he writes:

> I looked at my hands and they looked so new
> I looked at my feet and they did too.

> I looked all around me, it looked so fine;
> I asked the Lord if all were mine.

In Paul, the link with Christ is more intimate. Christ dwells in the believer and in the community. The believer is in Christ and the community is the body of Christ. The mode by which this mutual indwelling takes place, and by which Christ is made the life principle of the church and the church which is united to its head, is the spirit of Christ Himself.

> This new life which Christians share through grace, respond to by faith—i.e., the life of the resurrection anticipated in the present time—is a state of being in the Spirit.[31]

This does not only denote a condition of prophetic ecstasy. It includes the whole content of the Christian life, the deep personal union with Christ, made possible by grace. It is a state in which the Spirit of God dwells in the believers. The Spirit of God is now recognized as the Spirit of Christ.

To have the Spirit of Christ is the same as experiencing Christ Himself. If Christ is in you, your spirit is alive. The spirit is not substantially identical with Christ, but the Spirit mediates Christ to the church and the church to Christ. The Spirit make the risen Christ a glorified presence to the individual Christian and to the church collectively. It is in the Spirit that the believers and the church are united to the Lord. The Spirit is Christ's Spirit, the Spirit of the Son of God, and the Christian indwelt by the spirit enters into a new relationship with God, that of a son to his father. Through the Spirit with its assurances of Sonship toward God, the Christian has access to the Father and communion with Him. The indwelling of the Spirit gives man his peculiar dignity.

> It is this indwelling which is the mode of Christ's own indwelling.[32]

Participation in the spirit is the common experience of all Christians (Phil. 2:1) producing the fellowship of the spirit which Paul mentions in 2 Corinthians 13:14. The individual who is united to Christ enters into a union with Him in one spirit. He becomes one spirit with Him (1 Corinthian 6:17).

The one Spirit is thus the ground of the church's unity as the one body of Christ in which all wordly or fleshly divisions are transcended. Much of our effort to unite a divided Christendom fails because we put the cart before the horse. We start with doctrine, structure, and polity. We forget that our unity is in Christ. The only way to unite structure, polity, and doctrine is to fill the structure with the Holy Spirit.

This is also true with much of our labors in social, economic, and political strivings. We try to transform human society before we Christianize or evangelize human society. We forget that only the Spirit of Christ transforms human society. This does not mean that we should cease fighting for freedom and justice. It simply means that we must know that our struggle is in vain if we fail to confront society with the gospel of salvation. Only the Holy Spirit can transform men and society.

Present possession of the Spirit is a guarantee and first installment of the total redemption that is to be received hereafter. It is the ground of Christian unity.

The supreme manifestation of the working of the Spirit is love. Through the gift of the Spirit, God's love is poured into the hearts of Christians (Romans 5:5), and it is the source of the love which binds the Christian body together (Romans 15:30; Col. 1:18).

> The panegyric on love (I Cor. 13) is intended to show that, of all the manifestations of the Spirit, love is the climax.[33]

THE SPIRIT IN JOHANNINE THEOLOGY

In Johannine theology, Christ is uniquely possessed of the Spirit (John 1:32-33) as the Son and the enoy of God. The Christian is one who experiences a new birth of the spirit, i.e., a birth to a new life in the spirit, contrasted with the ordinary fleshly birth (3:5-8; 1:13).

This does not only denote a condition of prophetic ecstasy, it includes the whole content of the Christian life, the deep personal union with Christ made possible by grace. It is a state in which the Spirit of God dwells in the believers. The Spirit of God is now recognized as the Spirit of Christ.

The New Birth in the Spirit is not available until Christ's work is accomplished and He is glorified. The Spirit is to be the guide into all the truth, for He will mediate Christ to believers. All Christians are anointed as the people of the spirit-possessed Messiah, filled with the unction of the Spirit (1 John 2:20). The Spirit is the assurance of Christ's indwelling presence. The witness to the reality of Christ's incarnation, with the water and blood of His death and of the Christian sacraments (1 John 5:7-8), and the acknowledgment that Jesus Christ has come in the flesh are the criteria of the Spirit's inspiration in the church (1 John 4:2).

In the Book of Revelation, the Spirit is once again the inspiration of the prophet (as also in Peter), declaring a message through the prophet's utterances (Rev. 1:10;7; etc.; 4:2; 14:13; 21:1-10).

> The prophetic spirit being identified with the testimony of Jesus (Rev. 19:10) and in the expectant cry of the church to its Lord, "come" the Spirit himself is speaking (Rev. 22:17).[34]

The point of this historical survey is to show that the Holy Spirit, the third person of the Blessed Trinity, is He Who brings to the church a new awareness of the all powerful presence of God working in one's life. He gives to each receiving Him, one or more charismatic gifts. The outpouring of the Holy Spirit means the coming of life of the gift of the Spirit received at Confirmation and Baptism. It is not a special grace, but a renewal of the Spiritual life accompanied by a feeling of peace and joy hitherto unknown. It is a new and deeper awareness of one's Christian identity. The gifts of the Spirit will differ as the Will of God will determine. One person will receive one gift and another an entirely different one as God in His infinite wisdom will decide. Some will speak in tongues, others will prophesy, some will heal, others will administer, while some will teach. All of these are gifts of the Spirit. We must be careful not to limit God. We cannot catalogue His gift.

Where the Spirit of God is, there is freedom.[35]

CHAPTER V

The Concept of the Divine Spirit in African Religions

Ethnologists, social and cultural anthropologists, and Christian missionaries coming to Africa from Europe and North America have in one way or the other given various and divergent views of the African and his concept of a Supreme Being. Some of the preconceived conclusions of such globe-trotters confuse the mind rather than give an adequate assessment of the African's concept of the spiritual world and its interaction with the physical. Emil Ludwig, on a visit to Africa, is credited with asking the question:

> How can the untutored African conceive of God? . . . How can this be. . . . Deity is a philosophical concept which savages are incapable of framing.[1]

Ludwig is just one such voice of multitudes of his kind who disturbingly have suggested that the African is incapable of ethical and spiritual conclusions.

In his book *The Voice of Africa*, Leo Frobenius quotes a paragraph from a Berlin journal of the last century which strips the African of any higher knowledge outside of himself but himself:

> Before the introduction of a genuine faith and a higher standard of culture by the Arabs, the natives had no political organization, nor strictly speaking, any religion. . . . Therefore, in examining the pre-Muhammedan condition of the negro races, we must confine ourselves to the description of their crude fetishism, their brutal and often cannibalistic customs, their vulgar and repulsive idols. . . . None but the most primitive determine the lives and conduct of the negroes, who lack every kind of ethical inspiration.[2]

He further quotes a prominent church leader as saying, "Niggers have no souls and are burntout husks of men."[3] We can multiply the above quotations by countless others, which do nothing but create the atmosphere for spiritual and cultural exploitation of one race by another. For once it has been established that the African has no soul, and is insensitive to the spiritual world, the stage is set for mass exploitation of his dignity and the justification of the same. This was to be expected, because, in the period when Western theology itself had allowed the Christian church to become a civil religion, to do otherwise would have undermined the very ethos of Western exploitation of Africa.

It is gratifying to note, however, that a few serious writers tell a different story about the religious life of the African. E.G. Parrinder says:

> One of the greatest forces has ever been the power of religion. . . . Of course, Emil Ludwig's phrase "The Untutoured African" is out of date, if it was ever applicable, for all people have some traditions and skill if not book-learning.[4]

Africa has been partitioned when it comes to the question of its contributions toward civilization and religion. North Africa, before the Islamic conquests of the Seventh century A.D., is often disassociated from Africa, south of the Sahara, because it has been argued by most Western writers and historians that the black man was incapable of unique culture, and, for that matter, of any religious virtues of any consequence. Therefore, they assume that to associate the black man with North Africa would be to elevate him to a higher status of which he himself would be afraid. Modern archeological findings have refused to aid and abet this theory. Today the market is full of findings to the effect that Egyptian civilization was predominantly black. To write a dissertation representative of Africa as regards the concept of the Divine Spirit in African religions, Africa, past and present, with no middle wall of Africa partition, should be treated as a whole. If we can talk about Africa as one continent in terms of its economic explorations, the same rationale should guide us in talking about cultures and religion (to avoid partitions).

The African, it has been noted, is incurably and notoriously religious. His world view of life is one of a dynamic and pragmatic belief in the Supreme Being who governs and influences the course of human movements and human history. The religious contribution of black Egypt and so-called Africa, south of the Sahara, to world culture is immense. The existence of the Supreme Being has never been doubted by the African. Life is meaningful only as it relates to and finds roots in the Supreme Being. He ordains and sustains life. In giving life, he endows man with His eternal Divine Spirit, which leads and guides man in this life and the life hereafter.

It was about 4241 B.C. that the concept of the resurrection entered into

The Concept of the Divine Spirit in African Religions

the religious literature of Egypt. At this early date, they were affirming belief in life and the life after death. In his chapter on "The God-Consciousness of the Black Church" in *Quest For A Black Theology*, Dean Walter L. Yates of Hood Theological Seminary, Salisbury, notes about the concept of the resurrection and its implication for the religious and social life of the Egyptian, that ". . . this concept represented both the spiritual and physical resurrection." This was faith in life sustained by the giver of life . . . each candidate for the life after death had to account for his past actions. Could he honestly answer:

    . . . I have not done iniquity?
    . . . I have not robbed with violence?
    . . . I have not committed theft?
    . . . I have not acted deceitfully?
    . . . I have not made light the bushel?
    . . . I have not uttered falsehood?
    . . . I have not defiled the wife of a man?
    . . . I have not encroached upon sacred seasons?

"These expressions and many others," observed Yates, "are expressions of the God-consciousness in the nature and experience of all men." . . . This God consciousness may be summarized in the poem from Lewis Browne:

    Thy rising is beautiful,
    O Living Aton, Lord of eternity,
    Thou are shining, beautiful, strong.
    Thy love is great and mighty,
    Thy rays are cast into every face.
    Thy glowing hue brings life to hearts
    When thou hast filled the two lands with love.
    O God who himself fashioned himself,
    Maker of every land,
    Creator of that which is upon it.
    Men, all cattle large and small,
    All trees that grow in the soil,
    They love when thou dawnest for them
    Thou are the mother and the father of all that
    Thou hast made.

"These religious concepts," continues Yates, "were expressed not only along the Nile Valley, but in most of West, Central, and South Africa. The African along the Guinea Coast of West Africa expressed in his own speech and tongue his system of religion, which consisted of the universal, transcendent God, with lesser gods as his servants. Before the Bishops and Popes of the fourth century of the Christian era claimed universal control of man, body, mind, and soul, and, through the Petrine doctrine, subjugated man to a one-way ticket to heaven, purgatory, or hell, the black people on the West Coast of Africa had their own system of heaven under the auspices of their ebony black priests and wisemen. One need only to turn to the proverbs and theology of the people themselves to illustrate the point."[5]

To fully understand the concept of the Divine Spirit in African religious thought, we have to make a conscious effort to understand the African doctrine of man. What is man and what is the nature of his relationship to the Supreme Being? An honest objective answer to these inquiries will help us to grasp the functional operation of the Divine Spirit as conceived by African peoples; for African cultural and religious anthropology make it crystal clear that the Divine Spirit operates within the frame of human sphere and activity. The Divine Spirit does not operate in isolation from man the creature. In this relationship, the concept of the personality soul helps to unravel the seemingly hidden function of the Divine Spirit. Among the Anlo people of Ghana, West Africa,

> The complex soul has no name in its own right . . . but is often referred to paraphrasically as amea nuto, "the real person" or as ame ṅu si le ame me abe ya ene, "the person or thing that dwells in a body like the wind or air." But whenever the complex soul is named, it derives these names by metonymy, from names specially used for its two major component parts. A third name is athe Anlo for shadow.[6]

Dr. Gaba who gave the above analysis of the concept of the soul in Anlo thought further observes:

> The Anlo name for the life soul is Gbogbo. In its wider usage, Gbogbo may mean breath, spirit . . . Gbogbo as the life soul, has a direct origin from the Supreme Being and is regarded as the little bit of the Supreme Being that dwells in every human being. Coming therefore, from the Supreme Being, the life soul shares in the divine attributes of justness and goodness. In functional differentiation it is the same as Dzitsinya "The heart that forewarns," simply conscience. It is also the same as Se or Kla or *Dzogbese destiny* or Aklama, guardian genius . . . the life soul never loses its identity in the complex soul. It always remains, "wholly other fighting against man's lower psychic element in defence of the good and the beneficial to man in waking life as Dzitsinya conscience, and in sleep as Aklaman, guardian genius."[7]

Thus we discover that the African has had contact with the Divine Spirit from time immemorial. Similar ideas about the relationship of the soul of man to the Divine Spirit are held throughout and among all Africans, and, although expressed in different thought patterns and forms, they all converge to the one source of life, The Supreme Being. It is gratifying to note that the average African need not necessarily study the so-called classical Western philosophy or employ the tools of classical philosophical verifiability to understand his own relationship and that of the world to the Supreme Being, who occupies and operates in the center of his being, through his (the Supreme Being's) spirit. This concept of the Divine Spirit within the center of man's being makes it possible for the African, sometimes, in the absence of sarcerdotal priestcraft, to approach God directly. When and if he must pray to the Supreme Being via the ancestors, either by the pouring of libation or otherwise, the ultimate end of such religious exercise is to get in contact with the source of life itself.

This belief is widespread and is expressed through many thought forms, proverbs, philosophical systems, worship, etcetera. In worship, the African demonstrates his awareness of the Supreme Being. Since God is everywhere present, His manifestation is felt through His spirit made concrete in His confrontation with man as He answers his prayers and reveals Himself to man in many varied forms. An Akan proverb, which is expressive of the omnipresence of God, is "Wope Se Woka Asem Kyere Frama," if you want to talk to God, tell it to the wind.

> Through proverbs the Akan expresses his thoughts about God. The proverbs contain the wisdom of the ages and are a reflection of the philosophical and religious ideas of the Akan. All this wisdom the Akan believes, comes from God and the Akan expresses this by saying "Nsem Nyinaa ne Nyame," God is the source of all Wisdom. Through proverbs the Akan worship God by giving recognition to his power: "Asaase trew na Onyame ne Panyin," . . . the earth is large (wide), but God is the creator; and by telling of his many attributes of love and care for his creatures, of his dependability, of his omnipresence and invisibility, of His role as creator and sustainer of the universe, of His love of justice and fairness; "Since God does not like wickedness he gave every creature a name," and a potency of his omnipotence.[8]

In African religious thought, the Divine Spirit is apportioned to every man at his birth by God. This idea may appear out-of-joint to the Western mind because of the dychotomy existent in Western philosophical and religious thoughts. The African invariably holds the view that life is one entity. It is an indivisible psycho-physical totality. The spiritual lends meaning to the physical, and the physical portrays the spiritual and makes it pragmatic and concrete. This explains why the African approaches God whenever his life is threatened by external misfortunes. The Supreme Being is the source of all life, and man is the effect of God. Therefore if life is threatened, God must be approached. The Divine Spirit is not reserved exclusively for a special group of people. It is universal and at the disposal of man.

Man's destiny is lined with the telos of God. The will of God determines the end and purpose of man. Determinism in African religious and philosophical thought is not indentical with blind fatalistic determinism, which from an observational point of view, leaves man no freedom of choice.

African determinism is one that links man to God and makes God responsible for man. The religious implication of this thought is that man finds fulfillment only as his destiny is expressive of the divine purpose. This is expressed in such words as Nkrabea, Xove, "Desting." This face is also implicit in the opening words of this Igbo prayer: Chineke, Kelu mmadu; "God who created man"; Ndum, ndu ndi dkem; "the lives of my relatives." This attitude toward the Supreme Being makes it possible for the African to address God directly, to invoke his divine presence at the commencement of every worshipful action.

The dynamics of this worshipful action is the belief, noted earlier, that God is the source of all life. Take, for example, one of the Yoruba names for the Supreme Being, Orise. According to Professor E. Bolaji Idowu, Orise is an ancient name for God, which is not universally employed today. Among the Yoruba, though, it is commonly used among the Owo people (of Yoruba Land) and among the Ltsekiri and Western Ijaw. This name by derivation falls into two parts—Ori and Se. Ori is the essence of being and in the name of God means "the very source of Being" or "Source Being." Se is a verb meaning "to originate." Thus, the whole name means "the Source Being which gives origin to all being" or the Source of all beings. This name occurs in various forms in several parts of Nigeria and in Dahomey. The Igbo have a name which carries a similar or somewhat identical meaning and connotation. That is Chukwu. This also falls into two parts—Chi and Ukwu. Chi is a very pregnant word. It carries the connotation of an overflowing fullness, the Main-Source or Main-Essence of Being. Ukwu means great, immense; it has also the connotation of a bundle or "that which contains." Chi-ukwu thus means "the immense, overflowing source of Being." Both Ori and Chi are also the names of the essence of human personality; that which makes a person a person, that apart from which a person is not a living being, that upon which personal destiny depends.[9]

While it is true that the Supreme Being has endowed every man with his eternal Divine Spirit, making man responsive to him. There are times, however, when it is believed certain officers in the community, state, or village because of their theocentric nature are uniquely infested by the Divine Spirit of God. It is universally held among African peoples that the King or chief, by reason of his office as the political and sometimes spiritual leader of the community, is given more of the Divine Spirit, commensurate with his responsibilities. In this category are included the priests and other divinities who render service to the community on behalf of God. Since God is the founder of the community, the first ancestor, it follows logically that the King or chief who rules and has oversight over the community acts as God's representative. He, together with the High Priest, makes known the will of God to man in a given existential situation. Acting in such a unique capacity, they are in fact endowed sufficiently with the Divine Spirit for the judicious discharge of their responsibilities. Sometimes elders and leaders of homesteads are believed to be especially endowed with a plus of the Divine Spirit. By the constant exercising of their spiritual gifts of leadership, they are drawn much closer to the Supreme Being.

Not all African people have or had traditional rulers, but where Kings and chiefs existed, their office was usually regarded as having been divinely instituted or maintained. These Kings and chiefs are looked upon both as political heads and sacred personages, who symbolize the prosperity and welfare of their nations. In some societies, Kings lead or take part in religious ceremonies. In any case, the religious life of their people reflects this person and position . . . thus, for example, the Bavendas believe that when God is angry with their chief, he punishes the country with drought, locusts, or flood. . . . They also hold that God appears near the chief's house and makes his will known to the chief.[10]

We have heard stories of instances where priests were called by God and led to their vocation. Among the Fantes, it is commonly reported that the spirit of divinity calls a man or woman to be trained for the religious functions he or she is expected to perform. Expressions such as Okom Afa No (called by divinity) is used in reference to a man or woman called out by God. Whether he is called directly by God or dedicated to God through lesser divinities, the theology behind the "call" is that the Divine Spirit takes possession of the "called" and consequently sets him or her apart to render service on behalf of God to man and the community at large.

"Among the Lugbara, it is held that God calls a would-be diviner (mainly women) in her adolescence. She wanders about in the woods and after several days, returns with the power of the divine. The community then erects a shrine for her, which is referred to as the "hut of God. . . . The Turkanas believe that the diviner is God's chief representative, functioning as a doctor, purifier of age-sets, predicting raids, and soliciting rain. In time of war, it is the medicine-man who, among the Luo, makes sacrifices and prayers."[11]

The concept of the Divine Spirit as found among Africans has a positive, redemptive, salvific value, and the exertion of a tremendous dynamic influence over the whole nature of man. The absence of a so-called systematized theology in African religious thought should not be the unfortunate cause for the repudiation of the rich spiritual heritage of the African. In the apostolic church, the Christians did not have a systematized, well-wrapped-up theology, but one thing we can not do away with was the will and determination of the apostles under the influence and guidance of the Holy Spirit to successfully carry on with the witness of Jesus Christ.

The only criteria for our determining the workings of the Holy Spirit among the early primitive Christians are the exhibitions of a pragmatic faith which was indicative of the fruit of the Spirit. The fruit of the Spirit and the results of the labors of the early apostles, more than anything else, gave us the insight into the operations of the Holy Spirit (Divine Spirit) within the life of the early church.

I am not concerned so much with establishing a relationship between the early church and African religion, as I am with the relationship and relativity of the similarity of the concept of the Divine Spirit in the two. How are we able to explain the indomitable spirit of the African to survive? To attribute the will to survive in the face of the most awful degrading form of chattel slavery and its attendant dehumanization to sheer luck and mere determination would be to undermine and deny the very spirit and existence of God. The African's will roots deeply in the will of the Supreme Being, and fails to succumb to external forces because it is the very Spirit of the Supreme Being which is indestructible by mundane temporal powers.

The Divine Spirit operates whenever and wherever God wills it. There is no criteria to judge the modus operandi of the Divine Spirit. The best we can do is merely to observe the fruit of the spirit in the lives of Africans everywhere, who have refused to allow external extenuating circumstances to annihilate them from the face of the globe. Who can adequately explain the spirit that sustained and upheld Africans brought to America and other parts of the world in chains, to undergo the horrors of a slavery which even the lower creatures in the animal kingdom are ashamed of? Who can adequately explain the will to face the dehumanization and eventually reverse the process into a humanizing one? There must be something deeper in the center of the black man's being that enabled him to rise above the waters of oppressive society—something deeper and higher than sheer determination and luck. It must be, and it was, and is nothing short of, the Divine Spirit of God.

It is high time we repudiated the idea, once and for all, that chattel slavery gave the black man a higher form of religion. The African concept of the Supreme Being and the providential working of His Spirit within the soul of the black man produced the black will to survive, and also to transform the white masters' religion and God into the original spirit of the Gospel of Jesus Christ, which gives worth, dignity, humanity, and freedom to all people created in the image of God.

In an interview with Dr. Charles Shelby Rooks on the objectives of the Society for the Study of Black Religion, a staff writer of the Black Church magazine quotes him as saying:

> The major quesiton facing these new scholars is the assumption by some white historians that the black slave was a simple person who accepted and adopted the Christianity that his master taught and spoon fed him. These scholars must answer these questions: Was the black worship a simple adoption of the offering? Was there some input from the black experience into white Christianity? Did black people reinterpret what was handed them as religion? Otherwise how do you account for the tremendous thrust for freedom by not just the black people of today, but the old negro slave! If those blacks had the tabula rasa (black mind), why did they seek goals not taught them as slaves? Black minds had another source for the message.[12]

"Black hope then," according to Professor James H. Cone, "is neither derived from white religion nor white political structure, we do not believe our hope to be dependent upon Thomas Jefferson's Declaration of Independence or Lyndon Johnson's great society. Neither is it dependent upon the recent development of liberation theology among white theologians in Europe and America. Black hope is born out of black people's struggle and is connected with our African heritage and the Christian gospel. African heritage prevented black people from accepting the Christian gospel in any form that was unrelated to their fight for freedom. . . . Whatever we say about the gospel then, must be reconciled to our unwillingness to accept slavery as the will of God. Accordingly black slaves rejected white interpretations of Christianity which proclaims slavery as part of the gospel of Jesus." Cone further notes, "The power of the actualization of Freedom is what black people sometimes called the Holy Ghost. The Spirit is God's presence with us, who enables us to know that we were not created for slavery, but for freedom."[13]

This mind of the black man is deeply rooted in the center of his personality, the temple of Onyankopon, the Supreme Being. "Onyankopon onye Odamankoma Sunsum (God is an Eternal Spirit). . . . We now know the notion which corresponds to the Akan "Sunsum," namely, not 'spirit' as such, but the personality which covers the relation of the 'Body' to the 'Soul: (Okara). . . ." Sunsum, we know, is basically the e-su (phusis) which provides the possibility of the incipient individual's appearance in Nyankipon's presence, then and there to obtain his nkrabea, destiny or intelligence, his "message" to earth, to realize the essence or capacity of his particular soul (Okara). If, then, we are told that Nyankopon is the e-su or Sunsum of Odamankoma, we come face to face with the same dual entity in the Godhead which we had encountered in the study of the nature of the individual, namely, a being with an Okara, Soul, as well as a Sunsum individuality or personality, through the latter of which the Okara or Soul manifests itself in the world or experiencing being (Sunsum), and also a being who is to love the objective and destined life, or 'intelligence' of the conceived or spiritual being, the soul or Okara. . . . On this level Odamankoma is apprehended as the soul (Okara) of the totality, namely, the thing, of which Nyankopon is the Sunsum, or the experiencing individuality or personality. . . . As we saw in the case of the human individual, it was in the harmonizing or reintegration of the experience of the Sunsum with the ideality of the Okara that we get Honhom, the spirit of pure etherality that identifies or links up man with the Ideal Spirit, pure Honhom; not a Holy Ghost in the Christian sense, but a Spirit in reality—spiritus realitus."[14]

In the African concept of the Divine Spirit, we discover that the Supreme Being is both the cause and end of man. Without him, it is as impossible as it is impracticable for man to exist in any form. Datuah elucidates this belief when he notes:

> Through him each man, each soul, obtains his intelligence, his Okara the message to realize a destiny; to him the accounting is made by the honhom

of each man's Okara, till man attains full maturity of compeleted incarnation, whereby man becomes God's is absorbed into the interminable Odomankoma, and shares in divine immortality. He is in working harmony, with man, in cooperation with him for each Okara to become a honhom for each ideal to be realized . . . and all this was necessary for Nyankopan to be, because man himself has the dual nature of Sunum and Okara, man and not man; man and better than man. In Onyankopon man finds this duality exemplified, and the conception makes the passage from the earthly to the heavenly not impossible or inconceivable. The God-man is as necessary to life as the man-God. In the conception of Onyankopon as both Sunsum and Okara, the primal Onyame and the Final Odamankoma have a reconciliation that eases the way for the ascent of man from the terrestrial to the celestial. Onyankopon's value for life is any active value, a working value, the value for activity, of how best man should carry himself in conduct. Goodness implies values of something done. Onyankopon's doing is good. Onyankopon is good, is in fact the Supreme Good, the Akan God of Beneficence, practical content of the moral life.[15]

CHAPTER VI

The Nature of the Holy Spirit

The Holy Spirit is a divine mystery of the union of Christ with His people. It is the presence and power of Christ in the human heart. The church is the body of Christ. The Holy Spirit is the life and power within it. When, how, and why He chooses to operate in such a way is all a part of this great mystery.

Whatever is said by way of explanation or description is by its very nature limited by our finite expression. The Holy Spirit is a Heavenly Being. Any earthly description is, therefore, inadequate. Although our human description is inadequate; it is a genuine demonstration of truth, because it is grounded in Scripture and is meant to glorify God. Anything that is said about the Holy Spirit must be in the realm of poetry and song. It is the Holy Spirit that makes God real in the human heart. He makes the risen Christ also the living Christ. He empowers our Christian witness, He creates the Christian community.

It was on the day of Pentecost that the Holy Spirit transformed a band of fearful disciples into a fearless Christian community. It was on this day of Pentecost that the Spiritless message of the frightened disciples was taken as an arrow, feathered with the Good News of the glorious resurrection, and placed upon the string of the mighty bow of the Holy Spirit. Ever since that day it has been piercing the heart of an unbelieving world.

The Holy Spirit is a fact of human experience. He impinges upon the human senses through man's spiritual senses.

When He came to the early church, He impinged upon man's spiritual hearing.

> Suddenly there was noise from the sky which sounded like a strong wind blowing and it filled the whole house where they were sitting.[1]

It is not strange that the disciples associated this spirit-filled noise with the blowing of the wind. The wind has always been used to describe the working of the Spirit.

> And God breathed into man's nostrils the breath of life and man became a living soul.[2]

> The wind blows where it wishes, you hear the sound it makes, but you do not know whence it comes from or where it is going. It is the same way with everyone who is born of the Spirit.[3]

When the Holy Spirit comes, it impinges upon man's spiritual vision. Then they saw what looked like tongues of fire spreading. Tongues here symbolize a new knowledge—heart knowledge. The spiritual eyes began to see and the spiritual ears began to hear. Those disciples saw things that they could not see before. They saw tongues of fire. Fire is the source of light, and light is the source of life.

> And the light brought life to men.[4]

When the fire of the new life is sent from God, it impinges upon the human vision.

> In the year that King Uzziah died, I also saw the Lord.[5]

The human eye is here being used to witness the coming of the Holy Spirit. There will be those who will attempt to mythologize this passage. I am willing to accept it on faith. When the Holy Spirit came into the early church, man's spiritual eye was a witness to His power.

When the Holy Spirit came he impinged upon the sense of touch.

> And each person there was touched by a tongue.[6]

These tongues of fire impinged upon the human touch. Jesus often healed the sick by reaching out and touching them.

Here we see the risen Christ reaching down and touching His people. This touching was also a healing touch. It was a touch that empowered them to witness. The Holy Spirit here appeals to the sense of spiritual taste.

> I took the little book from his hand and ate it and it tasted sweet as honey in my mouth.[7]

It was on the day of Pentecost that the Holy Spirit came and impinged upon human speech. He sanctified human communication, "and began to talk in other languages, as the Spirit enabled them to speak."[8]

THE HOLY SPIRIT AND THE GOOD LIFE

The Holy Spirit is holistic in its approach to the good life. It changes the whole man. It transforms human society. Someone has said that the

The Nature of the Holy Spirit

modern church does not pray for the coming of the Holy Spirit; it does not feel the need of the Holy Spirit. The church no longer struggles against the power of wickedness in high places; therefore, the church has no need of power. The church no longer wants change; therefore, it no longer feels the need of spiritual power. God does not waste His gifts. Not until the church recommits itself to changing men and society will it receive the Holy Spirit. It is the presence of the Holy Spirit that enables the Christian to live the good life.

He helps to organize our priorities and assess our values. The Holy Spirit does not shield us from all wrong and all error. It empowers the will to will the will of God. While the Christian seldom reaches moral perfection, he is committed to righteousness, justice, and love.

Paul Tillich describes the role of the Holy Spirit in the living of the good life when he writes:

> The spiritual presence creates a theonomous morality. The term "theonomous" as applied to culture and morality has the meaning of the paradoxical phrases "transcultural cultural and transmoral morality". Religion, the self-transcendence of life under the dimension of spirit, gives self-transcendence to both the self-creation and the self-integration of life under the dimension of spirit.[9]

Christianity is a way of life that puts God at the center of life. Every believer must commit himself to follow Christ up the high road of Christian living. As rational beings, we must decide what it means to follow Christ. We must have a reason for the faith we declare. Our task is made difficult because there are many mysteries about our faith that we cannot explain. The only thing that keeps us from appearing absurd or false is the presence of the Holy Spirit within.

It is He who verifies the fact of spiritual reality and the truth of Christian mystery. It is the Holy Spirit within, who assures us that such great mysteries as the Holy Trinity are both true and relevant to the living of the Christian life.

Christian morality is made possible by the presence of the Holy Spirit.

THE GLOSSOLALIA, OR THE SPEAKING IN TONGUES

Luke's version of the happenings at Pentecost is that the church received the miraculous gift that enabled it to preach the gospel in the language of every nation under heaven.

> There are several indications in the story, and in the discourse that follows, that Luke has imposed his own interpretation upon a traditional version found in his sources.[10]

Many Biblical scholars believe that this speaking in tongues has reference to the Glossolalia. Speaking in tongues is an outburst of largely unintelligible speech under the influence of deep religious excitement. Paul does not think too highly of it. He does not condemn the practice, but considers it just another spiritual gift bestowed by the Holy Spirit upon some, but not upon all, Christians.

> Make love your aim and earnestly desire the spiritual gifts, especially that you may prophesy. For he who speaks in tongues speaks not to men, but to God for no one understands him, but he utters mysteries in the spirit. . . . He who prophesies is greater than he who speaks in tongues unless someone interprets so that the Church may be edified.[11]

In our time there are some Christians who insist that speaking in tongues is the only valid proof that one has received the gift of the Holy Spirit. This is not true, as not all who receive the Holy Spirit speak in tongues. Speaking in tongues must be judged by the life of the Christian. If speaking in tongues inspires one to bring forth the fruits of the Spirit, then and only then is it of the Holy Spirit.

> Ye shall know them by their fruits.[12]

> But the fruit of the Spirit is love, joy, patience, kindness, goodness, faithfulness, humility, and self-control.[13]

Paul Tillich places speaking in tongues in its proper theological context when he says:

> The church had and continues to have a problem actualizing Paul's ideas because of concrete ecstatic movements. The church must prevent confusion of ecstatic and chaos, and it must fight for structure. On the other hand it must avoid the institutional profanization of the Spirit which took place in the early Catholic church as a result of its replacement of charisma with office.[14]

This has also happened in Protestantism. It attempted to replace ecstasy with doctrine or moral structure. The church would do well to ever keep in mind Paul's teachings on the matter of speaking in tongues.

A church which attempts to ignore all ecstatic expression of spiritual charisma will wither and die. While at the same time, a church that makes ecstasy its chief concern, opens the door to the chaotic and disrupting forms of emotion that, in the end, will defeat its spiritual purpose. The ecstatic expression of religion must be balanced with the teaching of doctrine, the insistence upon order, and, above all, on the living of the Christian life—morality. The moral life is the best evidence of Christian emotion. Emotion must be

The Nature of the Holy Spirit

supported by both Christian ethics and Christian doctrine. Each dimension of Christian activity must be balanced by another. If not, Christian religion becomes degraded into something less than a true witness of the presence of the Holy Spirit. In the presence of the Holy Spirit, subject and object are united to form a new quality of unity that produces the new creature and the new society.

The Holy Spirit is not just a matter of subjective emotion alone, it is also objective reality as well. Therefore, speaking in tongues must be verified and substantiated by sound doctrine and moral behavior. The gift of the Spirit must be judged by the fruits of the Spirit.

The Holy Spirit produces the good life. The Holy Spirit enlightens our understanding and strengthens our moral judgment. Tillich says:

> The element of wisdom in the spirit makes such judgment possible. It is judgment directed toward what we have distinguished as the two poles in the self-integration of the moral self, self-identity and self-alteration. The spiritual presence maintains the identity of self without impoverishing the self's drive toward the attestation of the self, without disrupting it.[15]

What Tillich is emphasizing here is that man cannot save himself, he cannot pull himself up by his own spiritual bootstraps. Man, in order to live up to his own sense of morality, needs a power within greater than himself. The self cannot lift itself out of the quicksand of moral degradation. Man needs a power greater than himself. This power can be found only in the presence of the Holy Spirit. The Holy Spirit is the source of power for living the good life.

Throughout human history, man has tried to establish the beloved community. In spite of our scientific discoveries, we are still failing to live the good life. Human nature does not have the power to fulfill its self. Without God, even our quest for knowledge becomes tragically warped and twisted. Blackwood says:

> The quest for knowledge is good when directed Godward. But when it usurps the place of God, then good turns into evil. In our time, the outstanding triumph of civilization has been the hydrogen bomb. That was not produced by illiterate savages, but by the best minds alive. Scientific humanism has not yet produced a brilliant record of spritual achievements.[16]

It is not our striving after God that creates the good life, it is the Holy Spirit in us that produces the good life. It crucifies the flesh with its afflictions and lust. "Beyond that," they that are Christ's through the spirit are risen with him to newness of life. This new life brings forth the fruits of the Spirit. Jesus describes the nature of the Spirit when he says:

> The word that I speak unto you I speak not of myself, but the Father that dwells in me, He doeth the works.[17]

It is impossible for us to experience the same power that Jesus had in his life, except that the same spirit dwells in us that dwelt in him. If he could do nothing of Himself, no more can we; if he were dependent upon God for wisdom, for judgment, for power, no less are we. God's Spirit must dwell in us.

THE HOLY SPIRIT AFFIRMS THE LORDSHIP OF CHRIST

The Holy Spirit was given as a fulfillment of prophecy. This is what I will do in the last days, God says:

> I will pour out my spirit upon all men, your sons and your daughters will prophesy, your young men will see visions, and your old men will dream dreams, yes even my slaves both men and women, I will pour out my spirit in those days.[18]

The Holy Spirit was given as an act of divine grace. God was preparing his disciples to witness. He was preparing the new Israel. The coming of the Holy Spirit was an act of redemption. It was a part of His divine plan of salvation. The Holy Spirit comes from God through Jesus Christ.

> God has raised this very Jesus from the dead, and we are all witnesses to this fact. He has been raised to the right side of God, and received from him the Holy Spirit, as his Father had promised, and what you see and hear is his gift that he poured out on us.[19]

The coming of the Holy Spirit in this manner is proof of the Lordship of Christ. This proves He is the Messiah that was to come.

> All the people of Israel then are to know for sure that it is this Jesus, whom you nailed to the cross, that God had made Messiah.[20]

The Holy Spirit is God and must be viewed in the light of the doctrine of Trinity. This will be more fully discussed in another chapter.

The doctrine of the Trinity in many ways represents the crystallization of New Testament teaching. It is the Christian Gospel come to mature expression. It is an attempt to correlate, to understand, to clarify what the church means by Spirit, Lord, and God. It has to do with three divine manifestations of the God-head. It seeks to explain the mode and manner of Divine Revelation.

> The doctrine of the Trinity does not affirm the logical non-sense that three are one and one is three, it described in dialectical terms the inner movement of the divine life as an eternal separation from itself and return to itself.[21]

The Nature of the Holy Spirit

The divine life can be described as a Trinity within unity. It gives a dynamic description of the nature of the Deity. It reveals a God in the process of becoming, as he performs the work of creating, redeeming, and fulfilling. It points to a dynamic relationship between the structure of thought and the structure of being. The Trinitarian idea is paradoxical, but not contradictory. It attempts to describe the infinite creative tension of Christian reality. It attempts to express the fact of God's transcendent action, which excludes the necessity for all human preparation.

The Trinity surpasses but does not cancel out finite reason. In the understanding of the Trinitarian nature of God, finite reason is superseded, but not annihilated. It is supplemented by a higher reason. It is supported by ecstatic reality. The Holy Trinity is a paradox that transcends all human expectation and possibilities. It is the supreme mystery of religion.

> It breaks into the context of experienced reality, but cannot be determined by it.[22]

The doctrine of the Trinity is made imperative by the need for a balance between the concrete and the absolute. The Trinity points out the threefold manifestations of God as creative power, as saving love, and as ecstatic transformation. The Holy Spirit is the third person in the Blessed Trinity. He enables us to experience God as a living person and not as a dead identity. It is the creative ground of Being in every Being.

> The Divine Spirit is God Himself as Spirit in Christ, and through Him in the church and the Christian.[23]

Thus, the third person in the Trinity is the divine ground of divine creativity. It is the spiritual presence of the Divine. It is faith experiencing itself through ecstasy and love, denying itself in suffering and prayer, fulfilling itself in self-surrender. Thus, the Holy Spirit is the mysterious wonder-working power of God. It is connected with the normal religious acts of daily life as well as ecstatic experience of the divine. It empowers men to bring to pass God's divine purpose in history. It is proof that the living God is at work in the affairs of men. He is both a private possession and a community experience. He produces in men a new quality of life. He creates a society of love and joy and hope. This is the true nature of the Holy Spirit.

THE HOLY SPIRIT—A GIFT OF GRACE

In the soul of every Christian believer there are at work two kinds of laws. The law of nature as represented by the Ten Commandments, and the law of grace as represented by Jesus Christ. The law of nature condemns; the law of grace redeems.

In the eighth chapter of Romans, Paul refers to this law of grace as the law of the spirit.

> For the law of the spirit, which brings us life in union with Christ Jesus, has set me free from the law of sin and death.[24]

> It is the Holy Spirit working so that the righteous demands of the law might be fully satisfied in us who live according to human nature.[25]

It is the Holy Spirit that brings us into personal contact with God through Christ. He gives us life in a new dimension. Again, Tillich emphasizes the fact that the spirit takes us beyond the dimension of law.

> The spiritual presence shows the validity of the moral imperative unambiguously, just by showing its law-transcending character. The spirit elevated the person into the transcendent unity of the divine life and in so doing it reunites the estranged existence of the person with his essence; and this reunion is just what the moral law commands and what makes the moral imperative unconditionally valid.[26]

Only the Holy Spirit can keep the heart pure, by purifying our desires and sanctifying our motives. The heart is the seat of the motives and the desires. When the Holy Spirit takes over the heart, it cleanses the temple of our thought.

> As a man thinketh in his heart, so is he.[27]

When the Holy Spirit controls the heart, He brings peace, purity, power, and joy. When the Holy Spirit takes control, He empowers the human spirit. The human spirit is continuously drawing power from the Holy Spirit. It is feeding on the bread of life, and growing in ability to interpret the will of the Heavenly Father.

The Holy Spirit is constantly purging the human spirit of unwholesome, ugly thoughts of doubt, malice, passion, revenge, and supplanting them with good thoughts, pure motives, and noble desires. Christians are not exempt from nor immune to temptations; they are still subject to trials and testings, but the Holy Spirit gives power to overcome.

The Holy Spirit brings us peace through obedience to God. It reconciles man's spirit to the Spirit of God. This Holy Spirit is not another person, but is the spirit of the God-head. He is the Spirit of the Father and the Son.

> If the Spirit of God, who raised Jesus from death, lives in you, then He who raised Christ from death will also give life to your mortal bodies by the presence of His Spirit in you.[28]

The Nature of the Holy Spirit

The law of nature enslaves, but the law of the spirit liberates and sets one free.

> Those who are led by God's Spirit are God's sons for the Spirit that God has given you does not make you a slave and cause you to be afraid; instead, the Spirit makes you God's son, and by the Spirit's power we cry to God, Father, my Father. God's spirit joins himself to our spirit to declare that we are God's children.[29]

Thus, the Holy Spirit is the divine link connecting the Spirit of God and the spirit of man. It is the channel through which the power of God flows into human life. The power of God is the power of love. It is this power that creates the beloved community.

> Come Holy Spirit, heavenly dove,
> with all thy quickening power;
> kindle a flame of sacred love,
> in these cold hearts of ours.[30]

It is the Holy Spirit that gives us the power to live the Christian life.

> In the same way the Spirit also comes to help us, weak that we are. For we do not know how we ought to pray; The Spirit himself pleads with God for us in groans that words cannot express, and God who sees into the hearts of men knows what the thought of the spirit is for the spirit pleads with God on behalf of his people and according with his will.[31]

THE NATURE OF THE SPIRITUAL PRESENCE

Let us ask ourselves, what is the nature of the spiritual presence? Paul tells us:

> God saved us through the water of rebirth and renewing power of the Holy Spirit. For He sent down the spirit upon us plentifully through Jesus Christ, Our Saviour, so that being justified by grace, we might in hope become heirs to eternal life.[32]

Hans Kung describes the nature of the Holy Spirit in the early church as follows:

> In primitive Christendom how was the fact to be expressed that God, that Jesus Christ is truly close to the believer to the community of faith. Wholly real, present, effective? To this the writings of the New Testament give a unanimous response, but without regard to power claims for church theology, and piety. God, Jesus Christ are close in the Spirit to the believer, to the community of faith; present in spirit, present through the spirit and indeed

> as spirit. It is not then through memory, but through the spiritual reality, presence, efficacy of God, of Jesus Christ himself . . . perceptible and yet not, invisible, and yet powerful, real like the energy-charged air, the wind, the storm, as important for life as the air we breathe. . . . This spirit then is not as the word itself might well suggest the spirit of man, his knowing, and willing, living self. He is the spirit of God, who as Holy Spirit is sharply distinguished from the unholy spirit of man and his world. The spirit is no other than God himself. God close to man and the world as comprehending, but not comprehensible, self-bestowing but not controllable, life giving, but also directive power and force. He is then not a third party, not a thing between God and man, but God's personal closeness to men.[33]

The Holy Spirit is not another person independent of God. He is of the same essence, substance, and nature of God.

The Holy Spirit is available to all those who will seek him in prayer through faith. He will help us to quiet our desultory thoughts, desires, motives, and allegiance, while we open the innermost of our Being to the unseen power, to still our material thought and lustful passion, in order to know that the still small voice of the Holy Spirit is calling us to deeper depth and higher heights of spiritual reality. It is the nature of the Holy Spirit to transform the human spirit; to help one find God within and then to worship Him in spirit and in truth; to train the human spirit to respond to the divine will; to yield in joyous obedience to the divine command; to make Christ truly Lord and Master of life.

The Holy Spirit is always seeking for a medium through which to express Himself. He will not force his entrance into the heart, but if we will respond, He will come in, take control, and develop to the highest the natural gifts with which we have been endowed. He will make us blessings to ourselves and to mankind. He will guide us into new fields of creative service.

> But all these worketh that one and the self same spirit dividing to every man severally as he will.[34]

This is the mystery of the Holy Spirit which hath been revealed, though dimly, to all ages and generations, but was made clear in Jesus Christ. All the mystery, all the power is made clear to us when we confess a saving faith in Jesus Christ, the hope of Glory.

Then open your heart to Him, and He will grant you according to the riches of His glory to be strengthened with power by His spirit in the inner man.

CHAPTER VII

The Doctrine of the Trinity

The Holy Spirit is God dwelling within the heart of the Christian. He is everywhere present. In him we live and move and have our being. Wherever God is, the Holy Spirit is there. The Spirit upholds us, protects us, guides us, and empowers us.

The Holy Spirit within is life. This life is abundant, eternal, complete, and overflowing. It is the life of God. God shares this life with His children through the Holy Spirit. The Christian rejoices to know that the life that he lives is the gift of God through His Spirit.

The Holy Spirit is the final link that connects the divine with the human. He is the channel through which God flows into human history. The Holy Spirit is God, the Father, and the Son, proceeding into the spiritual community; redeeming and reconciling it. He is also the highroad upon which man returns to the city of God. Therefore, the doctrine of the Trinity must be more than a metaphysical discussion of the essence of God. It must be seen in the light of a correct understanding of the will of God and a clear perception of the purpose of God. This can only be found in the Bible which is the divine revelation of God. The only way to accomplish this is to return to the Bible as the Word of God.

> We need to go back to a more biblical and liturgical view of the Trinity as revealed history.[1]

The Trinitarian doctrine in the early church was arrived at through religious experience, not philosophical reflections. The failure of many theologians since that time, to grasp this truth is responsible for much of the failure to deal adequately with the subject.

The human mind can never of itself become the measure of this divine mystery. We can only know what God chooses to reveal to us through the Word and the Spirit.

The Holy Spirit brings divine light. He dispels the darkness of ignorance, prejudice, and fear. He brings understanding, wisdom, and light which illumines our every thought, and enables us to grasp divine truth.

The Holy Spirit is power. He is omnipotent and ever present. His omnipresence encompasses the cosmos. No person, place, thing, condition, or circumstance can hinder His divine will. This Holy Spirit is within the heart of the Christian. The human spirit is empowered to witness to the presence of the Holy Spirit; therefore creating that Blessed assurance of salvation history.

This Holy Spirit within is truth. He gives one the power to think truth, love truth, and seek truth. He no longer thinks falsely of any one. He knows the truth and it has set him free to receive that hidden knowledge revealed by the divine mystery proclaimed in the Scriptures, through the Holy Spirit.

The doctrine of the Trinity is an attempt to give human expression to this divine mystery. Divine mystery can never be fully explained or fully known by human reason. The nature of God, like the thoughts of God, is as high above man's understanding as the heavens are above the earth. Just as heaven and earth are linked together, so the divine and the human are united through the three divine Persons in the one Godhead. The doctrine of the Trinity is an attempt to explain and express this mystery.

Because of our finite limitations, we can never fully understand or express the modes and operations of God.

Man cannot discover God. He can only know Him as God reveals Himself to him. The sacred mystery of the Trinity is revealed truth. This revealed truth is beyond the full comprehension of the finite mind. The ladder of human understanding cannot reach the mountain peak of the divine nature. The Holy Trinity is knowledge that comes through faith.

> If any man will do his will, he shall know of the doctrine, whether it be of God or whether I speak of myself.[2]

God reveals himself to us as we seek to do his will:

> Off with our shoes, please, for the Holy Spirit is Holy ground. Away with figured syllogism and ordinary arithmetic: Here logic and mathematics do not suffice. The need is rather for a listening ear, and obedient heart, rapt adoration, and a careful engagement with the Holy Scriptures.[3]

Daniel Webster was once asked:

> How can you reconcile the doctrine of the Trinity with reason? He replied, "Do you expect to understand the arithmetic of heaven? We can never know all that it is to be known about the nature of the Holy Trinity. Yet, the Old Testament implies it, the New Testament declares it and Christian experience affirms it."[4]

We believe that the Lord our God, the Lord is one, and that there are three personal distinctions in the Godhead. We believe that within the unsearchable nature of God, there are three persons: Father, Son, and Holy Spirit. These three persons are one God. One in essence, one in will, and one in

The Doctrine of the Trinity

purpose. This truth is beyond the grasp of human reason, yet it is not contrary to human reason. It is at the heart of the biblical message. Dr. Herbert Lockyer says:

> Granted that there is not presented a formulated definition of the Trinity, yet the gathering together of allusions of such a three-foldness proves it to be a Scriptural doctrine as certain as any other. While the term Trinity is not found in the Bible, the truth of it is strewn across its sacred pages.[5]

THE ROLE OF THE HOLY SPIRIT IN THE GODHEAD

McDonald puts his finger on the essential role of the Holy Spirit in the Godhead when he writes, "The Spirit is the universal point of contact between God and history."[6]

It is impossible to understand the mission of the church without a clear view of the role of the Holy Spirit within the Godhead. This understanding will also determine the nature of both our Christology and our Ecclesiology. The understanding of the Holy Spirit forms the background and horizon for our interpretation of all the basic doctrines of the church.

> The sequence of the creed contains a logic of verification which is not accidental. "I believe in one God, in Jesus Christ, in the Holy Spirit." What is manifested in the third article can only be understood as an interpretation of the unfolding of what is said in the second and first. Revelation itself is an inchoactive pneumatology which later develops into the doctrine of the Holy Spirit.[7]

The doctrine of the Holy Spirit presupposes the doctrine of the Trinity. The word Trinity was first formally used at the Synod held in Alexandria in A.D. 317. From that day forward, it took its place among the great doctrines of the Christian faith. Long before this date, it was used by Theophilus, Bishop of Antioch; Lucian; Voltaire; and many of the early Christian writers. The word Trinity is derived from the Latin word "Trinitas" meaning three-fold. It here expresses the threefoldness of God. It describes God's threefold manifestation. It is distinct from the metaphysical term "Tri-unity." God is not a tri-unit. God is a trinity in unity. He is one divine life with three manifestations of that one divine life. The three persons are equal but one in essence.

> Believe that I am in the Father and the Father in me. . . . And I will pray to the Father, And He shall give you another Comforter that He may abide with you forever.[8]

The doctrine of the Trinity is as unique as it is profound. Lockyer says:

> Attempts have been made to find analogies to the Trinity. Man, example, is a tripart being, composed of spirit, mind, and body, but no three persons are structurally one. In nature, the universal presents itself to view as earth, sky and sea. Atmosphere is made up of light, heat and air. Matter itself is solids, liquids and gases. Water is found as snow, ice and liquid. From the sun we have light, heat and chemical effects. St. Patrick used the

illustration of the three green leaves of the Shamrock to convey to his congregation an intelligent conception of the three persons in the Godhead. Triads of divinities can be found in many religions, three being recognized as a sacred number. But in the Christian doctrine of the Trinity, there is nothing in common with the three of mythology.[9]

Since its first use by the Synod of Alexandria, many great minds, both Christian and non-Christian have pondered this mystery. But none has been able to fully comprehend its meaning.

One day St. Augustine was walking along the sea shore and saw a small boy digging a hole in the sand. "What are you trying to do?" he asked, "I am trying to empty the sea into this hole." Whereupon, Augustine said to himself, "Am I not trying to do the same thing as this child in seeking to exhaust with my reason the infinity of God and to collect it within the limits of my own mind.[10]

The Holy Trinity is the ineffable mystery of the threefoldness of the Godhead. It is the chief foundation of Christian doctrine. Irenaeus, in his treatise against heresies, turned to the Trinitarian doctrine as the cornerstone of his defense.

Complete faith in one God Almighty, of whom all things are, and in the Son of God, Jesus Christ, our Lord, by whom all things are, and all things shall be, and his disposition by which the Son of God became man. Also a firm trust in the Spirit of God who set forth the dispensation of the Father and the Son dealing with each successive race of men as the Father willed.[11]

The doctrine of the Trinity is an object of faith and not the product of reason. Faith tells us that God manifests Himself in three modes of eternal reality, namely, as God the Father, the great Creator, Sustainer, and Proposer of all things: as Son, the one and only Redeemer of mankind; as Holy Spirit, the Sanctifier and Enlightener of all. Thus we see that each Person of the Godhead has his own distinct role and spheres of influence. Yet, they are always found acting together in perfect unison.

There can be no relationship with God unless it is through the Holy Spirit. The Spirit is the point of contact for a two-fold movement; From God through Christ and the Holy Spirit to man, and from man in the Holy Spirit through Christ to God.

In one direction the self-giving unfolding of the Father through the Son in the Spirit which initiates the Trinitarian history of God's dealing with the Spirit through the Son is being lead back to the Father.[12]

The Trinitarian doctrine can best be illustrated by an isosceles right triangle encompassed in a double circle. It portrays in the three equal angles the equality within the Godhead. The double circle illustrates the double movement of the cosmos and God. Because of original sin, the cosmos falls from its state of original innocence into sin. Because of the new Adam, God through Christ invades the cosmos and, through the power of the Holy Spirit, redeems it and returns it to a state of holiness within the divine providence.

The Doctrine of the Trinity

No one can see the Word without the Spirit, and without the Son, no one can return to the state of blessedness in God. This truth does not defy or contradict human reason. It transcends reason, thereby enhancing and fulfilling the demand of reason. The reality of God is the very foundation of reason. If God is truly God, He must transcend reason and in so doing provide the very foundation upon which reason must build.

The theology of the Trinity does not violate human rationality or ontological reality. There are times, however, when one has to read between the lines in order to learn what the Holy Spirit has written there. Often what is written between the lines is of greater moment than what is written on the line. God, in His self-manifestation to man, is dependent on the way man receives His manifestation. This is why the Holy Spirit is of such vital importance to divine revelation.

> The role of the Holy Spirit is to bring the dispensation of the Father and the Son, dealing with each successive race of men, as the Father willed.[13]

The doctrine of the Trinity is an object of faith instead of a product of reason. Faith tells us that God manifests Himself in three modes or persons.

While the three persons are equal in essence, substance, will, and purpose, there is a distinction and even a subordination in roles or functions. The scripture teaches that the Father is first, the Son is second, and the Spirit is third. The Son is of the Father and the Holy Spirit is of the Father and the Son. The Father operates through the Son and the Son operates through the Holy Spirit. The Son does not send the Father, but is always said to be sent by the Father. Nor is the Holy Spirit ever said to send the Father or the Son, or to operate through them. Therefore, in the Holy Trinity, there is a subordination of the persons in terms of the mode of subsistence and function. In all things pertaining to essence and attributes, the persons of the Godhead are one; but in things pertaining to function or role, they are distinct.

According to the Scriptures, the Father created the world, the Son created the world, and the Holy Spirit created the world. Creation is a matter of essence; therefore, the three are one. On the other hand, there are certain acts or roles limited to one person of the Trinity, which are never performed by either of the others. Thus, "Generation" belongs exclusively to the Father, "Philiation" (Christ is the only begotten Son of the Father) to the Son, and "Procession" to the Holy Spirit. The Father creates, chooses, and calls. The Son redeems, reconciles, and saves. The Holy Spirit sanctifies, purifies, empowers, and guides. Each person in the Trinity has his peculiar function or role. The understanding of this arrangement is not a matter of logic, or metaphysics or philosophy. It is revealed truth obtained from the Scriptures through faith. This represents the biblical presentation of the doctrine of the Trinity. To say that the one divine substance can be manifested in three distinct persons with three unique roles is not unreasonable. It is super-reasonable. That is, it is beyond reason and can only be grasped by faith.

The terms Father, Son, and Holy Spirit, as applied to the persons of the Trinity, are relative terms. The relations which they express are mutual relations, relations in which the different persons stand one to another. The first person is called the Father, not because of his relation to his creatures, but because of his relation to the second person. The second person is called the Son, not because of any earthly relation, but because of his heavenly relation with the Father. And the third person is called the Spirit because of his relation with the first and second.

THE TRINITARIAN DOCTRINE IN OLD TESTAMENT TRADITION

The doctrine of the Trinity, while not explicitly stated in Old Testament writings, is firmly testified to on almost every page of the scriptures. The gradual unfolding of the doctrine is an example of progressive revelation. While no Old Testament writer makes the Holy Spirit the chief concern of his message, many writers assume His presence, imply His reality, and seek His guidance.

"Elohim," the divine term used of God at the beginning of the Bible, is a plural noun used over 500 times in the Old Testament and more than 5,000 times in the New Testament, accompanied continually by a verb in the singular. This is a term revealing the oneness of the Godhead and the plurality of persons in the Godhead. Further, this proper noun in the plural number meaning more than one, is associated with creation. God said: "Let us make man after our image and after our likeness."[14]

Not only is there a unity of essence in the Godhead, it is also a unity of operation.

> God who at sundry times in diverse manners spoke in time past unto the fathers by the prophets, hath in these last days spoken unto us by his Son, who he hath appointed heir of all things, by whom also he made the world.[15]
>
> If God who speaks in these passages uses the word us of himself, there is a perfectly clear statement to the effect that the Godhead is a plurality—whether that plurality be a duality or a Trinity, or some other number is spoken of.[16]

In the New Testament, God the Father, the Lord Jesus Christ, and the Holy Spirit appears as the joint object of all religious adoration and the Old Testament as the power, wisdom, and the Spirit of God.

> Doth not wisdom cry? And understanding put forth her voice? . . . The Lord possessed me in the beginning of his way, before his works of old. I was set up from everlasting, from the beginning, or ever the earth was.

The Doctrine of the Trinity

> When there were no depths, I was brought forth. When there were no fountains abounding with water, before the mountains were settled, before the hills were I brought forth.[17]

God communicates His will to his people through his word.

> After these things the word of the Lord came unto Abram in a vision saying, "Fear not Abram: I am thy shield and thy exceeding great reward.[18]

Here again we see the word of God imparting wisdom unto Abram. The term "Word of Wisdom" takes on the nature of personality. He can be seen and heard in a vision. He reveals the will and purpose of God. He is the means of divine communication. The word is often referred to as the mouth of God. It is the mouth of God that imparts his wisdom into the mouth of the prophet.

> With him will speak mouth to mouth, even apparently, and not in dark speeches: And the similitude of the Lord shall he behold: Wherefore then were ye not afraid to speak against my servant Moses.[19]

The word apparently means to become visible, to appear. The writer is saying that the word of God became visible to Moses. This is none other than Christ, the second person of the Trinity being foretold in the Old Testament. The word similitude means likeness, something that looks like but is not the same thing. It only resembles the real thing. The passage means not in speeches that are hard to understand. Not in images that resemble God, but the Word which is God himself. The Word is the real thing. The Word is God. God reveals his will to Israel through his Word. The Word is God:

> And there I will meet with thee, and I will commune with thee from above the mercy seat, from between the two cherubims which are upon the ark of testimony of all things which I will give thee in commandment unto the children of Israel.[20]

Here God is not only present in His word, but also in His Spirit. It is through His Spirit that His commandments become words to live by. They are living words.

> And I will dwell among the children of Israel and will be their God.[21]

Here God is promising to dwell among His people. He will dwell in the tabernacle and will commune with them when they come to worship. Not only will God dwell in the tabernacle, He will also dwell in the hearts of His people. They shall be filled with his Spirit.

And thou shalt speak unto all that are wise hearted whom I have filled with the spirit of wisdom.[22]

The center of Hebrew Theology is God's covenant presence in the midst of His people for the purpose of guiding, protecting, and providing. God dwells among his people, not in being, but in person, the person of his Holy Spirit. When prayer is directed toward the temple either by an Israelite or a stranger, God will hear it in his dwelling place in heaven and answer.

> Yahweh never "dwells" on earth as does man, he "tabernacles" in the midst of his people. The technical term for the tabernacle was drawn from the root and properly means "tent" but not "dwelling" in the ordinary sense. The center of priestly theology was the conception of God's convenant presence in the midst of the people for the purpose of revelation and atonement.[23]

The word Shakkan from which the word Shekinah is derived is used to express the reverent nearness of God to His people. The Shekinah and the Spirit, though not identical, are closely associated. It was through the Shekinah that God spoke to Moses out of the burning bush. The candelabrum that burned outside the veil was witness that the Shekinah abides in the midst of Israel.

In the Old Testament, the Shekinah is associated both with the wisdom of God and the glory of God:

> The Spirit, who makes known God's wisdom in the Crucified Christ brings freedom to those who turn to behold the glory of the Lord and are transformed from one degree of glory to another.[24]

Thus we see clearly that the doctrine of the Trinity is rooted firmly in Old Testament tradition.

> In the old covenant there was a cherubim of glory overshadowing the mercy seat, but in the new covenant the perfect revelation and the eternal purification for sin came through the Son of God who is the radiance of the glory of God.[25]

The Holy Spirit is the spirit of the risen Christ in the heart of the believers;

> Spirit of truth and love
> On thy redeeming wing
> Speed forth thy flight;
> Move over the water's face
> Bearing the lamp of grace
> And in earth's darkest place
> Let there be light.

The Doctrine of the Trinity

> Holy and blessed three
> Glorious Trinity,
> Grace, love and might
> Boundless as ocean tide
> Rolling in fullest pride
> Through the world, far and wide
> Let there be light.

THE DOCTRINE OF THE TRINITY IN NEW TESTAMENT WRITINGS

The doctrine of the trinity is presupposed in the New Testament. It is both implicit and explicit in New Testament thought. Everywhere it is presupposed that the doctrine was the fixed possession of the Christian community. While there are many hints and implied statements concerning the trinity in the Old Testament, with the coming of the Gospel and the new Testament, these implications become explicit and definite.

Donald Guthrie says:

> Of the trinity there are many adumbrations in the New Testament although it cannot be said the doctrine is expounded. Indeed it is significant that none of the New Testament writers see the need to speculate about such a doctrine. They are Christ and the Holy Spirit and which naturally gives rise to reflection about the unity of God. . . . Yet no presentation of section on trinitarian development.[26]

Guthrie points out four categoires of New Testament Scripture passages where trinitarian doctrine is implied.

1. Where trinitarian formulae are directly used (Matthew 28:19; II Corinthians 13:14; Revelation 1:4).
2. Where the formula is implied (Ephesians 4:4–6; I Corinthians 12:3–6; I Peter 1:2; Ephesians 1:3–14).
3. Where the three persons are mentioned (Galatians 4:4–6; Mark 1:9–11; Romans 8:1; II Thess. 2:13; Titus 3:4–6).
4. Passage that speaks of relationships.

McDonnel states that:

> At this point the Judeo-Christian (here this means non-Greek) and Syriac tradition have a contribution to make. One can ask whether a genuinely Semitic form of the gospel is attainable by exclusive dependence upon the New Testament written in Greek. Aramaic was one of the eminent languages of the civilized East from the sixth to the third Century B.C. Even after the conquest of Alexander the Great, Aramaic is one of its main dialects-Syriac, remained the chief spoken and written languages of the people. So there is alongside Greek and Latin Christianity, a Semitic form which in

its earliest expression was independent of Paul's theology and Hellenistic culture. Greek culture helped introduce non-Semitic elements into the New Testament.[27]

There is a vast difference between the presentation of truth through philosophical concepts as in Greek culture, and truth presented through pictorial imagery as in Semitic-Aramaic culture. We must remember that Jesus was a Semite who spoke Aramaic. It is this tradition that emphasized the creation theory of the Holy Spirit. Here we find a peculiar blending of the spiritual and the physical. It puts more emphasis on the common ground between the two. Aramaic theologians had no problem with God becoming man or the Holy Spirit entering into the human spirit.

> Tatian who was Greek educated (though later on he attacked Greek culture as corrupting), believed that the Divine Spirit who belonged to the original condition of humanity departed from the body-soul unity during the fall. The return to the fulness of humanity is only possible through the initiative of the Divine Spirit.[28]

In the Semitic-Aramaic interpretation of the Godhead, the Holy Spirit is not subordinated to the other persons in the Godhead. All persons of the Godhead are equal. The work of the Spirit is as important as that of the Father and the Son.

> Holy, Holy, Holy! Lord God Almighty
> Early in the morning our songs shall rise to thee.
> Holy, Holy, Holy! Merciful and mighty,
> God in three persons, Blessed Trinity.[29]

The teaching of Jesus is trinitarian in nature. He often dwelt not only on his own work, but on his Father's work and the work of the Holy Spirit. He claimed to be the Son of God and the Spirit-empowered one.

> All things are delivered to me of my Father: and no man knoweth who the Son is but the Father and who the Father is but the Son, and he to whom the Son will reveal Him.[30]

The Father sent the Son, and both the Father and the Son sent the Spirit.

> But the comforter, which is the Holy Spirit whom the Father will send in my name: He shall teach you all things and bring all things to your remembrance, whatsoever I have said unto you.[31]

The doctrine of the Trinity is the most distinctive mark of the religion called Christianity. This sketchy and brief survey of the place of the Holy

The Doctrine of the Trinity

Trinity in New Testament teaching emphasizes the fact that the trinitarian doctrine is founded firmly upon New Testament teaching. The Holy Trinity is one of the most profound, yet the most essential doctrine of the church. The New Testament contains evidence of both the transcendent and the immanent aspects of the nature of the Holy Spirit.

> Blessed and glorious King,
> To thee our praise we bring
> For this glad hour.
> Thou God of peace and love
> Thou Christ enthroned above
> Spirit whose fruit is love
> Display thy power.[32]

The Bible assumes that the trinity dramatizes a perfect unity, making the three persons one in holiness, love, wisdom, power, and eternal nature.

The Father is first in mode of operation, the original source of all things. "In the beginning God." He is the fountainhead of grace. He is the Father of the Lord Jesus Christ and the Father of all men, or the source of their being; and particularly the loving Father of all those redeemed by the blood of His Son.

The Son is second in the process of manifestation and the medium of all things, even judgment. He came as grace personified. He appeared and died as the Redeemer of mankind. It was through Him that God manifested Himself outwardly to all men.

The Spirit is third, seeing that He is the last revealed personality, and the one who came as the agent transferring the blessings of the Father and the Son upon the redeemed. He shares the attributes ascribed to God and Christ and is especially the helper and sanctifier of the saved. As the channel, the Spirit communicates, applies, and seals. The order of divine performance appears to be from the Father, through the Son:

> By the Holy Spirit
> So God the Father, God the Son
> And God the Spirit we adore,
> A sea of life and love unknown
> Without a bottom or a shore.[33]

In New Testament thought, The Holy Spirit was never limited to inward spirituality. He has to do with the restoration of the entire cosmos. He works through the whole of nature. As we have seen, He was with God in creation. The Eastern church seems to have become more aware of this cosmic scope of spiritual activity than the Western church. Hellenistic subjectivism and nineteenth century pietism have caused the Western church to overemphasize the inwardness of the Holy Spirit. The church must retain the concept of the Spirit as creator along with the Father. He must be viewed as the Spirit of the Father reconciling the world to Himself through the Son. The Spirit is more than just the mind of God as Hegel suggests. He is the Father in process of redeeming His world. The universality of the Holy Spirit is essential to any mature understanding of the trinity. McDonnell says:

> By restoring the Holy Spirit to creation one can both overcome the subjective style privatizing view of the spirit in pietism while evaluating the experiential dimension of pneumatology positively, and at the same time be on tract to theologize meaningfully about the Spirit of Christ in relation to resurrection and cosmic redemption.[34]

THE NATURE OF THE TRINITY

In spite of all the subjectivity surrounding the work of the Spirit, this work has a foundation in religious reality. In this sense we can say that the trinitarian symbols are a religious discovery which had to be made, formulated, and defended. What then, we ask, led to their discovery? One can distinguish at least three factors which have led to trinitarian thinking in the history of religious experience.

THE FUNCTION OF THE HOLY SPIRIT IN THE GODHEAD

The Scriptures teach, and this trinitarian doctrine presupposes, that the Holy Spirit is a gift from the Father and the Son. This presupposition is based upon the following affirmations:

a. That the gift belongs to the giver, and that it is of the same nature of the giver.
b. That the giver is free to give it. Giving is of the very nature of God. (God so loved the world that he gave . . .)
c. That the gift possesses the aptitude and essence to be given. Because the Holy Spirit is one in essence with both the Father and the Son, His will is always one with the will of the other two persons in the Godhead. Therefore, God the Father and the Son possess a giving nature. The Holy Spirit being one with them, possesses the aptitude to be given.
d. That the receiver can possess it. Only the believer can receive him. Only through faith in God through Christ, is the Christian empowered to receive Him. It is the Holy Spirit that creates saving faith in the believer.
e. That the giver will profit by it. God delights in saving souls. God is seeking to reconcile man to Himself. Whatever God desires is good for both God and man. Therefore in this sense, it does profit God to give His Holy Spirit.

The Doctrine of the Trinity

The Holy Spirit, in order to be the gift of the Godhead, must proceed from both Father and Son. Therefore, it is proper to refer to the Holy Spirit as a gift from both the Father and the Son.

A gift is not a gift until it is properly and unreturnably given. It is a thing which is not given with the intention of a return or a reward. It must be fully given. A gift freely given is always an expression of love. It is given for the benefit of the receiver. Therefore the Holy Spirit is the divine gift of agape love. It is God giving Himself to the believer in Christ. Since the Holy Spirit proceeds as love, He proceeds as the first gift.

> By the gift which is the Holy Spirit, many particular gifts are portioned out to the members of Christ.[35]

Since the Holy Ghost proceeds from the Father and the Son, He is properly called the first gift. It was the Holy Spirit that "moved upon the face of the deep." It is said of Mary, the mother of Jesus:

> The Holy Ghost shall come upon thee, and the power of the Highest shall overshadow thee: therefore also that holy thing which shall be born of thee shall be called the Son of God.[36]

While God's gift is free, it is not without conditions. Man must meet the requirements of receiving Him. Only when man meets the divine conditions is the gift bestowed upon Him. The conditions are repenting, confessing, and believing.

St. Thomas Acquinas says:

> Before a gift is given, it belongs only to the giver. But when it is given, it is his to whom it is given. Therefore, because the gift does not imply the actual giving, it cannot be called a gift of man, but the gift of God's giving. When however, it has been given, then it is the Spirit of man, or a gift bestowed on man.[37]

THE NATURE OF THE GODHEAD

Before we proceed to delve into this deepest and most profound of all religious mysteries, there are four words which need to be pondered hard, long, and prayerfully. They are *Spirit, Essence, Substance* and *Person*. Since we have already dealt with the word Spirit, we will proceed to examine the other three.

ESSENCE: What is essence? It is the Being of a thing. It is the primary quality that gives an object or person its identity; that which makes something what it is. It is the intrinsic, fundamental nature of a person or thing. It is that which makes perfume, perfume. Essence is reality in itself. It is that which gives persons and things the power of Being. It is that which makes reality real. It gives uniqueness to objects and persons. This is what Paul Tillich has in mind when he says:

> In whatever way the terminology may be changed; in whatever way the relation between true and seeming reality may be divided; in whatever way the relation of mind and reality may be understood, the problem of the truly real cannot be avoided.[38]

Essence is the father of reality and the mother of truth. Essence is the basic ontological reality. Essence is the power that enables something to be something in itself and of itself.

SUBSTANCE: Substance is the real or essential part of a thing—essence, reality, matter. It is that which gives character, meaning, and purpose. It is the essence or substratum, which underlies and is capable of having attributes or causing phenomena.

While substance is very similar to essence, it is not quite the same. Essence has to do with Being itself. Substance is that which unites being and non-Being. The Greek philosophers often confused essence and substance. There are times when these two terms are used synonymously. At other times, they are distinct one from the other, with essence applying to the state of pure being, and substance confined to that which unites being and non-being. Substance is found in both the positive and negative aspects of existence. There is no negative element in God. Therefore, essence is the quality of divine Being, while substance is the quality of all created being. Philo is right when he states that, . . . "substance is the predicate of Essence expressing itself on the level of existence."[39]

PERSON: What is meant by person? Person in the human sense has to do with the substance of human existence. It is that unity of Being and non-Being that forms the basic quality of the human individual. It is the merger of universality and individuality to form human existence. There is a difference between the human person and the divine person. The human person is finite, the divine person is infinite and absolute. Paul Tillich described the nature of the human person when he wrote:

> No individual spirit exists without participation and no personal being exists without communal being. The person as a fully developed individual self is impossible without other fully developed selves.[40]

This is not true of God. God is God all by Himself. He needs nothing outside Himself to fulfill Himself. This is the meaning of the Holy Trinity. In man, the self is individuality fulfilling itself by participating in the universality of God.

SUMMARY: Essence is pure Being. It is that which makes reality possible. Substance is that which unites Being with non-Being to create existence. The person is that which gives individualization to existence and enables the self

The Doctrine of the Trinity

to become aware of himself and his environment. There is a difference between the divine and the human person. The human person is finite and limited. The divine person is infinite and absolute. He is self-contained and self-sufficient. Therefore, in the Godhead, the essence is the same as person. Therefore, three persons do not presuppose three Gods. This is what St. Thomas Acquinas means when he says:

> Though the name of God signifies a being having Godhead, nevertheless, the mode of signification is different. For the name God is used substantively, but having Godhead is used adjectively. Consequently, although there are three having Godhead, it does not follow that there are three Gods.[41]

When we use the term persons we are not referring to the essence of God, but to the manifestations of that essence. The difference between the divine person and the human person is that the divine person is pure essence, while the human person is an ambiguous combination of Being and non-Being. When we speak of persons in the divine sense, we speak of the divine manifestation of the Godhead. When we speak of the one God, we speak of His essential nature, the unity of His Being and the unambiguous nature of that unity. This is the mystery of the Trinity, a mystery that can never be fully explained.

SUMMARY COMMENTS ON THE TRINITY

1. The doctrine of the Trinity is neither irrational nor paradoxical, but rather dialectical. Nothing divine is irrational.
2. There is only one paradox in the relation between God and man, and that is the appearance of the eternal or essential unity of God and man under the conditions of their existential separation—The Logos becoming flesh and entering time and space. The attempt to make the three equal is one of the worst distortions of the mystery of the Trinity. The Trinitarian Mystery is a part of the Christological Mystery. The Christ is the Spirit; therefore, Christology is not complete without pneumatology. The Holy Spirit is the actualization of the new Being in history. The doctrine of the Trinity comes at the end of the theological system because it is the final point of contact between God and human history. The trinitarian symbol is the church's answer to the question of the human condition. Man is finite. He is estranged—separated from, and rebellious against, God. Man's life is ambiguous. The doctrine of the Trinity is God's answer to man's estrangement. Only the Holy Spirit can enable man to experience God as a living person instead of a dead identity. The validity of the trinitarian symbol is not in philosophical speculation but in the revelatory experiences of the Father, Son, and Holy Spirit.

3. The trinitarian dogma is the work of many dedicated thinkers throughout many centuries, from the Old Testament redactors to the prophets, from the prophets to the apostles, from the apostles to the apologists, from the apologists to the system builders, from the system builders to the reformers, from the reformers to Ritschle, Harnack, Hagel, Dent, Schleiemacher, Barth and Tillich. They transformed philosophy and reshaped theology and formulated new doctrines. Old words were given new meaning—words like ousia, essention, substantia, hypostasis, physis, personae tritheism. This dogma has served a great purpose. It has given permanence, stability, consistency, contiguity, and some unity to Christian thought. It has preserved the mystery of the faith and protected the church from dangerous heresies.

In spite of the many assets it has produced some dangerous consequences:

1. The first one is a radical change in the function of the doctrine.

> While orginally its function was to express in three central symbols of the self-manifestation of God to man, opening up the depth of the divine abyss and giving answers to the question of the meaning of existence, it later became an impenetrable mystery put on the altar, to be adored. And the mystery ceased to be the eternal mystery of the ground of Beings: it became instead the riddle of an unsolved theological problem and in many cases as shown before, the glorification of an absurdity in numbers. In this form it became a powerful weapon for ecclesiastical authoritarianism and the suppression of the searching mind.[42]

2. It reduced Protestant Christianity to a tool for moral education, accepted by society for this reason.
3. It gave rise to the elevation of the Holy Virgin in Roman Catholicism.
4. The misuse of the trinitarian formula has tended to distort the unity in a manifoldness of divine self-manifestation.
5. The feminist revolution of our generation is questioning the all-male image of the Godhead and demanding a symbolism which transcends the sex alternative of male or female.

> The doctrine of the Trinity is not closed. It can be neither discarded nor accepted in the traditional form. It must be kept open in order to fulfill its original function—to express in embracing symbols the self-manifestation of the divine life to man.[43]

CONCLUSION

The doctrine of the Trinity does not contradict nor does it do violence to formal logic. Rather, it opens up new vistas of human understanding and

The Doctrine of the Trinity

leads to new horizons of human knowledge. It enriches the human quest with the sweet nectar of divine revelation. Paul Tillich puts it thusly:

> Nor is formal logic contradicted when in the dogma of the Trinity, the divine life is described as a trinity within a unity. The doctrine of the Trinity does not affirm the logical nonsense that three is one and one is three; it describes in dialectical terms the inner movement of the divine life as an eternal separation from itself and return to itself. Theology is not expected to accept a senseless combination of words, that is a genuine logical contradiction.[44]

The doctrine of the Trinity dramatizes the paradoxical reality of the eternal, conquering existence under the conditions of time. The doctrine of the Trinity is based upon three fundamental assumptions, namely:
   a. The tension between the absolute and the concrete nature of our faith.
   b. Our understanding of the nature of the divine life.
   c. The threefold manifestation of divine grace as power, love, and ecstatic transformation.

God in His power is thought of as Creator, Sustainer, Protector, and Judge. God in His love is thought of as Redeemer, Savior, and Revealer of eternal truth. God in His ecstatic transformation is the giver of the new Being, Regenerator, Comforter, Teacher, and Guide. This is what is meant by God the Father, Son, and Holy Spirit. The Holy Spirit must be seen in the light of this threefold manifestation of the divine nature. It is the Holy Spirit that enables us to experience the life of God. Through Him, God becomes a living God and not a dead identity. He enables us to experience God as ground of Being, God as form, and God as divine action. These are the assumptions that make trinitarian thinking meaningful.

Trinitarian thinking is dialectical in nature. It does not contradict reason. The Holy Spirit can only be understood in the light of the paradox of the incarnation. God becomes flesh through the power of the Holy Spirit. The seeming paradox of the Holy Spirit is only the out-working of the paradox of the incarnation.

Pneumatology cannot be possible without Christology. Christology needs pneumatology to make it complete. This is what Tillich menas when he writes:

> Like every theological symbol, the Trinitarian symbolism must be understood as an answer to the question implied in man's predicament. It is the most inclusive answer and rightly has the dignity attributed to it in the liturgical practice of the church.[45]

The trinitarian doctrine is best expressed not in the dogma of the church, but in its liturgical practice. In the theological struggle of the early church, one can see the development from the strict unitarianism of the Jewish church to a bitarianism, where Christ the Logos is one in essence with God, to a fully developed Trinitarianism, where there are three persons in the one

Godhead. This came to a head in the Council of Nicea, A.D. 325, and was finally affirmed in the second ecumenical synod.

The synod of Constantinople further refined the concept of the Trinity:

> Led by the Cappadocian Fathers, especially Gregory of Nazianzus, it made sharper distinctions between the concepts than were used in the trinitarian dogma. . . . The Father has the property of being ungenerated. He is from eternity to eternity. The Son has the characteristic of being generated. The spirit has the characteristics of proceeding from the Father and the Son. But these characteristics are not differences in the essence, but only in their relation to each other. . . . And in the Holy Spirit, the Lord and giver of life, who proceedeth from the Father, who with the Father and the Son together is worshipped and glorified.[46]

Thus we see the church struggling to frame a clear and true conception of what it is experiencing in its practice of the Christian faith. Practice creates doctrine, doctrine interprets faith, faith validates practice:

> The motive for it was again Christological. The Divine Spirit who created and determined Jesus as the Christ is not the spirit of the man Jesus: and the Divine Spirit who creates and directs the church is not the spirit of a sociological group. And the spirit who grasps and transforms the individual person is not an expression of his spiritual life. The Divine Spirit is God himself as Spirit in the Christ and through him in the church and the Christian. The consistency of this transformation of a bitarian strain in the early church into a fully developed trinity is obvious, but it did not help to solve the basic problems; How can ultimate concern be expressed in more than one divine hypostasis?[47]

Without the doctrine of the Trinity, the Christian religion becomes a mere tool for moral education. It is no accident that the Unitarian Church is excluded from the World Council of Churches.

The real meaning of the Trinity is that there is a manifoldness of divine self-manifestations. But the number three has prevailed because:

> Three corresponds to the intrinsic dialectics of experienced life and is therefore most adequate to symbolize the divine life.[48]

The chief function of the trinitarian doctrine,

> ". . . is to express in embracing symbols, the self-mainfestation of the divine life.[49]

A biblically based Trinitarianism must be grounded in a biblically based theology, Christology, and pneumatology that is theistic in nature, equally balanced and action-oriented. This must take into consideration a "Spirit Theism," a "Spirit Christology," and "Creation pneumatology." Each person of the Trinity enhances the other. There is no competition nor rivalry and no secondary or inferior member of the Godhead. The three persons of the Trinity are one in essence, one in purpose, and one in holiness.

CHAPTER VIII

Channels of Spiritual Power

What are the conditions which will induce the spiritual presence? What are the channels through which He enters the soul?

The Scriptures have not left us without guidance in this most important matter. While the Spirit of God is free to do as He chooses and to use whatever channel he desires, there is a pattern of spiritual activity that emerges on the pages of the New Testament. If one makes a careful study of the history of the early church, he will find there certain guidelines that direct one's soul to that kind of receptivity that enables the Holy Spirit to come into his life.

First, there must be a hungering and a thirsting after God. There must be a seeking and a desire for the Holy Spirit to come into one's life. This desire must be accompanied by an expectant faith and an urgent anticipation. This must be followed by fervent prayer, both individually and collectively. Finally, there must be a need and a purpose. One must ask himself, why do I want the Holy Spirit to come into my life? Do I desire Him for selfish reasons? If so, He will not enter into one's life.

The power of the Holy Spirit is different from other forms of power. Other forms of power are non-moral. That is, they may be used for either good or ill. The power of the Holy Spirit is only available to those who desire to glorify God. The Holy Spirit is the spirit of righteousness. It is the power to obey God. What is the nature and purpose of power? Power is the ability to change one's condition. It is the possession of strength to achieve one's desires: the ability to act, to sustain, and to build up. It is the physical, mental, moral, and spiritual capacity to act according to one's own discretion. It is the faculty of performing something. It is the ability to act and react to stimuli. It is influence and control over others. It is exerting authority. Power is freedom to be and to do. In order to be free, one must possess a degree of physical, mental, and moral power. It is being directed from within. Real power can only be measured by the internal quality of the person. There is a difference between force and real power. Real power must have both an intellectual and moral dimension. It must be grounded in the spiritual qualities of the human soul.

This brings us to the purpose of power. As to purpose, there are two kinds of power: Divine power and demonic power. Demonic power is the wanton, destructive, discreative use of power. It is power in rebellion against the Creator and the created. It seeks to maintain itself by turning in upon itself. By so doing, it becomes self-destructive. Demonic power carries within itself the seed of its own destruction.

Divine power is that which perpetuates itself by reaching beyond itself. It receives by giving of itself. It grows by sharing. It finds itself by losing itself. It brings order out of chaos, light out of darkness, and life out of death. The purpose of divine power is to make all things new.

> When anyone is joined to Christ, he is a new being; the old is gone, the new has come. All this is done by God, who, through Christ, changed us from enemies into his friends, and gave us the task of making others his friends also.[1]

This is the purpose of the Holy Spirit in the church. He renews our faith, rekindles our hope, reactivates our love, and makes effective our witness. The Spirit is Holy. This means that there is none of the demonic within Him. He is wholly good and entirely creative.

He contributes to our total well-being. He delivers us from the power of non-being. The Holy Spirit is the power of the presence of God in Christ working within the human heart. He is the power of God overcoming the demonic force within me. He is the power of God through Christ, recreating and redeeming the total personality. He is the Divine Spirit, creating and sustaining the spiritual community. He is the Holy Spirit that transforms the church organization into a living organism. It is through Him that the Christian church becomes the Body of Christ.

In the nineteenth chapter of Acts, we find a church that had not yet become the body of Christ.

> While Apollos was in Corinth, Paul traveled through the interior of the province and arrived in Ephesus. There he found some disciples and asked them, "Did you receive the Holy Spirit when you believed?" "We have not even heard that there is a Holy Spirit," they answered. "Well then, what kind of Baptism did you receive?" Paul asked. "The Baptism of John," they answered. The Baptism of John was for those who turned from their sins and John told the people of Israel that they should believe in the one who was coming after him—that is, Jesus. When they heard this, they were baptized in the name of the Lord Jesus Christ. Paul placed his hands on them and the Holy Spirit came upon them and they talked with strange sounds and also spoke God's word.[2]

These people were followers of John the Baptist, but they were not fully Christian. They lived in the twilight of the Christian faith. They had been baptized into a form of religious fellowship that was very close, but not quite Christian. They had not been baptized in the name of Jesus; that is, in the name of the Blessed Trinity. Here Paul puts his finger upon the requirement for receiving the Holy Spirit—baptism in the name of Jesus. Not only did Paul baptize them in the name of Jesus, he placed his hands on them, and the Holy Spirit came upon them. The clear implication here is that water baptism in the name of Jesus must be accompanied by the baptism of the Holy Spirit.

Baptism is the doorway into the spiritual community. The saving power of the Holy Spirit includes Christian baptism. The Holy Spirit creates faith in the Lordship of Christ. Then comes baptism as an expression of that faith. The Holy Spirit also empowers us to serve and to witness. Where the Spirit of God is, there is freedom. Who are we to hold God to a set procedure? God saves whom He wills in the way He wills. Notwithstanding, the New Testament pattern seems to be as stated above.

If one is saved by faith alone, how does this relate to the coming of the Spirit? Is the Holy Spirit essential to salvation? The Holy Spirit is necessary to salvation. Salvation must be seen as a process, not just an incident or an act. As Christians, we are being saved.

It is the Holy Spirit that makes our religion a living experience. Without Him, worship is empty. Ceremony is nothing more than a vain show and Christian ritual is meaningless. It is the Holy Spirit that transforms dead doctrine into living truth. He gives cohesiveness to the church. He makes our faith vital and our witness effective.

The Holy Spirit works through the Word to prepare the heart to receive the Gospel message. It is He who gives the Gospel its power. Before the day of Pentecost, Peter and John and the other apostles were a group of ordinary men. Once endowed with the Holy Spirit, they became giants of wisdom and power, who, by their preaching, laid the foundations for a new world religion. It was the Holy Spirit who created the spiritual community.

> Many of them believed his message and were baptized, about three thousand people were added to the group that day. They spent their time in learning from the apostles, taking part in the fellowship and sharing in the fellowship meal and the prayer. Many miracles and wonders were done through the apostles, which caused everyone to be filled with awe.[3]

This spiritual community was something new. It was not the work of the apostles alone. They were only instruments, channels, and agents through which the Holy Spirit worked to perform His new creation. The miracles that were wrought were done in the name of Christ. The Holy Spirit made them aware that Jesus, their resurrected Lord, was dwelling among them.

Not everyone who belonged to the early church was a member of the spiritual community. Only those who participated in the Pentecostal experience were able to live the Pentecostal life. There were those who were attracted to the church for sundry reasons. Some of them, no doubt, later shared the Pentecostal experience, thus becoming a part of the spiritual community. There were those who remained in the church but never became a part of the spiritual community. Luke tells us that:

> There was a man named Ananias whose wife's name was Sapphira. He sold some property that belonged to them but kept part of the money for himself as his wife knew, and turned the rest over to the apostles. Peter said to him, "Ananias, why did you let Satan take control of your heart and make you lie to the Holy Spirit by keeping back part of the money?"[4]

Ananias and Sapphira failed in their efforts to live the Pentecostal life, because they had not been changed by the power of the Holy Spirit.

Our first task as Christians is to get all of the members of the church to share the Pentecostal experience. Only by so doing will they be able to live the Pentecostal life. Only then can they become a part of the spiritual community. Only then will the church have power to transform the kingdoms of this world into the Kingdom of God and His Christ.

The church creates the spiritual community through the effectiveness of its witness.

> When people heard this, they were deeply troubled and said to Peter and the other apostles, "What shall we do, brother?" Peter said to them, "Turn away from your sins, each of you, and be baptized in the name of Jesus Christ, so that your sins will be forgiven and you will receive the Holy Spirit. . . . " Peter made his appeal to them and with many other words, he urged them saying, "Save yourselves from the punishment coming to this wicked people."[5]

The apostle's testimony was effective because it was Christ-centered and spirit-filled. The church today vacillates between individualistic pietism on the one hand and social gospel on the other. We need to realize that these are not mutually exclusive. They are both a part of the Christian gospel. Any effective testimony must include both. The church today needs to return to a Christ-centered, spirit-filled gospel. Such a gospel is both social and personal. It seeks to meet the needs of life in all of its varied dimensions.

How can one receive the Holy Spirit? How can we avail ourselves of this life-transforming experience? No man can save himself. The Holy Spirit is a gift from God to the believing heart. No man can earn it. No man is worthy to receive it. It is God's gift. God is at work in human history. God has a purpose for every life. Therefore, if we commit ourselves to Him in faith, He comes to us. He will reveal Himself to us. He will make his will known to us. We must believe that God is and that He will save all those who turn to Him in faith.

> This promise was made not because Abraham obeyed the Law, but because he believed and was accepted as righteous by God. For if what God promises is to be given to those who obey the law, then man's faith means nothing, and God's promise is worthless . . . The promise was based on faith in order that the promise should be guaranteed as God's free gift. . . . For we conclude that a man is put right with God only through faith.[6]

The Holy Spirit is the power of the presence of God in Christ. He is the promised gift that Christ sent to comfort His church.

> Nevertheless I tell you the truth; it is expedient for you that I go away; for if I go not away, the comforter will not come unto you, but if I depart, I will send him unto you. . . . Howbeit when he, the Spirit of truth, is come, he will guide you into all truth.[7]

Jesus taught his disciples many things. Because of the dullness of their spirit, there was much of His teaching that they could not understand. Therefore, Jesus promised to send them a comforter, a teacher, and a guide. The task of the Holy Spirit is to continue the work begun by Jesus. He is to continue and complete the unfinished training of the twelve apostles and Christian believers who would come after them. The Holy Spirit is not only a teacher and a guide; he is also an inspirer of prophecy. "He will declare to you things that are to come." The Holy Spirit is a spirit of prophecy. In the midst of all of the trials and tribulations of all of the ages to come, in spite of the apostasy, corruption, and persecution, He remains with the church, inspiring the sages of every generation with the vision of the Lamb of God who taketh away the sins of the world.

CHRISTIAN CONVERSION IS THE KEY TO A SPIRIT-FILLED LIFE:

> Jesus answered, "I tell you the truth; no one can see the Kingdom of God unless he is born again." How can a grown man be born again? . . . "I tell you the truth," replied Jesus, "that no one can enter the Kingdom of God unless he is born of water and the Spirit."[8]

This rebirth is called Christian conversion. What is Christian conversion? Harold DeWolf describes it as follows:

> The spiritual rebirth must come if the life in communion with God is to be entered. How it is to come cannot be determined by any formula. We cannot say when or how fast everyone must be reborn. Neither can we say that in everyone the new birth will appear as a radical reverse of direction.

Channels of Spiritual Power

> The Spirit works in many different ways in different lives. But let no one say that because the change may occur slowly or in the secrecy of the heart, it has not occurred at all. For if the soul is to enter into communion with God, then there must come sometime, somehow, the soul's awakening to solemn responsibility before God and the commitment of the soul to side with Him and by his grace to wage unceasing war against evil in the self and in the world.[9]

Although conversion is not the same in all persons, there are certain general signs that follow it. Usually, our deep feelings of guilt are removed. It increases our capacity to become concerned about the well-being of others. It makes one more cooperative with others. One becomes more interested in real achievement than in the praises of men. He becomes more interested in pleasing God than men. Conversion gives to one a new conception of himself. It settles once and for all the question of one's supreme allegiance. It gives to him an organizing principle for his life. This, in brief, is what we mean by conversion. Once this happens in the life of the individual, he becomes a new person. The Holy Spirit takes control of his life. It brings a new source of power.

When the Holy Spirit comes into our lives, our task is by no means over. We must keep the channels of the heart open to the guidance of the Holy Spirit. This is done by prayer. What is prayer? It is the work of the Holy Spirit within us. Prayer is based upon the belief that God exercises a guiding control over the affairs of every living creature—that He has a special interest in every human being. The God who maintains all the heavenly spheres in their courses is the same by whom, "Even the hairs of your head are all numbered."[10]

Modern science has created some difficulty in the belief that God can act upon a specific concern for particular individuals at particular times and places. Yet men still believe in special providence, in the very fact that God is the Lord of heaven and earth, that He has the power to work either through His laws or beyond them to carry out His living concern and purpose. Prayer keeps open the channel between God and the individual. Prayer keeps the soul receptive to the working of the Holy Spirit. Prayer has social benefits as well. When a man truly prays, he is more inclined to love his fellow man. It helps to create a benevolent social atmosphere. Prayer is one of the ways to expand the human consciousness without any lingering aftereffects. We are living in an age of psychedelic drugs. Modern man feels the need for the expansion of consciousness. To achieve this, men are turning to L.S.D., heroin, and other psychedelic drugs. Why is this so? Why do so many people feel the need so desperately? It is because middle-class religion in the Western world frowns upon any semblance of being fanatical about religion. Middle-class Protestant tradition does not emphasize prayer and fasting. We no longer have dreams and visions. The church needs to recapture the prayer and testimonial meetings. We need to teach our people to pray and to fast. We need to find ways of helping people to relieve their tensions during Christian worship. Prayer is the first step toward a therapeutic religion. Prayer opens the channel of religious receptivity.

What are the things that one can do to make himself receptive to the Holy Spirit? They are as follows: Have faith in Christ; Bible reading and private meditation upon it; earnest and sincere prayer; a hungering and thirsting after righteousness; fasting and praying; group prayer and corporate worship; and a desire to serve one's fellowman. If all of this is done in love, the Holy Spirit will come and dwell with you.

THE CHANNEL OF REPENTANCE

Repentance is the first channel of Spiritual Power.

> In those days came John, the Baptist, preaching in the wilderness of Judea, and saying, "Repent ye for the Kingdom of Heaven is at hand."[11]

There are three majestic mountain peaks in Christian history, namely, Jesus, Paul, and John the Baptist. John the Baptist is to the New Testament what the prophet Elijah is to the Old. He is the prophet of fire, the forerunner of the Messiah, and the herald of the New Age. He is the one who prepares the way for the advent of divine royalty. Jesus said of John:

> Among them that are born of woman, there hath not risen a greater one than John, the Baptist; Notwithstanding, he that is least in the kingdom of heaven is greater than he.[12]

One scholar calls John the "watershed" of religious history. He closes the old dispensation and opens the gate of a new era. The key to this new era is repentance. Thomas Carlyle said:

> Of all the acts of man, repentance is the most divine, the greatest of all faults is to be conscious of none.[13]

John the Baptist is the prophet of repentance. It is through the act of repentance that the soul is prepared to receive Christian salvation. Jesus said:

> I tell you nay, but except ye repent ye shall all likewise perish.[14]

It is the Holy Spirit who calls us to repentance. It reveals to us the ugliness and the treachery of our sins. It is sin that brings down upon us the divine wrath. Sin is the great destroyer.

REPENTANCE—A UNIVERSAL NEED

The Holy Spirit is calling us today to repentance. The Hebrew prophets were men of the Spirit. They were possessed by the Divine Spirit. They were used by the Holy Spirit to call the nations to repentance. Their words pealed like thunder into the ears of the nations.

Amos is one of the chief exponents of national repentance. As Amos stood in the marketplace and the temples of Samaria, he cried out:

> Thus saith the Lord, for three transgressions of Israel and for four, I will not turn away the punishment thereof, because they sold the righteous for silver, and the poor for a pair of shoes; they pant after the dust of the earth on the head of the poor.[15]

He was calling Israel to repentance. If Amos lived in America today, he would say to America, you need to repent. If you fail to repent, you cannot be saved. Because of your corruption, you shall perish like Babylon and collapse like Rome. The day of God is rapidly approaching. When that day comes, your dollar diplomacy cannot save you. Your technological know-how cannot shield you. Your stockpile of atomic weapons and guided missiles cannot protect you. I tell you, except you repent, ye shall all likewise perish. As a nation, America needs a spiritual transformation. This can be done only by the Holy Spirit. We have sown to the wind and now we are reaping the whirlwind. Repentance is the prerequisite for receiving the Holy Spirit and being transformed into a new life in Christ. It is through repentance that the Holy Spirit leads us into right relations with God, man, and society.

The Holy Spirit is calling us to personal repentance. He is calling upon us to repent of our religious hypocrisy and our spiritual indifference. Ours is an era of amorality that has given rise to hypocrisy in religion and corruption in government. It is a time of gangsterism and murder in high places. Crime is sapping the life and vitality from our economic system. The breaking of vows and the ignoring of contracts are destroying the public's confidence.

> There is no truth, no goodness, no knowledge of God in the land.[16]

Swearing, four-letter words, breaking faith, killing, stealing, adultery, superstition, prostitution, homosexuality, drunkenness, and dope have dimmed our reason and corrupted our spiritual understanding. One crime wave exceeds the other. The souls of men are corrupt; their minds, contaminated; and their consciences, dimmed. Crooked thinking and loose living have destroyed our sense of right. Our materialistic liberalism has destroyed our integrity. We respect no moral code. The dollar is our religion, and sexual pleasures are our God. Lawlessness is sweeping the nation from the highest to the lowest. A corrupt system has produced a corrupt people. If we fail to repent, this corruption will seal our doom. We have lost our sense of destiny.

> Ephraim is a silly dove, for Assyria is not able to heal you. He will not cure your wounds.[17]

Modern man has become a spiritual prostitute running after strange gods and forming philosophies and social alliances that have brought us to the very brink of destruction. When one reflects upon the economic injustice, political hypocrisy, social disintegration, and spiritual indifference in the modern world, it is impossible not to feel a profound concern for the future of modern civilization. We are no longer concerned about human freedom and social justice. Economic justice no longer demands our vigilance or motivates our actions. We have closed our eyes to the basic needs of our age. We have refused to learn the ultimate lesson of history; we have refused to heed the solemn warning of Lincoln when he said, "No nation can live half slave and half free."[18] This has a unique relevance to the modern world.

Can modern society survive; or shall it, too, like Greece and Rome, vanish like morning dew beneath the summer heat of racial bigotry and national tyranny? The only way modern man can survive is for him to repent. Shakespeare said:

> A true repentance shuns the evil itself, more than the external suffering or the shame.[19]

Repentance is the golden key that opens the palace of eternity. Our greatest glory consists not in never falling, but in rising every time we may fall. There is a future left to all men who have the virtue to repent and the energy to atone. Repentance is not just increasing our devotion but in improving our life. There is a common belief that the deathbed is the place for repentance. The man who is most likely to die a repentance death is the one who has lived a repentance life. He who takes the chance of waiting until he is ready to die to repent is playing Russian roulette with his soul. Deathbed repentance is burning the candle of life in the service of the devil, then blowing the ashes in the face of God. True repentance is being humbled for and not frightened at one's sins, and resolving to commit them no more. True repentance leads to reformation. It is to alter one's ways of looking at life. It is taking God's point of view instead of our own.

The best repentance is to get up and act for righteousness and forget that you ever had relations with sin. John Locke says:

> Repentance does not consist in one single act of sorrow, but in doing work meet for repentance, in a sincere obedience to the law of Christ for the remainder of our lives. To do it no more is the truest repentance.[20]

Channels of Spiritual Power

> Joy shall be in heaven over one sinner that repenteth more than over ninety and nine just persons, which need no repentence.[21]

Omar Khayyam writes:

> Come fill the cup, and in the fire of Spring, your winter garment of repentance fling; the bird of time has but a little way to flutter—and the bird is on the wing.[22]

Repentance is never out of date. It is as modern as the latest sin. It is the ever-present need of the soul.

Your first step in becoming a Christian is to repent of your sins. Unless one repents, everything else he does is meaningless. The Holy Spirit will not enter into an unrepentant heart.

THE NATURE OF TRUE REPENTANCE

Paul Tillich writes:

> The word "shubh" in Hebrew points to a turning around of one's way, especially in the social and political spheres. It points to a turning away from injustice toward justice, from inhumanity to humanity, from idols to God.[23]

Repentance suggests two elements. First, it means that one is going to stop being what one has been and stop doing what one has been doing. One is going to turn his life around and go in a new direction.

Just as John the Baptist prepared the way for Jesus, repentance prepares the way for Christian salvation. Without repentance, there can be no salvation. It is not enough to believe that there is a God. It is not enough to believe in the divinity of Jesus Christ. It is not enough to seek the Holy Ghost. The first thing that you must do is to repent of your sins. Salvation begins with repentance. Repentance is the gateway to salvation. It is a channel through which the Holy Spirit flows into the human soul.

True repentance consists in the heart being broken for sin and broken from sin. Some often repent, yet never reform. They resemble a man traveling on a dangerous path who frequently starts and stops but never turns back.

Repentance demands a radical change of mind, heart, and will. It looks at the past with honesty and remorse. It turns around and looks to the future with a resolve to make a new start. Repentance is the gateway to a new life.

There are two Greek words that describe two kinds of repentance. One is destructive and the other, constructive. The destructive kind has to do with simply regretting what has been done, but making no effort to undo it. It is said of Judas Iscariot that after he betrayed Christ, he repented and went out and hanged himself. This kind of repentance only compounds evil with tragedy. The Greek word used here is "apetresie," meaning simply to be sorry. There are many people who are sorry for their sins, but they do nothing to correct them. They, like Judas, only continue to compound evil with tragedy. The kind of repentance that leads to the remission of sins is that which was demonstrated by Peter on the night that he denied his Lord. When he heard the cock crow, it reminded him of the words of Jesus. He went forth and wept bitterly. This repentance was the first step toward salvation. It is expressed by the Greek word, "metanoia," which signifies a complete change of heart, soul, and mind. It is the beginning of a new life. It has to do with both a vertical relationship with God and a horizontal relationship with men. It makes possible love for God and man.

True repentance is a turning away from all forms of idolatry: racial, national, and materialistic. It is turning to God in total surrender. It means becoming a new person. Repentance is the golden key that unlocks the palace of eternity. It is making a positive response to redemption through Jesus Christ.

On the day of Pentecost, when the multitude asked:

> "What shall we do?" Peter answered, "Repent and be baptized, everyone of you in the name of Jesus Christ for the remission of your sins, and ye shall receive the gift of the Holy Ghost."[24]

St. Ambrose, one of the early church fathers, said, "True repentance is to cease from sinning."[25]

Repentance is rejecting the negative and embracing the positive. Paul Tillich says:

> The rejection of the negative with the whole of one's being is called repentance—a concept which must be freed from emotional distortion.[26]

REPENTANCE—A CHANGE OF ATTITUDE TOWARD SIN

Jesus died to make it possible for us to change. You no longer have to evade or cover up your sins. You can get rid of them. We spend much of our time and energy covering up and evading our sins. We try to evade our sins by pointing out the sins of others. We love to gossip about other people in order to take our minds away from our own faults. The thing we fail to realize is that when we have finished talking about the sin of others, our sins have grown worse. We turn to gossip and fault-finding because we do not have the courage to face our own faults. Stop wasting your time finding fault with others. Stop using the sins of others to justify your own. Only the Holy Spirit can sustain the good life. It is a human trait for man to look for someone else to blame for his sins.

The first thing that Adam did after he broke God's law was to try to find an excuse.

> God said to Adam, "Hast thou eaten of the tree whereof I commanded thee that thou shouldest not eat?" And the man said, "The woman who thou gavest to be with me, she gave me of the tree and I did eat."[27]

We, like Adam, are always looking for someone else to blame for our sins. I challenge you to stop blaming other people and repent of your sins. If your home is not happy, stop blaming the husband, or the wife, or the children. Repent of your sins.

>Get yourself right with God and He will show you how.

If your church is not what you think it ought to be, stop blaming the preacher, or the officers, or the choir, or the Presiding Elder, or the Bishop. . . . Get on your knees and cry, "It's me, it's me, it's me, O Lord, standing in the need of prayer." We spend too much time trying to whitewash our sins by blaming others. We make the mistake of trying to make our vices into virtues. If your neighbor has a fault, you will willingly call it what it is; but when you have a fault, it is only natural to try to cover up or justify it by calling it something else.

If your neighbor is stingy or not generous, you call him a tightwad or a scrooge; but if you are stingy, it's not so bad; why, you are just a careful spender and a good businessman. My friend, you cannot cover up your faults by blaming others. The only way to get rid of your sins is to repent.

Repentance is being sorry, not just because you were caught, but because you have sinned. Sin is not just against yourself or your fellow man; it is a sin against God.

When a married person breaks his marital vow, he not only sins against his mate, but he sins against God. When a church member refuses to support his church, he sins not against the church only, but against God. When one lies about another and degrades his character or causes enmity between friends, he is sinning against God. All human sin is ultimately sin against God.

The only cure for sin is Godly sorrow. If you can sin and feel good about it, then you are in spiritual danger. If you can lie about your neighbor and not feel a sense of guilt, you are in spiritual danger. Whenever you can sin and feel good about it, then you know that you are separated from God. You are in hell. The Holy Spirit will not enter your life until you repent.

The first step on the road to repentance is Godly sorrow. One must realize that every sin committed is a sin against God. Every time one sins, he breaks the heart of God. Every time one sins, he drives a nail in the hands of the crucified Christ. He thrusts anew the sword into his side. He presses the thorny crown on his head. When man sins, he crucifies Christ all over again. Not only do his sins destroy his inner peace, but they separate him from God. The only answer is repentance. Repentance is turning to God. He who turns to God must first believe that He is.

The life which you live is no accident. God made it for a purpose. It is sin that keeps us from fulfilling God's purpose for our lives.

>The soul that sinneth must die.[28]

All men are sinners. Each of us deserves to spend eternity in hell. The gospel is good news for us. Christ died for our sins. He took our place on the cross. He paid the debt we owe. If we will turn to Him in faith, Christ will forgive our sins. His blood that was shed on Calvary can cleanse us of all sins and make us Holy in the sight of God. Repentance is surrendering oneself to Christ. Even good men need to repent.

David was a man after God's own heart. He was a great King of Israel and a sweet singer of religious songs. He was a great deliverer of his people. One day, he discovered that he had committed a great sin. He had his friend Uriah killed in battle in order to get his wife. When the prophet Naaman confronted him with this awful sin, he did not try to deny it. He did not try to cover it up. He did not try to justify his faults. David repented of his sin. He went to the temple, fell down at the mercy seat before the horns of the altar, and cried out:

> Have mercy upon me, O God, according to thy loving kindness; according to the multitude of thy tender mercies, blot out my transgressions. Wash me thoroughly from mine iniquities, and cleanse me from my sin. For I acknowledge my transgression and my sin is ever before me. Against thee, thee only have I sinned and done this evil in thy sight, that thou mightest be justified when thou speakest, and be clear when thou judgest. Behold, I was shapen in iniquity, and in sin did my mother conceive me. Behold thou desirest the truth in the inward parts and in the hidden part thou shalt make me to know wisdom. Purge me with hyssop, and I shall be clean. Wash me and I shall be whiter than snow.[29]

David had the good sense to repent of his sins. It was on the Damascus road that Saul of Tarsus met Christ. Christ confronted Saul with his sins. When Saul was confronted with his sins, he turned to Christ and cried out, "Lord, what will you have me to do?"[30]

It is the duty of the church to challenge modern man to repent of his sins. The church must now allow modern man to fall headlong into the pit of destruction without warning. Where are the prophets of our modern era? Where are the John the Baptists, the Peters, the Pauls of the twentieth century? Must this modern Jerusalem fall without a Jeremiah to weep, or a Peter to preach, or a Paul to write a word of warning? Modern man has become a spiritual prostitute defiling his bed with racial animosity, secularistic imperialism, and religious indifference. The time has come for the modern prophet to call modern man to repentance.

THE CHANNEL OF SELF-SURRENDER

Self-surrender is God's answer to a world in revolution. The Holy Spirit will not enter a heart until it is surrendered to God.

> Then said Jesus unto his disciples, if any man will come after me, let him deny himself and take up his cross and follow me. For whosoever will save his life shall lose it, and whosoever will lose his life for my sake shall find it.[31]

The Holy Spirit is God's answer to a world in revolution. The Holy spirit creates a special kind of revolution, a revolution from within. The revolution from within is the key that can unlock the door to world peace and prosperity. It begins with the self. The perennial problem with the world is everybody thinks of changing humanity, but nobody thinks of changing himself.

Selfishness is the root and source of all social and moral evil. The thing that made Satan the devil was that he was so intensely selfish that he would rather reign in hell than to serve in heaaven.

It was St. Augustine who said:

> The world is controlled by two parties . . . those who have governed by love of self to the point of contempt of God and those who have governed by love of God to the point of contempt of self.[32]

Self-presevation is the first law of nature, but self-denial is the highest rule of grace. To exalt Christ is to reject self. Only the Holy Spirit can give us the power of self-rejection.

Mankind will never learn to live in peace and creative goodwill toward each other until he learns to reject self. Therefore, what we need in this world is a new kind of revolution: a revolution from within—a revolution created by the Holy Spirit. The trouble with our world is that it is forever changing and yet forever remaining the same. What our world needs is a new kind of revolution—a revolution that changes the inner man. This revolution can only be brought about by surrendering the self to Christ.

The Christian religion is a revolutinary faith. The Christian message seeks to revolutionalize the world by beginning with the self.

There are two kinds of revolutions: the revolution from within, and the revolution from without. The revolution from without changes the world, but leaves it basically the same. It changes the forms of government, social structures, the names of empires, and the rulers who govern them, but the world remains basically the same. History is filled with man's futile attempt to change human society in this way.

As we turn the pages of history, we are both startled and saddened by the vast number of idealistic and righteous revolutionaries who have become disenchanted, disappointed, and disillusioned because their best efforts to revolutionize society have failed.

The great French Revolution had its beginning in the noble ideas and high purposes expressed by Voltaire, Rousseau, and many of the Renaissance scholars. But in spite of this noble beginning, the French Revolution ended in Napoleonic despotism. The American Civil War was a magnanimous effort to realize the teachings of Christ and the dreams of the founding fathers. It was America's grand attempt to make itself truly the land of the free and the home of the brave. But it ended in white racism and black oppression, almost as vicious as slavery itself. Marxian socialism was a great dream—a lofty effort to eradicate oppression and achieve human equality—but this, too, ended in Russian imperialism and atheistic materialism.

Martin Luther King and the Civil Rights movement were the Black man's attempt to realize the beatific vision of a Christian society, but Martin Luther King was felled by a bullet in his head and the Civil Rights movement was brought to a standstill.

As we turn the pages of history, we are faced with the disturbing truth that mankind's most cherished dreams have turned to ashes. Why? Because he failed to begin at the beginning. He started in the wrong place. Every successful revolution, be it social, psychological, or economical, must begin with the human self at the foot of the cross. Only as the Holy Spirit works within us to change us, can we change the world. Holy Ghost power is the New Testament's answer to a world in revolution.

> Then said Jesus to His disciples, if any man will come after me, let him deny himself and take up his cross and follow me.[33]

When Jesus uttered these words, to what was He referring? What is the self? The self is the union of the basic elements that constitute individuality, identity, and personality. Someone has said that the human self is a blending of two worlds—the world of essence and the world of existence. The world of essence is the world of pure being, perfect spirit, and uncontaminated ideas.

It is the world in which all things fit together in harmonious relations. This is the kind of world to which Jesus was pointing when he taught his disciples to pray:

> Thy kingdom come, Thy will be done, on earth as it is in heaven.[34]

Paul gives us a glimpse of this world when he declares:

> When this earthly tabernacle is dissolved, I have a building of God, not made with hands, eternal in the heavens.[35]

John, the revelator, foretells the fulfillment of man's dream to live in this perfect world when he declares, "I saw a new heaven and a new earth coming down from God out of heaven."[36]

Man's sociology is often determined by his eschatology. He often strives to shape his present world to conform to his dream of spiritual utopia.

The human self, however, is not only the product of man's beatific vision; it is a composite of two worlds—the world of essence and the world of existence. This world of existence is the one in which we live. It is one that is buffeted about by the contending forces of being and nonbeing, good and evil, right and wrong, joy and sorrow, light and darkness, smiles and tears.

It is the world in which goodness is engaged in a bloody conflict with evil. The human self is caught up in this bloody struggle. The human self must find a way to emerge victorious from the struggle. It must find the strength to continue to engage in the struggle. The Holy Spirit teaches us that the only way that the self can win the victory is through surrender to Christ. Then said Jesus to his disciples, "If any man cometh after me, let him deny himself, take up his cross and follow me."[37]

Every human problem can be solved at the foot of the cross. Every human need, every human desire, every human guilt, all of our human aspirations, longings, strivings, and fears can be rectified, purified, and glorified by the power of the Holy Spirit.

The self is man's greatest problem. Your greatest problem is yourself. All of your sins are rooted in the self as the fingers are rooted in the palm of your hand. All of the crimes in the nation, Watergate, violence in the streets, corruption in high places, racism, tribalism, nationalism, religious animosity, and class struggle can all be traced to their roots in the self.

E. Stanley Jones puts it this way:

> Why do we get angry and blow our top? Because someone has crossed the self. Why do we lie? Because we think it would be of some advantage to the self. Why are we dishonest? For the same reason. Why are we impure? Because we think it will be of some pleasure to the self. Why are we jealous or envious? Because we think that someone is getting ahead of the self. All of these outer sins are only symptoms of a diseased self. The sin-sick self is humanity's greatest problem.[38]

The poet must have been struggling with this problem when he wrote, "I have to live with myself and so I want to be fit for myself to know."[39]

How does one make himself fit for himself to know? This is the most complicated riddle of all history. He who unravels the riddle of the self discovers the key to both time and eternity.

The most searching and most provocative question that you can ask is, What shall I do with myself? The self is your greatest problem. It is your inevitable and eternal challenge. Only the Holy Spirit can solve this problem. He enters into the human spirit and transforms the self from a battleground of emotional conflict into the city of God in miniature.

There are three classic answers that have been given to the eternal question of the self. The first was formulated by Socrates, the father of Greek philosophy. The second was given by Marcus Aurelius, the most noble soul of Rome. The third is offered by Jesus of Nazareth, the most sublime spirit in all history. Let us take a look at these classical answers for a moment.

It was Socrates, the father of Greek philosophy, who said, know thyself.

The chief study of man is man. Man's chief concern is not mathematical abstraction as the Pythagoreans would have us believe. It is not the atomic properties of nature as Democrates would have us think. The chief study of man is not the great galaxies in the starry heaven, nor the lesser creatures that crawl upon the earth, nor the great monsters that swim in the deep, nor the fowls that inhabit the stratosphere. The chief study of man is man. Know thyself, says Socrates.

This saying of Socrates has much truth in it. It is a wise insight. It represents one of the great revolutions in the world of human thought. It is a deep insight into the nature of human reality. This answer by Socrates, as full of the truth as it is, is not sufficient. It is the truth, but not the whole truth. It is based upon three false assumptions. Socrates assumed that: (1) By the power of the human understanding, man could reveal himself to himself. (2) By the searchlight of human reason, man can discover what is wrong with himself. (3) By the enlightened and determined will, man can make right that which is wrong with himself.

The Bible teaches us that these are false assumptions; therefore, the writer of the book of Proverbs reminds us:

> Trust in the Lord with all of thine heart and lean not unto thine own understanding. . . . In all thy ways acknowledge him and he shall direct thy path.[40]

Job says:

> Acquaint now thyself with him and be at peace; Thereby good shall come unto thee.[41]

The searchlight of human reason cannot reveal the depth of human depravity. Only when we see ourselves through the eyes of God can we see how sinful we are. An enlightened and determined will cannot lift us to the height of divine potentiality. Man cannot lift himself out of the quagmire of sin. He can only be lifted by the power of the Holy Spirit.

The answer to the riddle of the self is hidden in the secret pavillion of divine wisdom.

> The fear of the Lord is the beginning of wisdom—a good understanding have they who keep his commandment.[42]

These false assumptions of Socrates are at the heart of man's failure to build a better world. For more than two thousand years, the Western world has acted upon these false assumptions. Age after age, man has been preoccupied with the study of man. He has written history, collected data, performed diagnosis, prognosis, and psychoanalysis. He has philosophized, theologized, psychologized, and socialized; yet the problem of the self remains unsolved and human society remains corrupt. Jesus Christ is saying to his modern disciples, you shall receive power after the Holy Spirit has come upon you. The first thing that the Holy Spirit does is to lead one to surrender himself to God.

Marcus Aurelius, another great philosopher, the wisest and most courageous soul of Rome, went about teaching men the need of self-control. He believed in the power of the will to correct and control the self. He thought that the enlightened and resolute will could cure the disease of the self. Marcus Aurelius assumed that man had power to will, the will of God. He misunderstood the nature of man; rather, it is the self that controls the will and not vice versa. Therefore, if the self is diseased, the will is also sick. Only the power of the Holy Spirit can cure the diseased will by transforming the self. The self can only be redeemed and controlled by the spirit of the risen Christ within us.

This is what the Apostle Paul is trying to teach us when he writes:

> For I know that within me dwelleth no good thing. For to will is present with me, but how to perform that which is good, I find not, in the good I would, I do not; but the evil which I would not, that I do. . . . I find then a law that when I would do good, evil is present with me.[43]

Yes, the self is sick unto death, and no amount of human effort can change that. No amount of human medication can cure that. This was true in the days of the Roman Empire. It is still true today. Only the power of the Holy Spirit can change and purify our corrupt self and our corrupt society.

Our society, like Rome of old, is dying from the lack of self-control. Our ship of state has been cut loose from its moral moorings and is floating dangerously in the midst of hiding rocks and treacherous shoals of moral degradation.

We live today in a permissive and promiscuous society. Anything goes. Homosexuality, lesbianism, wife-swapping, divorce, stealing, lying, cheating, gambling, drunkenness, dope addiction—you name it, we have it.

The sins of modern society would make Sodom and Gomorrah look like child's play. What is the answer? The only answer is Christ. Jesus said, "Ye shall receive power after the Holy Spirit is come upon you."[44]
Then, and only then, will we be able to change our society.

All of the new laws that are passed, all of the new methods of crime prevention and detection will avail for nought unless men are controlled from within. Only Christ can give us that something within that holds the reins. That something within is none other than the third person of the Holy Trinity.

If you would learn self-mastery, begin by yielding yourself to the one great master, Jesus Christ.

We live in an age when self-control is a hateful thing. We place our emphasis upon achievement. Self-control without achievement is nothing. But, achievement without self-control is worse. Until a man learns to conquer himself, he is still a slave to all things. The domain of one's self is the greatest empire that a man can conquer. To be a slave to your own passion is the most abominable kind of slavery. He who is the king of himself and the master of his own passion is the greatest conqueror that the world has seen.

This brings us to the final classical answer to the problem of the self.

> And Jesus said to His disciples, "If any man will come after me, let him deny himself and take up his cross and follow me."[45]

Our world is sick. It is sick with sin. It is sick unto death; Jesus is the only balm of Gilead that can heal the sin-sick soul. The blood of Jesus is the only medicine that can make the wounded whole. The Holy Spirit is the only power that can change the world. Your greatest problem is not your husband, nor your wife, nor your children, nor your relatives, nor your boss, nor your co-workers, but you. Not your school, but you. Not the teachers, but you. Not your church, but you. Not the neighbor, but you. What you need to do is to bring your sin-sick self to the foot of the cross and cry out, "It's me, it's me, it's me, O Lord, standing in the need of prayer."[46]

When Jesus met the Samaritan woman at the well, she was willing to talk about many things. They talked about racism:

> Then saith the woman of Samaria, how is it that thou being a Jew asketh drink of me which am a woman of Samaria?[47]

They talked about religious bigotry:

> Our fathers worshiped in this mountain and you say in Jerusalem is where men ought to worship.[48]

They talked about their common heritage:

> Art thou greater than our father Jacob who gave us this well?[49]

As important as these things were, Jesus knew that the most important thing in this woman's life was herself; therefore, Jesus kept on talking to her until he got her to see herself. It was only after Jesus got her to see herself, was this woman able to go back into the city and cry out, "Come, see a man which told me all things that ever I did, surely he is the Christ."[50]

The Holy Spirit within us is the only complete and sufficient answer to the problem of the self. The only way to solve the problem of self is by surrendering the self to God through Christ and the empowerment of the self with the Spirit of Christ. The prophet Isaiah was among the elite of his day. He was a man of noble heritage and much learning, but he spent many of his years in the twilight zone of religion. He declares that:

> In the year that King Uzziah died, I also saw the Lord sitting up on a throne high and lifted up and his train filled the temple.[51]

In response to the divine call, Isaiah surrendered himself to God; it was then that God introduced Isaiah to himself. For the first time in his life, Isaiah saw himself as he really was.

> Then said Isaiah, "Woe is me for I am undone because I am a man of unclean lips and I dwell in the midst of a people of unclean lips. For mine eyes have seen the King, the Lord of hosts."[52]

The Holy Spirit is God's answer to a world in revolution. Do you want a better family? A better society? A better church? A better nation? Then bring yourself to the foot of the cross—and let the blood of Christ wash and make you clean.

Open your heart to the Holy Spirit and pray with S. Longfellow:

> Holy Spirit, truth divine,
> Dawn upon this soul of mine;
> Word of God and inward light,
> Wake my spirit, clear my sight:
> Holy Spirit, love divine,
> Glow within this heart of mine,
> Kindle every high desire,
> Perish self in thy pure fire.
> By thee may I strongly, bravely, bear and nobly strive;
> Holy Spirit, right divine,
> King within my conscience reign,
> Be my Lord, I shall be forever bound, forever free.[53]

A SPIRIT-FILLED LIFE

How can one know when the Holy Spirit is working in his life? The one way to know is by studying the lives of spirit-filled men. There are many spiritual biographies recorded in sacred scripture.

Nowhere in sacred scripture is the power of the Holy Spirit demonstrated more vividly than in the life of the apostle Paul (or Saul of Tarsus).

Saul is exhibit A of a soul in rebellion against God (before his conversion). He represents the demonic forces at their strongest. Saul was not what the world would consider an evil person. He was a decent, well-educated, deeply moral, highly religious, culturally refined, brilliant, young man. He was a Pharisee of the Pharasees. He was brought up in the strict observance of the Hebrew faith. If there were one person who could get to heaven without being born again, Saul was that person. Yet, Saul represented a soul in rebellion against God. He was rebelling against God in the name of God. Saul was trying to live by the law and not by grace. He thought man could save himself by knowing the law. He sought salvation through the keeping of the law. This produced a deep sense of guilt and tension that drove Saul to a kind of religious fanaticism that caused him to participate in the persecution of the Christians. The supreme religious danger is that we who are religious may find ourselves fighting against God and persecuting God's people, all in the name of religion.

Much of the frustration and tension of our times are due to this same contradiction. Jews persecute Christians and Christians persecute Jews, Catholics persecute Protestants and Christians persecute Moslems, and Moslems persecute Christians, all in the name of God. History is filled with incidents where the demonic forces of evil use the religious institution to fight against God. Whenever this occurs, it creates tension and frustration. Yet, God is at work in history. The Holy Spirit works among the tension and frustrations of human society for the purpose of calling man and society to repentance. The Holy Spirit was at work in the life of Saul bringing him to the point of conversion. Saul was on his way to Damascus to search out Christians and to bring them bound to Jerusalem. He describes what happens as follows:

> . . . and as I was traveling and coming near Damascus about mid-day, a bright light suddenly flashed from the sky around me. I fell to the ground and heard a voice saying to me, "Saul, Saul, why do you persecute me?" "Who are you Lord?", I asked. "I am Jesus of Nazareth whom you persecute," he said to me. The men with me saw the light but did not hear the voice of the one who was speaking to me. I asked, "What shall I do, Lord?" And the Lord said to me, "Get up and go into Damascus, and there you will be told everything that God has determined for you to do." I was blind because of the bright light and so my companions took me by the hand and led me into Damascus.[54]

Someone has said that the lightning that does the most damage is not that which we see in the sky. That is only a thin and weak streak. The lightning in the sky is called the leader, but that which follows is from the earth below. It is this that is most powerful. The light from heaven was the leader; it gave rise to the lightning from below in the heart of Saul. The Holy Spirit from above generates the Holy Spirit within. This broke the chain of demonic power within the heart of Saul and caused him to discover his spiritual blindness.

The physical blindness of which Saul spoke is only symptomatic of a deeper spiritual blindness. Saul realized that this was no ordinary experience—that he was for the first time face-to-face with God. Saul knew that this was a divine human encounter that would change his entire being. When Saul heard the voice, he knew that it was the voice of God. He also learned that the voice of God is at once the voice of Jesus of Nazareth. It was here that Saul learned that God was in Christ reconciling the world unto himself. This is why Saul could reply, "Who are you Lord?" Saul's statement is both a question and an affirmation. The one whom he met on that Damascus road is Lord and Savior. That Jesus of Nazareth is also God of human history and Lord of human life. How did Saul know this? The Holy Spirit taught him. It was the Holy Spirit that revealed to Saul his spiritual blindness. The tragedy of spiritual blindness is that the person does not know that he is blind. Saul had many previous opportunities to accept Christ and refused. Any man who refuses to accept Christ is blind. Only the light from heaven can reveal the darkness within. Saul was spiritually blind but did not know it. Man, in his fallen state, is deficient both in mind and in will. He cannot know the will of God; neither does he have the will to obey God. Saul, with all of his powerful intellect and great learning, did not know God. With all of his dedication to the law, he could not obey God. He could not will to will the will of God. When the Holy Spirit, as the light from heaven, invades the soul, it enlightens the mind and empowers the will. Saul became a changed man. The Damascus road experience dramatizes what happens when the light from heaven invades the human soul. This light may come suddenly or gradually. In either case, the results are the same. When it comes, it reveals to us our blindness, our lostness, and our sinfulness.

> Come Father, Son and Holy Ghost
> And seal me Thine abode.
> Let all I am in Thee be lost.
> Let all be lost in God.
>
> The sanctifying power pour,
> To quench my thirst and wash me clean.
> Now saviour let the gracious shower
> Descend, and make me pure from sin.[55]

It teaches us that in spite of our lostness, our sinfulness, God loves us and gave himself for our salvation. If we will only stop to listen, we can hear God speak to us as he spoke to Saul on that Damascus road. He is calling us to surrender, to repentance, and to a new life.

In this Damascus road experience, we see a soul in transition—a personality in process of change. On that Damascus road, God spoke his final word to Saul. God speaks to us in many ways. He speaks to us through nature.

> The heavens declare the glory of God; the firmament showeth forth his handiwork.[56]

God speaks to us through the human consciousness. God speaks to us through his word, the Bible. God speaks his final word through his son, Jesus Christ. When God spoke to Saul, he stopped him in his tracks and he fell to the ground. Sometimes, God has to knock us down before we will stop and listen. Sometimes, he knocks us down with sorrows.

> In the year that King Uzziah died, I saw the Lord.[57]

God knocked Isaiah down with sorrow. God knocked the nation of Judah down with Babylonian captivity. As Saul lay prostrate and blind upon the ground, he felt the need of knowing God. He cried out, "Who art thou, Lord?" As he lay there, God revealed Himself to Saul. "I am Jesus of Nazareth, whom thou persecuteth." When God introduces Himself to you as the Christ, He gives you a new outlook, a new purpose, and a new philosophy of life. Saul says that those who were with him saw the light. They knew that a change had taken place in the life of Saul. When the Holy Spirit comes into your life, people around you can see a change in your life.

The Damascus road experience dramatizes the miracle of a soul transformed by the indwelling spirit.

> It is no longer I that live, but Christ that liveth in me.[58]

Saul became a new man.

> Behold old things have passed away; all things are made new.[59]

Saul received a new direction for his life.

> I asked, "what shall I do Lord?" And the Lord said to me, "Get up and go into Damascus and there you will be told everything that God has determined for you to do."[60]

God gives direction through His church.

The Pentecostal movement is a gift of God to His church. It needs the guidance and the counsel that the church can give. The Pentecostal experience must be judged by the church. Without the sanctifying influence of the church, the charismatic movement becomes corrupt, narrow, and nothing more than empty emotion. When a soul is filled with the Holy Spirit, he seeks the fellowship of Christian believers. He is willing to be led by the man of God. He hungers for the fellowship of Christian believers.

Nothing is more effective than a life filled with the Holy Spirit. The apostle Paul is exhibit "A" of what the Holy Spirit can do with one life that is filled with the Holy Spirit. Paul was lost in Christ with God. He, more than any other one person in history except Christ himself, has done the most to spread the Gospel of the Christian Church.

Any life that is totally surrendered to God in Christ can become an effective channel of spiritual power.

A SPIRIT-FILLED CHURCH

> But ye shall receive power after the Holy Ghost is come upon you. And ye shall be witnesses unto me both in Jerusalem and Judea, and in Samaria, and unto the uttermost parts of the earth.[61]

The most pressing need of our age is a Spirit-filled church. It is the only organism that can give birth to a new and better civilization. We are living in the twilight of history. Our world today is suspended between two civilizations: one is sick and dying, and the other is powerless to be born. Ours is a sick world. It is sick with sin, stifled by racism, and handicapped by nationalism. The "have nations" are suffocated by capitalistic abundance, while the "have not nations" are being betrayed by communistic promises and neocolonialistic intrigue. They are being bewitched by atheistic materialism and abject poverty. Our modern culture is dying because we are cut off from our roots. No amount of racist backlash, generated by reactionary demagogues and hatemongers, can restore its tarnished grandeur. Our civilization needs to be renewed, reformed, and revolutionalized by the power of the Holy Spirit.

There is a new world developing in the womb of divine providence. At the moment, there seems to be no power sufficient to deliver it. There is no midwife to cut the umbilical cord. Many martyr saints and sages have tried to give birth but failed. Ghandi, Nkrwmah, John and Robert Kennedy, Martin Luther King, Medger Evers, and a host of others have given their lives to bring this new world into being, but it is yet to come forth. Only the Holy Spirit working through the church can deliver it. Why is the Christian church failing to give birth to this new world? Because the church is too weak, too sterile, and too complacent. The church itself needs a rebirth in Spirit. Only the Holy Spirit working through the church can give birth to a new age of ethnic unity, and economic and social justice. Only the Holy Spirit can fill the human soul with love. Only He can teach each nation and tribe how to love each other. A Spirit-filled church going forth to witness to the Lordship of Christ is the greatest need of our age. The church has been weak too long. It needs power—Holy Ghost Power.

ON BEING FILLED WITH THE HOLY SPIRIT

> And it came to pass on the morrow, that their rulers and elders, and scribes, and Annas the high priest, and Caiaphas, and John and Alexander, and as many as were of the kindred of the high priest, were gathered together at Jerusalem. And when they had set them in the midst, they asked, "By what power, or by what name, have ye done this?" Then Peter, filled with the Holy Ghost, said unto them, "Ye rulers of the people, and elders of Israel, if we this day be examined of the good deed done to the impotent man, by what means he is made whole; Be it known unto you all, and to all the people of Israel, that by the name of Jesus Christ of Nazareth, whom ye crucified, whom God raised from the dead, even by him doth this man stand here before you whole. This is the stone which was set at nought of you builders, which is become the head of the corner. Neither is there salvation in any other: for there is none other name under heaven given among men, whereby we must be saved."[62]

In this chapter, we see Peter, who is being filled once more with the Holy Spirit. He had been filled on the day of Pentecost, and now he is being filled again. Why? Because a fresh refilling was necessary to accomplish this new and specific task. He had refused to obey the order of the authorities and kept on preaching Christ. This annoyed the Jews. Instead of Peter kowtowing to the authorities, he stood up with holy boldness and continued to preach Christ. It was because he was filled once more with the power of the Holy Spirit that he was able to defy the status quo.

David M. Howard tells this story:

> I had a friend in Columbia named Lupercio Tabe, who was a fearless pastor. One Sunday, he was preaching from his pulpit when a man appeared at a side window of the church, aimed a pistol at Lupercio and ordered him to stop preaching. The Congregation, seeing the danger, dove to the floor and hid under the pews. Lupercio, however, never flinched. He went right on preaching the Gospel. The man fired four times at him. Two shots went past his head, one on one side, one on the other, and lodged in the wall behind him. Two shots went past his body, one under one arm, one under the other, and also lodged in the wall. The would-be assassin then dropped his gun and fled, Lupercio, still unmoved, continued to preach.[63]

Such a reaction is not natural, to put it mildly. It could only have been a special filling of the Holy Spirit which enabled him to face the danger of death with unflinching coolness and continue the preaching of the Word with boldness.

The history of the Christian religion is filled with the heroism of men and women who have been filled and refilled with the power of the Holy Spirit.

Christian history abounds with incidents and achievements caused by the church's having been refilled with the power of the Holy Spirit. In our own American history, just before the Great Awakening, a deterministic, rigidly scholastic puritanism had caused dry rot to undermine the power of the church. The church was lifeless and ineffective. The Gospel, itself, was suffering. It was during this time that the church went back to the Bible and rediscovered the dynamics of New Testament living. The church was filled once more with the power of the Holy Spirit. It was then that they realized a new type of dynamic evangelism, that provided one of the greatest achievements of Christian expression since apostolic time.

The church today needs to be refilled with the power of the Holy spirit. The church cannot stand still. Our evangelistic efforts and our theological explanations must be based upon our personal encounter with God. It must be driven by the power of the Holy Spirit. The greatest need of our age is a Spirit-filled church, which inspires boldness in witness, holiness in living, and soundness in doctrine.

Once we have come to our best definition and clearest interpretation and understanding of the great doctrines through prayerful study, let us still sing with the poet:

> In inward baptism of pure fire,
> Wherewith to be baptized I have
> Tis all my longing soul's desire
> This, only this my soul can save.
>
> Love, mighty love, my heart o'er power
> Oh, Why dost thou so long delay!
> Cut short the work, bring near the Son
> And let me see the perfect day.[64]

Only the Holy Spirit can purify religions if the church must go forward. It must continue to perform its threefold task of preaching, teaching, and sanctifying human society. This must always be done under the power and guidance of the Holy Spirit and the Holy Word. The Word and the Spirit are sufficient to correct our deficiencies and balance our interpretation. Very often, the church sought to flee excesses, only to discover that it has left all of its cherished possessions behind. The church must ever seek to be a faithful steward of those priceless possessions entrusted to it by its Lord. It must strive to present a clear, dynamic, and spirit-filled understanding of its biblical, theological, and historical tradition. Faith must always be connected with life. Biblical exegesis and biblical understanding must always seek to bring the gospel to bear in the solution of present-day problems. It must seek to answer the question and fulfill the quest of men in society. It must also seek to transform human society. The Word must always be interpreted in such a manner as to make possible the fulfillment of the promises of the new covenant of full salvation in Christ, and to encourage a life of holiness by faith in the here and now.

A spirit-filled church must act as the leaven that purifies the whole loaf of human society. Without the Holy Spirit, the church is lifeless and ineffective. The church must always affirm through its witness that the same Spirit who spoke the Word through inspired men is working out that Word in the life of individual Christians and in the beloved community with both power and grace. Any pattern of theological presentation or ethical teaching which does not have practical results to this end must be brought into question. Both justification and sanctification must be kept at the heart of any Christian theology.

> Transform my nature into thine
> Let all my power thine impress feel;
> Let all my soul become divine
> And stamp me with thy Spirit's seal.[65]

The greatest miracle of a spirit-filled church is the church itself. With Christ as its head, the early church was able to perform many miracles. The greatest of all miracles is the Assurance of Personal Salvation. When the individual Christian becomes convinced that he is forgiven of his sins and that he is a new born child of God, he becomes a source of spiritual power. It is the Holy Spirit within the human spirit that gives one the Assurance of Salvation. It is true that we are also assured by the Word of God as declared in the New Testament, but this New Testament Assurance is both objective and general. It is the promise to man in general. The Holy Spirit working within the human spirit individualizes one's witness and clarifies one's assurance. The New Testament assures me that he who believes in Christ shall be saved. The Holy Spirit working within my human spirit assures me that I have been saved. This is what John Wesley means when he writes:

> The eyes of His understanding are open. . . . And He who of old commanded light to shine out of darkness shining on his heart he sees the light of the glory of God, His glorious love, in the face of Jesus Christ. His ears being opened he is now capable of hearing the inward voice of God, saying "Be of good cheer. Thy sins are forgiven thee. Go and sin no more." He . . . in his heart the mighty workings of the spirit of God . . . and now he may be properly said to live; God having quickened him by His Spirit he is alive to God through Christ.[66]

It is the duty of the church to lead each believer into this experience of inward assurance of salvation. Their assurance can only be obtained through a personal experience of saving faith. John Wesley describes this saving faith when he writes:

> The faith I want is "a vital trust and confidence in God that through the merits of Christ, my sins are forgiven, and I reconciled to the favour

of God . . . I want that faith which none can have without knowing that he hath it . . . He is free from doubt having the love of God shed abroad in his heart through the Holy Ghost which is given unto him; which Spirit itself beareth witness with his spirit that he is a child of God."[67]

A spirit-filled church is a church made up of persons who have this beloved assurance. Only then can the church have the power to transform human society. The relation between the church and society must be motivated and directed by the power of the Holy Ghost. The quality of life in human society will be determined by the nature and extent of their spiritual relationship. If the church is spiritually weak, it will be compelled to conform to the standards of the world. If the church is made strong by this blessed assurance, it will have the power to transform the world.

While the church is called to live in this world, it must never be "of this world." This world is an egocentric unit of human existence. The church is a Christo-centric organism. It is primarily concerned with witnessing to the new life in Christ. It is empowered by the presence of the Holy Spirit who abides within it. While the church seeks to serve the world, it is never subservient to the world. It is only subservient to Christ the Lord. Only a spirit-filled church can glorify God through service to humanity. It is the Holy Spirit that empowers the church and enables it to serve humanity and transform society. There are many ways that a spirit-filled church can serve humanity to the glory of God.

It may act as a lump of yeast, leavening the whole loaf. It may serve as the ax at the root of the tree to cut it down. It may serve as God's pruning hook, cutting away the dead branches of corruption. Only as the church is empowered and guided by the Holy Ghost, can it glorify God and transform human society.

Only those whose hearts have been converted by the Holy Spirit can become a vital link in the chain of spiritual power. A spirit-filled church is a converted church. Harold DeWolf describes the nature of this conversion when he writes:

> The spiritual rebirth must come if the life in communion with God is to be entered. How it is to come cannot be determined by any formula. We cannot say when or how fast everyone must be reborn. Neither can we say that in everyone the new birth will appear as a radical reverse of direction. The Spirit works in many different ways in different lives. But let no one say that because the change may occur slowly or in the secrecy of the heart, it has not occurred at all. For if the soul is to enter into communion with God, then there must come, some time, some how, the soul's awakening to solemn responsibility before God and the commitment of the soul to side with him and by his grace to wage unceasing war against evil in the self and in the world.[68]

Although conversion is not the same in all persons, there are certain general signs that follow it. Usually, our deep feelings of guilt are removed. Conversion increases our capacity to become more interested in real achievement than in the praises of men. One becomes more interested in pleasing God than men. Conversion gives to one a new conception of oneself. It helps one to resolve one's inner conflicts. It gives one a new set of values. It settles, once and for all, the question of one's supreme allegiance. It gives one an organizing principle for one's life. This, in brief, is what we mean by conversion. Once this happens in the life of the individual, he becomes a new person. The Holy Spirit takes control of his life. It brings a new source of power.

When the Holy Spirit comes into our lives, our task is by no means over. We must keep the channels of the heart open to the guidance of the Holy Spirit. This is done by prayer and Christian service.

CHAPTER IX

The Five Plateaus Leading to the Summit of Spiritual Power

The Spirit-filled church is powerful, unstoppable, unconquerable, incorruptible, and victorious. The Holy Spirit made the early apostles irresistible and awesome in face of oppositions. How did they acquire such awesome power? They did so by climbing the mountain of Spiritual power.

There are five plateaus leading to the mountain peak of Spiritual power, they are:

1. Repentance.
2. Self-surrender.
3. Seeking after the Spirit.
4. Total Commitment to Christ.
5. Christian Service to Humanity in the Name of Christ.

REPENTANCE

The first act of repentance is accepting the Christian view of the human predicament. Man is a child of God who is in rebellion against the Will of the Father. This rebellion has alienated, separated, and caused him to become estranged from God. Yet God's love is ever seeking to restore mankind. God is in Christ, reconciling the world to Himself. Repentance is responding to God's overture of love. It is experiencing Godly sorrow for our sins. It is refusing any longer to travel the downward road. It is turning around and turning to God. It is accepting God's overture of divine reconciliation. Repentance is more than an act that is performed once and for all. It is an attitude toward God. It is a view of man. It is demonstrating a willingness to be recreated by the Holy Spirit. Repentance is stopping, turning around, and embracing a new divine relationship.

SELF-SURRENDER

Self-surrender is submitting the self to a power greater than oneself. It is making oneself available to God. It is seeking to become God-like. Jesus said,

> Seek and ye shall find, but if from thence thou shalt seek the Lord thy god thou shalt find him, if thou seek him with all thy heart and with all thy soul.[1]

David also experienced this spirit of self-surrender when he said,

> O God thou art my God, early will I seek thee in a dry and thirsty land, where no water is.[2]

Isaiah expressed the need for self-surrender when he wrote, "Yes, with my spirit within I will seek thee early."[3]

God has given to every man the freedom of choice. Therefore, the Holy Spirit will not possess a man against his will. Self-surrender, therefore, is a prerequisite for salvation. Self-surrender is, "Fruit meet for repentance." It is kneeling at the foot of the cross and crying out:

> All to Jesus I surrender, all to him I freely give. I will love and trust him, in his presence daily live.[4]

SEEKING AFTER THE SPIRIT

In order to receive spiritual power, you must desire it enough to seek it with all your heart. The Holy Spirit waits to be invited. He searches the heart to see if all things have been ready for him to enter.

Receiving the Holy Spirit is a matter of the will. The human will must will to will the will of God.

> Whosoever will, let him come and drink of the water of life freely.[5]

If you truly desire and sincerely seek the power of the Holy Spirit, he will come and dwell within you and possess your entire personality. The desire for the Holy Spirit must be motivated by the desire to do God's will.

> Seek ye the Lord while he may be found, call ye upon him while he is near.[6]

TOTAL COMMITMENT

Total commitment is an important plateau that leads to the mountain peak of spiritual power. Saving faith leads to Total Commitment, it opens the flood gate of Spiritual power.

The early disciples received power because they were totally committed to Christ. They had decided that come what may they would follow the risen Christ. They had gathered in the upper room, seeking to better understand the nature and demand of this commitment.

> And suddenly there came a sound from heaven as of a rushing mighty wind, and it filled all the house where they were sitting and they were all filled with the Holy Ghost and began to speak with other tongues as the Spirit gave them utterance.[7]

There are many who profess Christ but are not totally committed to him. What is Total Commitment? It is going all the way with Christ and believing that he will go all the way with you.

It is making our feet into hind's feet and climbing to the high places of the spirit. It is taking God at His word. It is daring to stand on the promises of God. It is forsaking all to follow Christ. When this is done, the Holy Spirit comes and dwells within you. He'll empower you, instruct you and guide you.

CHRISTIAN SERVICE

Christian Service is service to humanity in the name of Christ. Christian Service is the key to spiritual power. God is the greatest conservationist. He never wastes His gift. He increases our power as we increase our desire to use it in His service. Dietrich Bonhoffer describes the nature of Christian Service when he writes:

> It is nothing else than bondage to Christ alone, completely breaking through every program, every set of laws, no other significance is possible, since Jesus is the only significance, beside Jesus nothing has any significance. He alone matters.[8]

Christian Service is always rendered to man in praise to God. There is a German proverb that says:

> What I spend I had. What I saved I lost. What I gave I have. Whatever you give in Christian Service you still have. Whatever you give of your hopes, your enthusiasm, your tears, your labors, that and that alone is yours and yours forever.[9]

Wilberforce spent his life fighting slavery and the slave trade. After Parliament had passed the bill, a member referring to Wilberforce, said, "that the pillow upon which he could rest his head at night, and know that the slave trade was no more, was a greater thorn of splendor and glory than that of the Emperor Napoleon." Wilberforce was rich in what he had done for mankind. This is the reward of Christian Service. This is not, however, the greatest reward. The greatest of all rewards is the privilege of walking with God in service to man and experiencing His power to overcome the forces of evil.

It is to know His comfort in times of trouble, to know His peace in times of strife, and to know His joy in times of sorrow.

WE MUST DARE TO SERVE

 A. Give of Yourself
 B. Prepare Yourself
 C. Improve Yourself
 D. Self-Dedication

GIVE OF YOURSELF

Christ gave of Himself. Christ was one in the beginning with God. He is God's only begotten; He is one in essence with God, yet he gave of Himself.

> Let this mind be in you which was also in Christ Jesus who being in the form of God thought it not robbery to be equal with God: but made Himself of no reputation, and took upon him the form of a servant, and was made in the likeness of men.[10]

We often emphasize the giving of Himself on the cross, but of equal importance is Christ giving of Himself in His incarnation. It was Christ giving of Himself in His incarnation that made the cross meaningful and possible.

SELF PREPARATION

Giving of oneself must eventuate in self-preparation. Luke tells us that:

> Jesus increased in wisdom and stature and in favor with God and man.[11]

Growth through preparation is the fundamental requisite for Christian Service. Preparation demands effort. It requires willingness to change one's attitude and readjust one's scale of values; it demands growth. The Holy Spirit nurtures the believer and gives him the power to grow in Grace. This growth is made possible by prayer, study, reevaluation of ones priorities and loving ones neighbor as oneself.

SELF-IMPROVEMENT

Self-Preparation is what man does with himself, but Self-Improvement is made possible by the power of the Holy Spirit. He is our teacher, guide, and protector. It was the Holy Spirit that transformed Peter from an impetuous liar on the night of Christ's crucifixion to a powerful preacher and flaming envangelist on the day of Pentecost. When the church submits itself to the power of the Holy Spirit, He improves its power and capability. It is the Holy Spirit that inspires us and empowers us to serve, and leads us into a Totally Committed life that only He can make possible. Total Commitment should lead to Total Dedication.

Total Dedication is not something that comes easily. Even after Pentecost, the disciples had more growing to do before they could entirely dedicate themselves to the Christian way. Total Dedication is the stirring within the soul of every latent power of doing, it is the stoking of all the slumbering fire, the quickening of muscles and stretching of sinew, and the burning scintillating struggle of the brain, the whole of one's being—might of body, mind and soul—thrown with total abandonment into one's chosen field of endeavor.

Ananias and Sapphira are examples of what happens when persons strive to live the Pentecost life without first sharing the Pentecostal experience. Absolute dedication is freedom from detachment. It is man's total involvement with the whole of his existence, with his fears, his anxiety, his self-constradictions, and his despair, with the paradoxes in him and in his social situations. It is persistent involvement without regard to the outcome. It is the Holy Spirit that produces the entirely dedicated life. It is the absolutely dedicated life that produces Spiritual power. Power to become the light of the world, the catalyst of society and the maker of national destiny.

As the light gleaming in the bulb throws its rays in every direction and engulfs the bulb itself with the light which it radiates, so our letting the Holy Spirit, who is the light of the world, shine out from the center of our being, fills not only our whole being full of light, but this light radiates from us in every direction and becomes an ever-increasing influence in the world.

The Holy Bible is filled with men and women of both the Old and New Testament who were leaders in their age and accomplished great things in their generation, because they permitted themselves to be possessed by the Holy Spirit. This power is available to all of us today, if we will meet the conditions. If we will believe God and take Him at His word, even when it is contrary to our own experience and to all human reason. We will know of his power if we can only believe in the unseen power working in us. We can say with Job, "Though He slay me, yet will I trust him."[12]

No man begins this faith fully mature; he must be willing to grow. Christian growth is often painful, frustrating, and sacrificial, but if we obediently yield to the Holy Spirit within us, we will grow into the stature of Pentecostal power. This power does not come at once. Like seeds hidden beneath the earth's mold, that grow long in silence and darkness before coming to light, so these giants of the spirit grow silently, unobtrusively into mighty warriors of the spirit. The Holy Spirit has His roots so deep in eternal wellsprings of the human spirit that it takes many years of Christian nurturing to develop His power and to prove His existence. But when the giant is developed he leaves eternal footprints in the sands of both time and eternity.

> I'm pressing on the upward way new heights
> I'm gaining everyday still praying as I'm
> onward bound Lord plant my feet on higher ground.
>
> I want to scale the utmost height and catch
> a glimpse of glory bright but still I pray
> till heaven I
> Lord lift me up and let me stand, by faith
> on heaven's table land; a higher plane than
> I have found Lord plant my feet on higher ground.[13]

CHAPTER X

The Holy Spirit in Human Life

THE NATURE OF LIFE.

Life is a unity of multidimensional expressions. The multidimensional unity of life partakes of both being and nonbeing. Therefore, it is ambiguous in nature.

Life is composed of two basic elements, namely Essence and Existence. Life has diversity within unity. It has a unity of meanings and a multitude of functions. Each function is made possible by the quality of life it possesses.

There are many intellectual approaches to the understanding of life. In continental Europe, we find the "Philosophy of Life Approach." In the United States of America, we find the "Philosophy of Process Approach." Each of the great religions of the world has its own peculiar approach to the understanding of life.

One cannot know God unless God abides within him and reveals Himself to him. Therefore, the religious approach is the key to divine revelation. In all true religions, God takes the initiative. The initiative is made possible through the Holy Spirit working within the human spirit. Kilian McDonnell puts his finger on the core of the problem of modern thought when he writes:

> We need to go back to a more biblical and liturgical view of the Trinity as revealed in history. Who is the Spirit we meet in history and why specifically was the spirit sent? Does the spirit have any personal specificity in history, any unrepeatable role? The key to pneumatology, if there be any, is salvation history, God working through Christ, in the Holy Spirit, who is the point of contact with our religious, moral, political and social life. One cannot salvage pneumatology and leave trinitarian doctrine an abstract reflection on eternal essences. When pneumatology looses the horizon and become⌐

decorative it is because it has lost its trinitarian rootage. The proper study of the Holy Spirit is both the Trinity and the culture.[1]

The Holy Spirit has the power to transform both the quality of human life and the purpose of human culture. It transforms both life and death. Death is no longer the end of life, but a point of transition. The quest for the key to the understanding of life is the source of all true religion. To know God is to know life.

Life includes its own negation, therefore, death is part of life. Because life has the power to resurrect itself, death becomes only an interlude in the transitional manifestations of life. Death is only the change from one form of life to another. This is what Paul was referring to when he wrote:

> When this earthly tabernacle is dissolved I have a building of God not made with hands eternal in the heavens.[2]

The secret of life is its ability to overcome and transcend its own negations. Life is a polarity of creativity and decay. There are three phases of life: birth, death, and resurrection.

Living beings are also dying beings, and dying beings are also resurrecting beings. This idea has its counterpart in the scientific concept of the conservation of matter. There are two basic concepts of life, the ontological and the generic. Tillich says:

> This generic concept of life is the pattern after which the ontological concept of life has been formed. The observation of a particular potentiality of beings, whether it is that of a species or of individuals themselves in time and space, has led to the ontological concept of life. Life is the actualizing of being.[3]

Life has the power to transform itself from potential to the actual. There are two basic elements of life: essential, and existential. The essential has to do with potentiality; the existential has to do with actuality. Life is always seeking its ultimate fulfillment. This is what the Apostle Paul is referring to when he says:

> For in this life we groan, earnestly desiring to be clothed upon with our house which is from heaven, if so that being clothed we shall not be found naked. For we that are in this tabernacle do groan, being burdened; not for that we would be unclothed, but clothed upon, that mortality might be swallowed up of life. Now he that hath wrought us for the selfsame thing is God, who also hath given unto us the earnest of the spirit.[4]

Life is a mixture of these essential and existential elements that possess the power of actualization. All forms of existence do not possess the power of actualization.

The Holy Spirit in Human Life

There are three basic forms of life, namely: inorganic, organic, and spiritual. Spiritual life is that form of being which the New Testament calls eternal life. It has a qualitative difference. Eternal life is free from the structure of existence. It is life free from finitude, estrangement, conflict, and death. It is unambiguous life sustained by pure being. It is unstructured and therefore free from the limitations of existence. It is not limited by time and space, nor is it subject to death and decay.

> The distinction of the Potential from the Actual implies that all dimension are always real if not actually, at least potentially, a dimension's actualization is dependent on conditions which are not always present.[5]

There is a difference between natural life and spiritual life. Natural life is limited by time and space. It is also imperfect and subject to death. It is limited by non-being.

THE NATURE OF THE SPIRIT

The spirit written with a small letter refers to the essential nature of an object or person. It is that which gives meaning and power to a person or thing. It is that which gives the object its integrity. On the human level, it is that which makes man, man. This is what the Bible refers to as the human soul. The soul of the man is the Spirit of the man. The soul has to do with life manifested on the human level.

> And God breathed into him the breath of life and man became a living soul.[6]

Tillich says:

> It was in the experience of breathing and above all in the cessation of breathing in the corpse that man's attention was drawn to the question, what keeps life alive? His answer was breath. Where there is breath there is power of life; When it vanishes the power of life vanishes.[7]

The divine breath or spirit is the giver of life. All life is good because it is both created and sustained by the divine spirit.

> And God saw every thing that he had made and behold, it was very good, and the evening and the morning were the sixth day.[8]

> In the beginning was the word, and the word was with God, and the word was God. The same was in the beginning with God. All things were made by him; and without him was not anything made that was made. In him was life, and the life was the light of men.[9]

Paul completes this picture of the nature of the divine life when he writes:

> Now he that hath wrought us for the self same thing is God, who also hath given unto us the earnest of the spirit.[10]

It is the Divine Spirit that creates the human spirit. The Divine Spirit is not identical with the human spirit. The human spirit is finite and therefore subject to the ambiguities of human life. The Divine Spirit is infinite, and therefore free from life's ambiguities. The Holy Spirit is beyond sin; therefore, it alone can redeem and sanctify the human spirit.

Only as the human spirit is possessed by and filled with the Holy Spirit can man please God.

> Now a man who should be in like manner possessed by the spirit of God so that he should not know what doeth or leaveth undone, and have no power over himself, but the will and spirit of God should have the mastery over him and work and do and leave undone with him and by him, what and as God would: such a man were one of those whom St. Paul saith: "for as many as are led by the spirit of God they are the sons of God and they are not under the law but under Grace," and to whom Christ saith; "for it is not ye that speak, but the spirit of your Father which speaketh in you.[11]

The Holy Spirit is available to all who will meet the conditions to receive him. These conditions are simple. They are Repentance, Faith, and Love. These conditions can only be met by those who diligently give themselves wholly to God. It is then that God prepares the human spirit to receive His Divine Spirit. It is only then that God pours out His Spirit upon the human spirit.

The Holy Spirit is that which animates life and purifies the human spirit. It is the Holy Spirit who preserves life in all of its varied dimensions. This is done, as far as we can tell, without any form of inner awareness of the abiding of the Divine Spirit. The lower dimensions of life are not aware of the indwelling of the Divine Spirit. This awareness is made possible in men because of the special quality of the human spirit. The human dimension of life, while having much in common with the lower dimensions is unique in that it can become aware of the presence of the Divine Spirit within the human spirit.

To distinguish between the Holy Spirit on the one hand and the spirit in the lower dimensions of life on the other, we will refer, from this point on, to the human spirit as the human soul. It is the Holy Spirit that creates and preserves the human soul. It is the Holy Spirit that reconciles the soul to God. It gives the soul the power to enter into the Kingdom of God. It gives the soul power to overcome all moral and psychological impediments. The Holy Spirit cleanses the soul from sin, thereby making it Holy.

The human soul and the human spirit are one and the same. It is here that I disagree with Paul Tillich who insists that they are not.

> In any case, while the word "soul" is alive in Biblical, liturgical, and poetic language, it has lost its usefulness for a strict theological understanding of man, his spirit, its relation to the Divine Spirit.[12]

I am certain that one can make a strong case for the oneness of the human spirit and human soul. The creation of the human soul is different from the creation of the human body. The human body was created from the dust of the ground, but the human soul was created by the Spirit of God. When the body dies, it goes back to the dust from whence it came. At death the soul goes back to the God who gave it. Therefore, the soul and the human spirit are essentially one.

The Bible abounds with passages equating the human soul and the human spirit.

> And the Lord formed man of the dust of the ground, and breathed into his nostrils the breath of life; and man became a living soul.[13]

In this passage of scripture we discover two distinct actions of God: one is an act of creation, man is created out of the dust; the second is man's elevation. Not only is man created, but he is also elevated by being given the divine image. It is this image in man that the bible refers to as the soul of man. The soul of man is both unique and eternal. It makes him qualitatively different from the rest of God's creation. The human soul is kept alive by the indwelling of the Divine Spirit. When man sinned, the human soul was separated from the Divine Spirit.

> Therefore, the Lord God sent him forth from the Garden of Eden. . . . so he drove out the man; and he placed at the east of Eden, Cherubims, and a flaming sword which turned every way, to keep the way of the tree of life.[14]

It was sin that separated man from the source of spiritual life. Although he continued to exist physically he was dead spiritually.

Only the Holy Spirit can bring this spiritual change in the heart of the believer.

> Wesley believed that any change wrought within the heart of the believer was by the inspiration of the Holy Spirit and that until this holy love was "shed abroad in the heart" no one could enter heaven.[15]

This teaching of Wesley may appear strange to some who insist that the Holy Spirit is given subsequent to regeneration at the time of the "so-called second blessing," but in this concept, Wesley is at one with most reformed teaching.

There can be a little doubt that Wesley considered regeneration the work of the Holy Spirit. On the day of Pentecost, it was the Holy Spirit who performed the work of regeneration when they first believed. This in no way denies the future outpouring of the Holy Spirit upon the same believers. There is no doubt that this indwelling presence of the Holy Spirit is mediated to the believer at the time of his baptism, but that personal presence comes to be more fully understood and more deeply experienced as the believer proceeds to live the Christian life. This is what John Wesley means by "going on to perfection."

It is the work of Christ that restored the human soul to its spiritual source, thereby restoring in him the quality of eternal life. It is the Holy Spirit that maintains this quality of life by indwelling the human soul. When man sinned, his soul was not taken away, but it lost its divine quality of life. Therefore, his life was a living death—a spiritual death.

The relation between the Holy Spirit and the human spirit (soul) is one of life giving on the part of the Holy Spirit and life receiving on the part of the human soul.

> Whosoever believeth on Him should not perish but have eternal life.[16]

Man is a spiritual being. This means that he is the only organism in which this dimension of life is dominant.

> But man can partly miss that creative act in which the dominance of the psycholgoical is overcome by the dominance of the Spirit.[17]

This is what the New Testament calls unbelief. Man, because of his unbelief, denies his birthright.

Contrary to some modern theologians, we have dared to equate the human spirit with the human soul. The human soul experiences the spiritual presence as meaning and power. Spirit is the actualization of power. It unites the power of God with the nature of God to create the highest dimension of life.

It is the Holy Spirit that works in the human soul. It is the Holy Spirit that enters into the human soul and enables the self to transcend itself. When the soul is grasped by the Holy Spirit it creates a state of "Ecstasy" and produces saving experience. This state of Ecstasy may express itself in a diversity of ways. No expression ever contradicts the spirit of Christ.

> Ecstasy does not destroy the centerness of the integrated self. Should it do so demonic possession would replace the creative presence.[18]

THE HOLY SPIRIT WITHIN THE HUMAN SOUL

The soul must learn to receive the Holy Spirit by practicing his presence. H. Thillicke describes the working of the Holy Spirit within the human spirit as follows:

> In Paul the connection between present and future eschatology is precisely that the spirit is here already, the power of the angel of grace on the world which already gives eternal life now (Romans 5:8) but whose goal is that everything becomes subject to Christ. . . . But now the spirit has been given and has given and has permeated our hearts with love (Romans 5:5) transferring us from the distance of servanthood to the immediacy of sonship . . . to be and he will also lead into truth and reveal what is now still cancelled.[19]

The Holy Spirit is the creator of all that is, the life of all that lives, and the wisdom of all the wise. For all things have their being in the fulness of the Divine Spirit. He is the source of all power, knowledge, life, and rest. In the Holy Spirit all things consist. It is the Holy Spirit within the human spirit that enables the soul to reach so high as to cast a glance into eternity.

> For the beholding of the hidden things of God shalt thou forsake sense and the things of the flesh, and all that the sense can apprehend, and that reason of her own power can bring forth, and all things created and uncreated that reason is able to comprehend and know and shalt take thy stand upon an utter abandonment of thyself and as knowing none of the aforesaid things, and enter into union with Him who is, and who is above all existence and all knowledge.[20]

It is the Holy Spirit within the human spirit who enables man to perceive what God wills to do with him, and that his blessedness lieth alone in God. It is the Holy Spirit that imparts within the human spirit that true essence of divine love. He enables him to truly love God, under all circumstances, in having and not having, in sweetness and bitterness, in good or evil report, for he seeks alone to honour God in all things. It is the Holy Spirit that brings man inward peace. It is a peace that the world cannot give. It is divine peace. It is that peace that Christ promised his disciples.

> My peace I leave with you. My peace I give unto you not as the world giveth, give I unto you.[21]

The Holy Spirit brings Christian joy. This joy is unlike that of the world. The joy that the world gives is based upon temporal experiences that are subject to outside circumstances: material acquisition, gratifying sensations, satisfying pleasures, the wielding of political or economic power, wealth, fame, position, and the things of this world. All of these forms of human gratification cannot eternally fulfill or everlastingly satisfy. They are as temporary as they are temporal. They are fleeting as they are false.

The human soul must learn the art of receiving the Holy Spirit.

> To learn an art which thou knoweth not, four things are needful. The first and most needful of all is, a great desire and diligence and constant endeavor to learn the art. And where this is wanting, the art will never be learned. The second, is a copy or example by which thou mayest learn. The third, is to give earnest heed to the master and watch how he worketh, and to be obedient to him in all things, and to trust and follow him. The fourth, is to put thy own hand to the work and practice it with all industry.[22]

Christian joy is the only joy that satisfies. It fulfills the human spirit by filling it with the Divine Spirit. Christian joy is not subject to temporal conditions. It does not seek to satisfy by gratifying human desire. It fulfills the human spirit by purifying human desires and sanctifying human motives. It lifts the self beyond itself and by so doing enables the human self to transcend itself.

It is a joy that comes through the realization that the human spirit is at one with the Divine Spirit. There is no more estrangement, separation, and hostility between the human spirit and the Divine Spirit. This is joy in the midst of human adversity and life's vicissitudes. Because God is with us, trouble won't last always; suffering will be redemptive; tribulation will turn to jubilation; trials will eventuate into triumphs; and persecutions will be transformed into peace—a peace that passeth all understanding. Tribulation teaches patience, and danger teaches us hope, and hope makes us unafraid. Christian joy is an enthusiastic tranquility that can withstand the storms of life.

When John Wesley sailed from England to Georgia, on board the ship was a band of Moravians who sat singing in the midst of a mighty storm. While the rest of the crew were overcome with fright, they sang songs of praise to God. This amazed John Wesley. These Moravians were able to sing in the midst of the storm because they possessed Christian joy that gave them a peace that passed understanding.

A GOOD CONSCIENCE TOWARD GOD

When the Holy Spirit comes into the human soul, it brings a joy that is maintained by a good conscience toward God and a steadfast hope.

This good conscience tells me that I am right with God. I am doing the will of God. I am being guided by the will of God. It assures me that I can depend upon the promises of God. Christ lives in me.

> What a wonderful change in my life has been wrought since Jesus came into my heart . . . . .[23]

The Holy Spirit in Human Life

This good conscience within me is non other than the Holy Spirit accusing me when I am wrong and leading me to repentance. It forgives me when I repent. It encourages me in the struggle against evil and leads me in the paths of righteousness. It enables me to regret the wrong and rejoice in the right. This good conscience toward God gives me a keen sense of right and a steadfast hatred of wrong. It endows me with a strong moral sense. It keeps me aware of the ethical implications of my conduct. It enhances my sense of human worth.

When the Holy Spirit dwells within the human soul, one can see the image of God in every person he meets. Others are brought to God through him.

The Holy Spirit purges the human conscience. The human conscience can become corrupted and tarnished by sin. The light of truth can be put out, and the human conscience can become a place of utter darkness—so dark that right seems wrong, and wrong seems right, sweet tastes bitter, and bitter tastes sweet, good becomes evil, and evil becomes good. It is the Holy Spirit within the soul that brings light to the human conscience. For many, the light of Christian morality has gone out. The human conscience has become a place of utter darkness, violence, crime, racism, economic injustice, and social corruptions are filling the lives of this modern technological society. The sins of our age make Sodom and Gomorrah look like child's play. Only the Holy Spirit dwelling within the soul can reverse this unholy trend. A good conscience is a faculty of the Holy Spirit. It is a gift from God to the soul. It is created by making God our only criterion for human conduct. It is impossible to possess a good conscience toward God without a living and vital faith in Jesus Christ. Faith in Jesus Christ enables one to live a God-centered life. We are called upon to make our Christian witness in a sinful and hostile society.

The Holy Spirit brings a steadfast hope. What is hope? Christian hope is steadfast expectation and spiritual anticipation. It is standing in the midnight hour believing in the coming of the morning. It is expecting the best from God, and giving the best to God. It is the assurance that God is still in control of this world. In His own time, He will bring in His Kingdom. It is believing that all is well because God is still in control of His Universe.

THE WORK OF THE HOLY SPIRIT

The Holy Spirit is the third person of the Holy Trinity. He is the power of God and of Christ. He proceeds from the Father through the Son. He is the power of God through Christ, redeeming the world from sin and reconciling the world to God. He convicts men of sin, justifies men before God, and brings man to a saving faith in Jesus Christ. He empowers man to accept Christ as the Lord of Life. He reveals to us the truth about Christ and our relation to him. He gives to the believer the blessed assurance of Christian Salvation. This assurance is made available through the illumination of the human soul by the indwelling of the Holy Spirit. This comes through listening to the preached word, the reading of Scriptures, and the inner witness of the Spirit. The Holy Spirit performs both a secondary and a primary work. Some theologians call it prevenient and Saving Grace.

HIS SECONDARY WORK

Let us consider first the secondary work of the Holy Spirit. It is to bring man to a knowledge of God. God is revealed to man through His creation.

> Heavens declare the glory of God and the firmament showeth His handiwork. Day unto day uttereth speech, and night unto night showeth knowledge.[24]

It is the Holy Spirit that teaches man to behold God in nature. God makes Himself known to us through our moral sense or our awareness of the oughtness of things. This is the working of the Holy Spirit within the human soul. God reveals Himself to us through our awareness of order and beauty. All of these are instruments through which the Holy Spirit makes us aware of the reality of God. This is what theologians call natural or prevenient grace. All of the true religions of the world would fall within this category. The Holy Spirit, through prevenient grace, prepares the soul to receive God's saving grace.

THE PRIMARY WORK OF THE HOLY SPIRIT

The primary work of the Holy Spirit is to bring man to a saving faith in God through Christ. Christianity is a religion, but it is much more than that. It is faith-saving faith. There are many religions and a multitude of faiths, but there is only one "Saving Faith." That is the faith in God through Christ. What is faith? It is belief, intellectual assent, and trust. The Bible tells us of three kinds of faith. The faith of the devil. The devil believes in God. He believes and trembles, but he is not saved. The non-Christian believes in right, goodness, justice, and peace, but he is not able to live up to the teaching of his faith. Therefore, he is not saved. Saving faith is commitment to God in Christ. It is the combining of the emotions and intellect, through the will, in an act of commitment to Christ. It is accepting God's work of justification by faith alone. It is experiencing the New Birth in Christ. It is being born from above through the indwelling of the Holy Spirit. It is growing in grace and going on to perfection through the power and guidance of the Holy Spirit.

There are three major steps in the act of Saving Faith. First, there is an act of God. It is God who justifies. He makes us right with himself by his acceptance of the atoning work of Christ. It is Christ's life, work, death, and resurrection that causes God to accept us as righteous. In Christ, God accepts the unacceptable. He reckons the sinner righteous in His sight.

The second step is our acceptance of Christ. When we accept Him in faith, the Holy Spirit enters into our souls and performs the miracle of the second birth. We are regenerated thorugh Christian Baptism. We become redeemed through the blood of Christ. Blood here is a symbol of divine love. As sinners, we break the divine laws of God. The love of Christ restores the broken relationship and we become reconciled—"at one and at peace with God."

The Spirit dwells within us and we are sanctified by the Holy Spirit. The Holy Spirit, working through us, leads us to perfection. The New Birth is that work of the Holy Spirit through which our innermost souls are changed so that sinners become saints. It restores the image of God in us. It frees us from the power of sin.

Thus the twofold function of the Holy Spirit is to save the sinner and sanctify the saints.

THE HOLY SPIRIT IS LOVE

He brings into being the new man and the new society. One of the most tragic experiences of the church throughout its history has been the confusion, strife, bitterness, and division that has occurred, (all) in the name of the Holy Spirit. The Holy Spirit never does anything contrary to the Word of God nor the Spirit of Christ. That which is contrary to the teaching of Christ is not the work of the Holy Spirit. That which divides and destroys the church is not the work of the Holy Spirit. *Spiritual ecstasy never disrupts structure.* The Holy Spirit is love to God and man. It is suffering all things, believing all things, and hoping all things.

The work of Christ and the work of the Holy Spirit are one and the same. The incarnation of Christ is itself the work of the Holy Spirit:

> And the angel answered and said unto her, "The Holy Ghost shall come upon thee, and the power of the highest shall overshadow thee, therefore, also that holy thing which shall be born of thee shall be called the Son of God."[25]

It is the Holy Spirit that teaches the Christian how to pray. We of ourselves do not know how to pray as we ought. Therefore, every prayer that reaches God is the work of the Holy Spirit. The Holy Spirit prays through us. Such a prayer is impossible for the human spirit, because man does not know how to pray; but it is possible for the Holy Spirit to pray through man, even if man should not use words.

The formula—"being in Christ"—which Paul often uses, does not suggest a psychological empathy with Jesus Christ; rather, it involves an ecstatic participation in the Christ who "is the Spirit," whereby one loves in the sphere of spiritual power. The Holy Spirit does not create confusion.

> For God is not the author of confusion, but of peace, as in all churches of the saints.[26]

Paul Tillich clearly defines the role of the Holy Spirit in the church organizations and fellowship when he says:

> The church had and continues to have a problem in actualizing Paul's ideas, because of concrete ecstatic movements. The church must prevent the confusion of ecstasy with chaos, and it must fight for structure. On the other hand, it must avoid the institutional profanization of the spirit which took place in the early Catholic Church as a result of its replacement of charisma with office. Above all, it must avoid the secular profanization of contemporary protestantism which occurs when it replaces ecstasy with doctrinal or moral structure.[27]

In order to maintain a well-balanced and holistic approach to the Christian faith, one must keep the elements of ecstasy, structure, doctrine, and psychology in proper perspective. This approach is one that will provide a unity of all aspects of religion. It must be the kind of unity that is both enchanting and correcting. It is the Holy Spirit who enables us to approach God as both object and subject. While the Christian prays to God, God prays to himself through us.

The spiritual presence is often accompanied by emotional expression. However, every emotional expression is not the spiritual presence. There is always the danger of mistaking emotional excitement for the presence of the Holy Spirit. True religious emotion is that which eventuates in holy living.

There are two types of religious emotions. One that is entirely subjective and void of spiritual meaning and another which is both subjective and objective and filled with spiritual creativity and divine reality.

Subjective emotion is to the human soul what alcohol and certain other drugs are to the human body. It creates an unreal state of existence, which leaves the individual empty, letdown and depressed.

Spiritual emotion is both subjective and objective. Because of the reality and unity of this experience it is creative, therapeutic, morally cleansing, and spiritually enchanting. It administers to the whole person. It does not leave the worshiper empty and exhausted.

Those who are responsible for Christian Worship must be careful to see to it that Christian Worship does not degenerate into empty emotion.

Spiritual emotion creates a new unity between the subject and the object—God and man become one, with man's self-awareness enhanced and magnified. Man is able to see himself, his neighbor, and God in a new divine light which enriches his whole being.

Empty emotion is nothing more than subjective intoxication, void of creativity. Spiritual emotion is holistic and creative. It does not depend solely upon rhythm and sound alone. Its chief elements are the Word and the

The Holy Spirit in Human Life

Sacraments. These are the twin pillars of the Christian experience. They are the bedrock of the church. Without them, one might have an organization or an assembly of people, but not the church. Without them, worship becomes an ineffective and empty ceremony, void of creative power.

The Holy Spirit is communicated through the Word and the Sacrament. These are the two pillars upon which the church is founded. They are the church. Everything that is done in the church revolves around them or emanates from them. They are the media of the Holy Spirit. They are used to communicate the Holy Spirit to the human soul.

> The duality of Word and Sacrament would not be as significant as it is if it did not represent the primordial phenomenon that reality is communicated either by the silent presence of the object as object or by the vocal self-expression of a subject to a subject.[28]

The Holy Spirit is divine reality encountering human reality. This happens through the signs of the silent word in the Sacraments, through sounds that become words under the dimension of the Spirit.

We are using the term Sacraments here in its more comprehensive meaning. The argument as to the number of sacraments is irrelevant within this broader context. We mean by sacrament everything through which the Holy Spirit acts, and all relationships through which the spiritual community experiences the presence of the Holy Spirit. It is an act or object through which the spiritual community comes into being. Human life is a multidimensional unity. The Holy Spirit reveals Himself through the subconscious as well as through the conscious; therefore, spirit-bearing objects and acts are, or may be, materials through which the Holy Spirit reveals Himself.

One, however, must be on his guard against the tendency to distort the use of Sacrament in the manner of the Roman Catholic Church of the Middle Ages and the early reformation period. We must not turn religion into magic and primitive superstitions. The uncritical reliance upon sacrament may lead to the omission of the role of the human will in the religious life. When this happens religion becomes magic and the Sacraments become demonic. In spite of this danger, there is validity in the sacramental mediation of the Holy Spirit.

There is also a second danger—the intellectualization or moralization of the Holy Spirit. The Holy Spirit is more than an idea. It is not limited to human cognition. The Holy Spirit is more than a moral awareness or moral consciousness. The Holy Spirit is holistic in its approach to human experience. He grasps the total man.

> In religious terminology, one could say that God grasps every side of the human being through every medium. The formula unites Protestant principle and Catholic substance, refers definitely to the sacrament as the medium of the Spiritual Presence.[29]

Any act or object or person that can be used to glorify Christ can become material for sacramental mediation of the Holy Spirit.

The most important medium of the Holy Spirit is the "Word." The Bible is the Word of God in the sense that it contains the Word of God. The Bible is the document of the Divine Revelation. The Bible speaks to the human soul. Only when the Bible speaks to the human soul does it create ultimate concern that may lead to man's reconciliation to the ground of his being. The branch that had been cut off by sin is grafted once more into the vine, and becomes a living part of the spiritual community.

> Again, however, we must establish a criterion to use against the false elevation of human words to the dignity of the Word of God. The biblical words are this criterion. They constitute the ultimate touchstone for what can and cannot become the Word of God for someone. Nothing is the Word of God if it contradicts the faith and love which are the work of the Holy Spirit and which constitute the new Being as it is manifest in Jesus as the Christ.[30]

The Holy Spirit works through prayer. It is through prayer that the Holy Spirit reveals the soul to itself. Because of sin, man does not know himself. It is through prayer that the Holy Spirit reveals to the soul its true desires. Because of man's estrangement from God, he is out of touch with himself. He seeks to fulfill false desires. He is directed by false motives and pursues false goals.

It is only by prayer in the spirit that man can know the reality of answered prayer. Because of his sin, man prays amiss. Therefore, he needs the Holy Spirit to make intercession for him before the throne of God.

> Likewise the Spirit also helpeth our infirmities for we know not what we should pray for as we ought: but the Spirit itself maketh intercession for the saints according to the will of God.[31]

It is the Holy Spirit that serves as the connecting link between the human spirit and the Heavenly Father. This is what the Negro spiritual means when it says, "Every time I feel the spirit, moving in my heart I will pray."[32] There are four stages in the prayer life of a Christian believer:

    (a) That of Belief.

> He that comes to God must believe that he is.[33]

    (b) That of Trust. We must be willing to act upon the promises of God. This is what is meant by praying in the name of Christ.

> And whatsoever ye shall ask in my name, that will I do, that the Father may be glorified in the Son. If ye shall ask anything in my name, I will do it.[34]

(c) The prayer of fulfillment. We come now to the point of growing.

> And this is life eternal that they might know thee, the only true God and Jesus Christ whom thou hast sent.[35]

Prayer has now become realization. We know in whom we believe.
   (d) Oneness and joy. Our prayer is fulfilled when the soul becomes one with God.

> Holy Father, keep through thine own name those whom thou hast given me, that they may be one even as we are one.[36]

When the Holy Spirit leads us into oneness with God, oneness in Christ, and oneness with each other, our prayers end in satisfaction. We become an inlet and an outlet for the power of the Holy Spirit. The Holy Spirit flows unhindered into our souls and out into the souls of others. We become a channel of divine grace. We are channels for the power of the Holy Spirit that brings this new life into being. We are saved by grace through faith. Faith begins with belief. The world in which we live is the sum total of our beliefs. It is through our beliefs that we claim our divine heritage as children of God.

Before we can reap the fruits of the spirit, we must sow the seeds of the spirit. The seeds of the spirit are the desires of the soul. The desires which we plant in the soul will determine the fruits of the human spirit. Desires in the soul are like seeds which reproduce after their kind. They become the fruits of the human spirit. The only way the human soul can produce the fruits of the Holy Spirit is for the Holy Spirit to plant the seeds of right desires. These desires will become realistic in our experience. It is in the secret pavilion of the soul that the realities of life are produced. If the desires are good, the realities will be good. It is through prayer to God that true desires are planted in the human soul. The divine law of cause and effect is at work within the human soul. It cannot uproot the false desires that grow in the polluted soil of our sinful condition. This law only produces that seed that is sown; it cannot change the seed. This can only be performed by the Holy Spirit as He invades the human soul. With the instrument of faith, the Holy Spirit uproots seeds of false desire and plants the seeds of spiritual truth. He thereby makes possible the production of the fruits of the spirit.

Glenn Clark calls these seeds the soul's sincere desire. The describes the soul's sincere desire as follows:

> I believe that our sincere desires are placed in our hearts, are molded and fashioned by the hand of God—. Our dreams in the first place rise from desire. They are indexes of what in our deep subconscious self, we seek and crave. And what a person seeks and craves, other things being equal, is

> something that is good for him to have, provided he can take it in a way that will do no violence to ones accepted moral or social code.[37]

Once the Holy Spirit has revealed to you your soul's sincere desire, the only thing that remains is for you to pray in the name of Jesus. What does it mean to pray in the name of Jesus? It is to use the Jesus method of prayer. What is this method of prayer? It is like a son confiding his secret desires and deepest hope into the ears of a loving father. It is a personal, loving desire, confided to the God of love. It is becoming one with God in prayer. When the human soul becomes one with God through Christ, we can be sure that our prayer is answered. This is the greatest truth in the universe. It is the very foundation of our Christian faith. Jesus said:

> In that day ye shall know that I am in the Father and ye in me and I in you.[38]

This threefold oneness is our assurance that our prayers will be answered. Jesus is the vine. The father is the caretaker, and we are the branches, Jesus is our point of contact with God. His life is that point where humanity and divinity meet in a reconciling experience. Therefore, we must pray in the name of Jesus. That means that we use the Jesus method of praying. Glenn Clark describes it as follows:

> Prayer with Jesus was very "simple." You take your own or your brother's need deep into your heart, and identify with it. Then forgetting your brother and yourself as best you can, and above all forgetting your trouble, then turn completely in thought to God and rise into the high consciousness of oneness with the Father through the consciousness of your oneness with Christ and having risen to that high place, you pray until the peace of God comes upon you. Then your prayer is answered.[39]

Jesus was aware of his own helplessness, therefore, He trusted completely in God the Father. It is the feeling of helplessness and trust which gives Christian prayer its power. This kind of praying is not the work of the human soul alone. It is the work of the Holy Spirit making intercession for us before the throne of God.

When we climb the ladder of prayer, opinion becomes conception, and conception develops into belief, and belief issues forth into trust, which matures into faith. That faith is transformed into conviction, develops into realization, and realization becomes knowledge, and knowledge leads to oneness. When this stage is reached, the Holy Spirit takes all our problems and all our needs and presents them to the Father, knowing that he will care for us in his own good time. We can rest in the knowledge that God's time is always the right time.

When the Holy Spirit enters the human soul, He enables us to experience

The Holy Spirit in Human Life

a new beginning. We turn away from life's problems and start with life's answers. This is what Jesus means when he says:

> What things soever ye desire when ye pray believe that ye shall receive them and ye shall have them.[40]

This advice comes following one of the greatest promises in the New Testament.

> Whosoever shall say unto this mountain, be thou removed, and be thou cast into the sea: and shall not doubt in his heart, but shall believe that these things which he saith shall come to pass; he shall have whatsoever he saith.[41]

What a mighty promise. What a blessed assurance. Too often we start with our problem and never get away from the problem. Therefore, we become more deeply sunk in the quagmire of our own doubts. When the Holy Spirit takes control of the soul He causes us to turn away from our problem and start with the answer. He enables us to concentrate upon the soul's sincere desire. He increases our faith in God. He teaches us to believe in our desires and in the power of the Holy Spirit working in us to bring it into expression. If you truly believe in it, it will some day come to pass.

The Holy Spirit teaches us to believe in God, in our fellow man, and in ourselves. Ask the Holy Spirit to guide you. He knows what is best for you. He will help you make right choices. We so often permit ourselves to be limited by our doubts. This is why Jesus said:

> What things soever ye desire, when ye pray, believe that ye receive them and ye shall have them.[42]

> For since the beginning of the world men have not heard nor perceived by the ear, neither hath the eye seen what God, hath prepared for him that waiteth for him.[43]

God wants us to have the best. Men of faith do not have to choose the second best. God will give us that which we can accept for ourselves. We do not have to become grasping, greedy, or egotistical. Life will not hold out on us. The more we put into life, the more life will give to us. The Holy Spirit is the Spirit of love. Love rules the world. The power of the Holy Spirit is an expression of divine love. He gives us the necessary wisdom, insight, and understanding to achieve our soul's desire. The Holy Spirit enables one to know what is right for him. What is right spiritually is also right mentally and materially. God is not a God of poverty and illness. It is the will of God that we live an enthusiastic, happy, radiant, and fulfilled life. The Holy Spirit will give us power to overcome the adversities, withstand the tribulations and sorrows of life through answered prayer. "It is the Father's good pleasure to give you the Kingdom." God's will for us is always for our good.

MANIFESTATIONS OF THE HOLY SPIRIT

Every prayer that is answered is a manifestation of the spirit. Each answered prayer has the following levels:

1). The prayer is first placed in the soul by the Holy Spirit. The human soul does not know how to pray as it ought, therefore, it must be taught by the Holy Spirit. Therefore, answered prayer must be first manifested in the human soul by the Holy Spirit. The Holy Spirit not only teaches us what to pray for, but also how to pray. Every answered prayer is a seed sown in the soul by the Holy Spirit. It is the Holy Spirit that teaches us to pray in faith. It is He who pleads for us before the throne of God. The human soul does not cause the prayer to be answered. It is the Holy Spirit that plants it, cultivates it, and fertilizes it with faith. This is the first manifestation of spiritual prayer. How can one know when he is praying in the spirit? The Holy Spirit is the Spirit of Christ. When we pray in the spirit we pray in the attitude of Christ—of love and faith.

2). The prayer that is answered is communicated to the mind by the Holy Spirit. This second step is important because it is with the mind that we serve God. The mind is the instrument that gives birth to answered prayer. Answered prayer is conceived in the soul, but it is born in the mind. It is in the mind that one expresses the true nature of the soul's sincere desire. It is in the mind that prayer receives the quality of motivation that enables it to become a reality. Prayer in the soul is potentiality. Prayer in the mind is actuality. The human mind is the lens that projects the prayer on the screen of human cognition. It is at that point that the individual becomes aware of his soul's sincere desire. He knows what he is praying for. He visualizes his desire. It becomes a concept of the mind.

3). The conscious mind then deposits it into the subconscious mind. Here it is ready to become manifested in the material world. The Holy Spirit works within the conscious and the subconscious to bring the prayer to material manifestation in the right way and at the right time. Once the prayer is deposited into the subconscious mind, it becomes a part of the universal mind. It takes its place alongside of the multitudes of prayers in the mind of God. It is the Holy Spirit that preserves its identity and brings it to actuality.

4). The final level is that of visible and material reality. It takes its place on the physical planes. It then becomes answered prayer. It is only now that we know whether this desire is a soul's desire and that it is the fruit of answered prayer.

Thus we see that answered prayer first takes place in the human soul. It is a seed planted in the soul by the Holy Spirit. It is then projected on the screen of the human mind. It is stored in the soil of the subconscious until it is ready to take its place on the physical plane.

THE ROLE OF THE HUMAN SPIRIT IN PRAYER

The human spirit has veto power over every prayer of the soul. It can affirm or disclaim every human desire. It is through the human will that the human spirit affirms or rejects the soul's sincere desire. The Holy Spirit will not coerce the human will. The Holy Spirit awaits the approval of the human will before He continues his work of answering prayer. The human will can reject the soul's sincere desire at any stage of its manifestation. The Holy Spirit makes it happen but the human spirit must let it happen. This is why Christ said, "Whosoever will, let him come."[44]

God made man free. The human spirit through the human will must certify human prayers. When the human will, wills to will the will of God, then the Holy Spirit guarantees answered prayer. The gardener does not make the seed grow. He must choose the seed, and he must do the things that are necessary to help it to grow. He must prepare the soil, cultivate the soil, and keep out the weeds. But only God can bring the increase. If our prayers are to be answered, then we must cooperate with the Holy Spirit to bring it to pass. How can one know when he is cooperating with the Spirit instead of working against the Holy Spirit? The Holy Spirit works for us through us. But we must learn to follow the promptings of the Holy Spirit. We cannot compel the answering of our prayers. We cannot force the outcome. We must not be afraid to work with God. When we learn to work with Him, things are accomplished. Our soul's sincere desires are realized without strife or difficult striving. We must pray and work. Pray as though it all depends upon God, and work as though it all depends upon us. There is no difficulty, confused situation, or human problem to which the answer is not known to the Holy Spirit. As we become aware of the power of the Holy Spirit within us, all conditions and all things are possible. We do all things through the Spirit of Christ who strengthens us. If one does not know the right answer, all he needs to do is to turn to the power of the Holy Spirit within him and he will find the answer. The Holy Spirit guides us in making the right decisions. The burden of making the right decisions is not left to us alone. The Holy Spirit is always present to guide us. Let us seek the wisdom of the Holy Spirit in making the right decisions, in everything we do.

CHAPTER XI

The Guidance of the Holy Spirit

> In all thy ways acknowledge Him and He will direct thy path. Commit thy ways unto the Lord: trust also in Him and He will bring it to pass. How be it when He, the Spirit of truth is come, He will guide you into all truth: For He shall not speak of Himself, but whatsoever He shall hear that shall He speak: And He will show you things to come.[1]

THE ASSURANCE OF DIVINE GUIDANCE

God does not leave us alone. We do not have to grope through uncertain paths and travel unchartered seas as we journey through the tangled maize of life. The Spirit of God is with us to comfort, strengthen, protect, and guide us. The Christian believer is assured of Divine Guidance. The Christian is blessed with a threefold source of Divine Guidance; namely, the sacred scriptures, the Christian fellowship, and the Holy Spirit.

The Christian must at all times seek to be the instrument in the hands of God. He does not do anything of himself. He must at all times seek Divine Guidance. Christ has promised to be with us to guide us.

Many times, we do not avail ourselves of Divine Guidance, because we fail to examine our motives, sanctify our desires, and clarify our goals. Very often we seek to glorify ourselves instead of God. We put selfishness and pride at the center of our activities. We spend our energy outmaneuvering, outwitting, and circumventing others, instead of seeking to do the work of God.

When we put God first, when we seek to do His will, accomplish His purpose, and exemplify His Spirit, we can be assured of His eternal favor and Divine Guidance. The only way to perform our missionary task is to seek Divine Guidance.

The Guidance of the Holy Spirit

Jesus in, His farewell message to the disciples, emphasized two important facts that assures them of the continued and valid nature of the Divine Guidance which they were to receive after His departure. First, that what He had given them was of the same quality and nature of the prophetic revelation of the sacred scripture. He shared with them that which He had heard from His heavenly Father. Yet, because of their lack of Spiritual maturity, they had failed to learn much of what Jesus had tried to teach them. They were still in the *kindergarten* of the spirit. He assures them that His incarnate revelation will be continued by the Holy Spirit, who will bring them into the full stature of spiritual maturity. The Holy Spirit's authority is the same as that of Jesus. It is from God. "For whom God hath sent speaketh the word of God: For God giveth not the spirit by measure unto him."[2] God the Father is the source of Divine Guidance. Jesus is God incarnate who possessed the fulness of God's nature. The Holy Spirit partakes of the fulness of this divine nature and therefore glorifies both the Father and the Son. Jesus was taught by the Spirit of God in Him.

> And the Jews marveled saying, "How knoweth this man letters, having never learned.[3]

Jesus answered them and said:

> My doctrine is not mine, but his that sent me: If any man will do his will he shall know of the doctrine whether it be of God, or whether I speak of myself.[4]

Jesus did the work of God, and the Holy Spirit continues the work of Jesus Christ. The guidance that the Holy Spirit gives never contradicts the nature and the work of Christ. The Holy Spirit is Christ guiding and instructing the believer. The substance of His guidance will be the same as that of Jesus, for He will take what is Christ's and reveal it to His followers. Therefore, the Holy Spirit, who is Christ within, glorifies the Incarnate God. Just as the son glorifies the Father, so the Holy Spirit glorifies the Son. This truth had yet to be fully grasped by the disciples and through them proclaimed to the world.

The Spirit will continue and complete the unfinished training of the followers of Christ. Yet one more office of the paraclete is to be named: "He will declare to you the things that are to come." The Spirit of Christ is the spirit of prophecy. Amid all the gloomy forebodings in days of persecution and apostasy, the spirit continues to inspire Christian souls with the vision of the lamb seated upon the throne—the symbol of the victory of the cross. The Holy Spirit is God through Christ guiding His church.

HOW TO RECEIVE SPIRITUAL GUIDANCE

How does one avail himself of the guidance of the Holy Spirit? One must seek harmony. What is harmony? Harmony is based upon order. In music, harmony is a tone whose rate of vibration is a precise multiple of that of a given fundamental tone. Harmony in society is to exist in peace and friendship. It is peaceful existence.

> Blessed are the peacemakers for they shall be called the children of God.[5]

The Holy Spirit brings peace by leading us into harmonious living. It is the Holy Spirit that enables us to see the harmony as it is revealed in nature. Shakespeare describes it as follows:

> How sweet the moonlight sweeps upon this bank! Here we sit and let the sounds of music creep in our ears: Soft stillness and the night becomes the touches of sweet harmony. Sit Jessica, look how the floor of heaven is thick inlaid with patios of bright gold; There's not the smallest orb which thou behold'st, but in his motion like an angel sings, still quiring to the young-eyed cherubime; Such harmony is in immortal souls; But while this muddy vesture of decay doth grossly close it in, We cannot hear it.[6]

It is the Holy Spirit that enables us to transcend for a brief moment this "muddy vesture of decay" to get a foretaste of heaven's harmony within the soul. In order to know this harmony, we must seek it not only in art and beauty, but also in the daily rounds of the common life. Harmony is the prelude to spiritual power. Luke tells us!

> When the day of pentecost had fully come, they were with one accord in one place and suddenly there came a sound from heaven as of a rushing mighty wind and it filled all the house where they were sitting.[7]

Almost two thousand years have passed since this event; yet mankind has done little in his effort to utilize this power to solve human problems. We are enslaved by human habits and harassed by diseases that science cannot cure. The social atmosphere is made stale and heavy by anxiety, fear, worry, and hate; all because we seek conflict instead of harmony, war instead of peace. Jesus came to show the way to harmonious living. He sent the Holy Spirit to enable us to find the way to immortal harmony. He proved that the power of the spirit is greater than that of all the sealed tombs and human discord. The church teaches us to believe in his omniscience. We proclaim the worth and power of prayer, yet we are helpless to apply His power to our everyday problems. All because we do not seek harmony. Paul Tillich describes the Protestant concept of harmony when he writes:

> In their thoughts harmony does not mean that everything is sweetness and light. It means that a law of harmony works 'behind the back' of people and their egotistical intentions. . . . The law of harmony regulates the innumerable conflicting trends, purposes, and activities of all individuals without human interference.[8]

The Guidance of the Holy Spirit

This progressive optimism may be exaggerated, but it points to the eternal truth of the saying that "Right is right since God is God and right alone must win." The idea of harmony is based upon the belief that there is a Divine directing creativity in the world.

> God directs the processes of individual social and universal life toward their fulfillment in the kingdom of God. Revelatory experiences are imbedded in general experience. They are distinguished from it but not separated from it. World history reveals its mystery.[9]

The search for harmony will ultimately lead to God. God is Spirit and God is Holy. Therefore, to search for harmony leads to the quest of the Holy Spirit to guide us into the kingdom of God, which is the Supreme expression of harmonious existence. Divine guidance is not only an inner experience, it is also an outward manifestation. This guidance is not always pleasant. This is what Paul means when he writes:

> . . . and not only so, but we glory in tribulation also; knowing that tribulation worketh patience; and patience experience; and experience, hope; and hope maketh not ashamed; because the love of God is shed abroad in our hearts by the Holy Ghost which is given to us.[10]

SEEKING CONSENSUS THROUGH THE HOLY SPIRIT

It is wise to seek consensus when solving group problems. Getting on one accord is the gateway to spiritual power and institutional success. To seek for consensus is a Christian virtue of great magnitude.

> Behold how good and how pleasant it is for brethren to dwell together in unity; It is like the precious ointment upon the head that ran down upon the beard, even Aaron's beard: that went down to the shirts of his garment; as the dew of Hermon, and as the dew that descended upon the mountains of Zion; for there the Lord commanded the blessing, even life forever more.[11]

Consensus is the basis of all Democratic government and the cornerstone of national existence. Seeking consensus is another way of accepting the guidance of the Holy Spirit.

Consensus in society must be preceded by inner calmness within the human soul. In the quietness of the mind, one can find the peace that passes all understanding. The Holy Spirit will come to us and guide the human spirit in ways of peace. He will express Himself in every part of one's existence and in every moment of one's life. The Holy Spirit within me knows what is good for me. He will make the decisions and tell me what I should do. In the calmness of my soul, I am made to realize that God is my supply and that the Holy Spirit will provide all my needs. He will lead me to good friends and material prosperity. As I open my heart to the Holy Spirit, He will make my desires known to God and He will meet all my needs.

> Be strong and of good courage: be not afraid neither be thou dismayed: for the Lord thy God is with thee whither soever thou goest.[12]

There is no problem, no difficult situation, no insurmountable obstacle, no moral contradiction to which the answer is not already known to the Holy Spirit. He knows what to do and how to do it. He will reveal to you the right answer if you will willingly follow His promptings.

As I listen to the Holy Spirit within me, I am guided in making right decisions. He makes them for me; therefore, I am protected from error. Only when I ignore His promptings do I fall victim to error in sin. When I turn again to Him, the burden of making right decisions is shifted from my shoulder to His. He points the way and I walk once more in plain paths.

> Trust in the Lord with all thine heart and lean not unto thine own understanding. In all thy ways acknowledge Him, and He shall direct thy path.[13]

Everything that has ever been known or ever will be known is known by the Holy Spirit. When my human spirit is in tune with Him the things that I need to know will be revealed unto me. All of life cooperates with the power of the Holy Spirit within me. When one's life is led by the Holy Spirit, his life is God's life. Therefore, there is nothing too insignificant to take up with the Holy Spirit. When your life becomes God's life and your business becomes God's business, the task becomes easy. "Take my yoke upon you and learn of me and I will make your yoke easy and your burden light." There are no depressions or recessions in the economy of the Holy Spirit. When your business becomes God's business, it is from thence forward good business.

OBEDIENCE

The final step in spiritual guidance is obedience. The hallmark of religion is obedience. "Obedience is better than sacrifice." When the Holy Spirit takes control of our lives we obey not because of fear, but because of love. It was said of Jesus, "He was subject unto them." Philip Brooks said:

> Obedience must be the struggle and desire of our life Obedience, not hard and forced, but ready, loving and spontaneous; the doing of duty, not merely that the duty may be done, but that the soul in doing it may become capable of receiving and uttering God.[14]

Christian obedience is the ability to say with the poet:

> I'll go where you want me to go, dear Lord.
> O'er mountain or plain or sea.
> I'll say what you want me to say dear Lord, I'll be what you want me to be.[15]

The Guidance of the Holy Spirit

A man soon tires of riding a horse which will not obey his reins. So the Holy Spirit will not dwell in a person who will not obey His commands. The Holy Spirit's guidance will come less often to the one who refuses it when it does come. Sometimes, when we seek a big promotion, the Holy Spirit leads us to a small promotion. But, if we are obedient enough to accept the small one, it will become a direct stepping stone to the higher promotion. The secret is to follow the guidence of the Holy Spirit and trust Him to fulfill your heart's desire. Sometimes God demands us to put our past in order before He opens the larger door to the future. The Holy Spirit enables us to see in our disappointment, God's appointments. The Holy Spirit is God. He is nearer, than breathing, closer than hands and feet. God is spirit and they that worship Him must worship Him in spirit and truth. The Holy Spirit is the spirit of love. Only by hating, resenting, and criticizing our fellow beings can we separate ourselves from the Holy Spirit.

The Holy Spirit will guide us into paths of peace.

CONCLUSION

The Holy Spirit will guide the Christian believer into the fulfillment of life. The fulness of life rests in one's becoming what God meant him to be. Each man is different; therefore, the Holy Spirit deals with him differently. However, there are certain basic principles involved in spiritual guidance. When one follows these basic guidelines, he receives Divine Guidance.

Harmony, consensus, and inner calmness are the spiritual pillars of Divine Guidance. Harmony is the pearl that beautifies all of nature. Consensus is the cornerstone of human society. The Holy Spirit is the source of Divine Guidance. Relaxation and inner calmness are the sources of spiritual peace. The Holy Spirit will not force His guidance upon you. You must seek it. You must accept and obey it when it comes to you.

Guidance comes to us in many ways. It comes through other people, through a job to be done, a duty to perform. Sometimes the Holy Spirit will teach us to accept less than we desire while we await God's future Blessings. It teaches us to trust God for the future.

If we are to be guided by the Holy Spirit, we must be willing to wait on God. Waiting on God is not sitting down and doing nothing. It is paying the price of guidance by spending time in quiet meditation, accepting our failures, engaging in purposeful activity, and trusting God for the future. Guidance comes more readily when we get rid of all bitterness, dare to see life as a whole, refuse to succumb to self pity, and accept our disapointments as God's appointment. By doing these things, we put our past in order. Then God is ready to put our future in order.

> Holy Spirit, faithful guide ever near the Christian's side. Gently lead us by thy hand pilgrim in a desert land. Weary souls forever rejoice while they hear that sweetest voice whispering softly, Wanderer, come follow me. I'll guide you home.[16]

CHAPTER XII

The Holy Spirit Will Give You Health

"I will restore health unto thee and I will heal thee of thy wounds," saith the Lord.[1]

And Jesus said unto Him, "go thy way, thy faith hath made thee whole," and immediately he received his sight and followed Jesus in the way.[2]

Your body is the temple of God. The Holy Spirit is the presence and power of God in you. Sickness and disease are evidence of a failure of the human spirit to cooperate with the Holy Spirit within you.

What? Know ye not that your body is the temple of the Holy Ghost which is in God, which ye have of God, and ye are not your own. For ye are bought with a price. Therefore glorify God in your body, and in your spirit which are God's.[3]

Sickness, pain, and suffering are contrary to the Supreme will of God. The body is meant to be clean, healthy, and happy. The key to health is wholeness. Wholeness is made possible only through total commitment to the god within. Therefore, the first requirement for health is to love the spirit of health, which is wholeness. Wholeness leads to holiness and holiness leads to health. The way to have a healthy body is to love the body in a pure, holy, and spiritual way.

This spiritual love for the body expresses itself in three ways. First, it is a love of physical activity. One must think of the body as the masterpiece of physical creation. It is the most articulate thing that God has ever made. Therefore we must love seeing people use their bodies to skate, dance, swim, and engage in body building activities. All of this should be done to the

The Holy Spirit Will Give You Health

glory of God and the happiness of man. The body should be used to expand and develop the mind. The Greek philosophers held that the chief function of the body was to help develop the mind. They were aware of the close relationship between physical development and mental growth. For them the goal of a sound body was to produce a sound mind. Therefore, contemplation was the supreme goal of a healthy body. For the Christian, the chief function of the body is to express the Spirit of God. Our personal bodies are merely receiving sets for manifesting the message of divine love through the channel of human experience.

Glenn Clark says,

> If one is sick he does not see a sick body, he sees merely a perfect receiving set catching a message from the great broadcasting station of God, and the moment the message is decoded and obeyed, instantly the sickness will vanish away.[4]

Human sickness is like the ringing of a telephone. When you pick up the phone to receive the message, the phone will stop ringing. Sickness is an annoying vibration received by our sensitive and miraculously responsive receiving station called the human body. This vibration will cease as soon as the message is received and obeyed.

Some of God's greatest messages to the world have come to the human race through sickness. Sickness is universal disharmony, expressing itself in physical terms. God speaks to man through harmony and disharmony. God prefers to speak to man through harmonious manifestations of His presence. Because man is rebellious and sometimes refuses to listen, God uses the avenue of disharmony to convey His message. The Holy Spirit brings us health by enabling us to listen to and obey the divine message. Glenn Clark says:

> I know personally that some of the most effective direct messages that God has ever sent to me, He has sent in the form of temporary illnesses. One message was that I was to take more time to be still with Him. Another time He told me that I must throw out all of my worthless baggage of fear.[5]

The chief function of the human body is to express the love of God. When we clog the channel with selfishness, we take cold. When we clog the channel with anger we have indigestion. When we clog the channel with tension, we have high blood pressure. When we clog the channel with anxiety and hate, we have heart attacks, etc. It is the Holy Spirit that helps us to unclog the channel of divine love thereby bringing us health.

The second requirement of a healthy body is to love the whole of the body. We must learn to view the body in its totality. The human body is a vital part of the universal mechanism of God's creation. It is God's little world. It is the minute expression of God's universal creation. Man is God's little God. Man's body is God's little world. It is a minute, external, concrete and tangible expression of the intangible attributes of God. Glenn Clark says:

> Every organ of the body has a spiritual counter-part in the great soul of God. For example the heart is but a spiritual manifestation of the spirit of love; the blood flowing through the veins and arteries is but the spirit of joy flowing through our channels of consciousness. Our lungs represent inbreathing and outbreathing of the spirit of life: the secretions of liver represents the spirit of truth and the action of the stomach symbolizes the receiving and the assimilating of spiritual harmony and power.[6]

Seeing the body as a whole is to view it within its universal context and to view each organ of the body in its relation with every other organ of the body. To love the wholeness of the body is to love the physical, moral, intellectual, emotional, and spiritual aspects. It is to realize that spiritual disease such as fear, jealousy, prejudice, pride, and hate can cause physical disease. To love the whole body means that you love all of God's divine attributes. To do otherwise is to sin against the Holy Spirit. The body is the manifestation of the spirit within. A healthy spirit creates a healthy body.

The third requirement for a healthy body is willingness to pay the price of human service. You must be willing to give your life away in human service. This is what Jesus had in mind when he said:

> But it shall not be so among you; but whosoever will be great among you, let him be your minister, and whosoever will be chief among you, let him be your servant.[7]

The best way to preserve your health is to give it away. To spend it as fully as the need for it calls. Just as one should be willing to sacrifice his lower appetites for the welfare of his body, and to preserve his body through a program of exercise and carefull eating, he should be willing to express that energy and health in service to his fellowman. Self-preservation must give way to the need to serve the higher good. There are many physicians and psychologists who contend that all sickness is merely congestion in some form. It is a stoppage. Something is clogging the channel of divine love. Unselfish service is one of the best ways to unclog the spiritual channel and permit the power of the Holy Spirit to flow through us. Love is the greatest thing in the world. It is the secret of a healthy body.

Health is the natural birthright of every human being. Health is both physical and mental well-being. God created man in His image and likeness and declared the creation was very good. Good health is not just the absence of illness, it is spiritual well-being. It is because man separates himself from his spiritual source that he becomes sick. God is not the source of sickness.

The Holy Spirit Will Give You Health

If you are not enjoying perfect health, it is because for some reason you are failing to express wholeness in spirit, mind, and body.

If you will turn in faith to the power of the Holy Spirit, He will restore your divine well-being. Life is a trinity of spirit, mind, and body. The spirit is the key. True health must begin with the spirit. The well-being of the human spirit depends upon the Holy Spirit. The human spirit receives its health from the Holy Spirit in the same way that the metal object receives its drawing power from the magnet. The way a magnet receives its power may help to make clear the growth process of the human spirit. A magnet can be made by putting a piece of hard steel near a magnet and letting it rest there for a time. Nothing will be seen to pass from the one into the other. Yet that piece of steel will catch something from the magnet that gives it the power to attract just like the magnet. The steel does not strain after the power, nor in any way force it to come in, but just rests passively near it, and quietly the subtle power of the magnet possesses it. When it is possessed by the power, it can attract objects to itself. The first step in spiritual healing is to let one's spirit rest in the conscious presence of the source of power which is the Holy Spirit, and allow His power to be infused into you. This is what Jesus meant when he said:

> If you abide in me, and my words abide in you, ye shall ask what ye will, and it shall be done unto you.[8]

What is disease? It is the absence of ease of body, mind, and spirit. The body is a trinity. When there is an absence of ease in one part, there is an absence of ease in all parts. Just as when the foot is injured, the heart feels the pain, so it is when the body is sick, the spirit shares that sickness. In order to regain health, the whole man must be treated. To treat the foot is simply to alleviate the condition that will pop up somewhere else. Man is a trinity; therefore, a healthy body demands a healthy mind and a healthy spirit. The human spirit receives its health from the Divine Spirit.

Down through the centuries, man has believed in spiritual healing. It is based upon the premise that the spirit has power over the mental and the physical. The Holy Spirit can give us victory over evil thoughts and evil habits. This same spirit has power over every physical weakness. If we will dare to trust Him, He will give us the victory. The modern man who reads the account of Jesus' work with the blind, the halt, the lame, and diseased of every kind is made to marvel over Jesus' power to accomplish great things through Spiritual healing. The church has need for such power today. This power is still with us. This gift has not been taken away. Being ignorant of this truth, we neglect the cultivation of this gift. We fail to test it in our own experience. Because we have not tested it, we have no assurance that it exists. When Jesus said, "I have come that ye might have life and that ye might have it more abundantly," He was referring to the entire gamut of human experience—the body, mind, and spirit. The Holy Spirit can heal us physically if we will dare to turn to Him in faith. We do not conquer disease by just ignoring it or refusing to employ the service of a physician or refusing to take medicine, but rather by recognizing the need of the help of a higher power to stimulate the vital forces within us. This is necessary to enable us to overcome the evil of sickness. We need to take time in the quietness and assurance of our inner being to draw to us more of abundant life that Jesus promised.

The power of the Holy Spirit can be brought to bear upon any human condition. If we dare to trust ourselves to that unseen physician, if we possess an unfaulting faith in the power of the Holy Spirit to heal, this faith will bring abundant reward. Healing faith does not come at once. It takes time and effort. It takes much prayer and fasting.

> Then came the disciples to Jesus apart and said, "Why could not we cast him out." And Jesus said unto them, "Because of your unbelief. For verily I say unto you. If ye have faith as a grain of mustard seed, ye shall say unto this mountain, remove hence to yonder place; and it shall remove and nothing shall be impossible unto you. Howbeit this kind goeth not out but by prayer and fasting."[9]

Christ assures us that there is an unseen reservoir of healing power available for our use, and when we learn through the spirit how to connect with it, we will find power to rise above the limitations of the flesh, to find freedom from pain and sickness. The promise of healing is made over and over again in the Bible:

> For I am the Lord that healeth thee.[10]

> Bless the Lord O my soul, and forget not all his benefits; Who forgiveth all thine iniquities; who healeth all thy diseases.[11]

The Holy Spirit has the power to heal physical ills, Paul assures us:

> If the Spirit of Him who raised Christ from the dead shall also quicken your mortal bodies by His Spirit that dwell in you.[12]

My friends the Holy Spirit has power to heal. According to your faith so shall it be unto you. The Holy Spirit is ready to heal you right now. If you will only dare to believe.

CHAPTER XIII

The Role of the Holy Spirit in Missions

When they therefore were come together they asked of him, saying, "Lord wilt thou at this time restore again the kingdom of Israel?" And he said unto them, "It is not for you to know the time or seasons, which the Father hath put in his own power, but ye shall receive power, after that the Holy Ghost is come upon you. And ye shall be witnesses unto me both in Jerusalem, and in all Judea, and in Samaria, and unto the uttermost part of the earth." (Act 1:6-8).

Our first responsibility as a missionary is to be a witness for the Lord. It is our duty to bring in the Kingdom through our Christian witness.

After the resurrection of Christ, His disciples came to Him expressing their concern about the restoration of the Kingdom of Israel. They had grandiose ideas of thrones and empires; armies marching to victory; navies mastering the seven seas; kings and potentates bowing before the majestic grandeur of a newly rising power with Jerusalem as its capital. Jesus attempted to answer their question by redirecting their vision. Instead of focusing their attention upon marching armies and sailing fleets, He called them back to their responsibility. "But ye shall receive power, after that the Holy Ghost is come upon you; and ye shall be witnesses unto me both in Jerusalem, and in all Judea, and in Samaria, and unto the uttermost part of the earth." Not a world conquest, but a universal witness. Not world domination, but world redemption. This is the Christian task. How is this to be achieved through our Christian witness? We are called to be a witness for the Lord.

BEHOLD THE NATURE OF THE WITNESS

It is a spiritual witness. It is not of this world. It is a task that can only be performed by individuals who have received power from on high. The

Holy Spirit empowered men and women who are inspired to share their knowledge of the saving Grace of the Lord, Jesus Christ. A true witness is one who has something to share.

On a battlefield, a soldier had an artery of his arm shattered severely by the fragment of a shell, and was fast bleeding to death. A passing physician bound up the artery and saved his life. As the physician was leaving, the man cried, "Doctor, what is your name?" "Oh, no matter," said the doctor. "But, doctor, I want to tell my wife and children who saved me." So when Christ comes to us binding up our spirits and saving our dying souls, there is a longing to tell others what he has done for us. When Christ saves your soul, you will want to tell others. A Christian witness is one who finds a peculiar joy in sharing his faith with another. Do you have enough faith to share with someone else? The world needs Christian men and women who have enough faith to share with others. A true witness is one who shares his faith.

How do we witness? We witness through fellowship. The Christian church is a fellowship. There is a tie that binds us together. It is a tie of Christian love. Christians ought to love each other. They ought to live together in such a way that people in the world will want to become a part of the fellowship. It is a fellowship of suffering. There are times when we will have to suffer for the right. Christ suffered, and we too will have to carry the cross. Must Jesus bear the cross alone and all the world go free? No, there is a cross for everyone, and there is a cross for me.

THE POWER TO WITNESS

In order to be a witness for Christ, you must have the power. Jesus promises, "But ye shall receive power, after that the Holy Ghost is come upon you." Without the power of the Holy Spirit, your witness will not be effective. If you are to be an effective witness for Christ, you must experience the power of the Holy Spirit in your life.

The church's witness today is weak and ineffective. Why? Because the church lacks power—spiritual power.

A few years ago, I saw a cartoon which all too accurately illustrated the predicament of the church. A family was leaving on vacation. The car was loaded with baggage and fishing poles, but when the driver stepped on the starter, the car would not start. Somebody had disconnected the battery. Therefore, there was no power. The church today is like that car. Somebody has disconnected the battery. We have a nice looking car—well streamlined, and with plenty of baggage—but no power. We are all dressed up to go, but we are not going anywhere. Only as the church is connected with the power of the Holy Spirit, can we hope to have the victory. The most urgent question facing the church today is, "How can it avail itself of this power?" The answer is simple. We must pay the price.

It will cost you something to obtain the power of the Holy Spirit. It costs self-surrender and humiliation, and the yielding up of the most precious things to God. It costs the perseverance of long waiting, and the faith of strong truth. But when we are really in that power, we shall find this difference; that whereas before it was hard for us to do the easiest things, now it is easy for us to do the hardest things. James Harvey, the friend of the Wesleys at Oxford, describes the change that took place in him through his anointment by the Holy Spirit.

> That while his preaching was once like the firing of an arrow, all the speed and force thereof depended on the strength of his arm in bending the bow; now it was like firing a rifle-ball—the whole force depending upon the power back of the ball, and needing only a finger-touch to let it off.—A.J. Gordon.

The church needs the power of the Holy Spirit. God has no respect of person. What he has done for the early disciples, he will do for you. What he did for Peter and John, Wesley and Moody, he will do for us. The power of the Holy Spirit is available to all believers in Christ. All we have to do is to tap the source, connect the battery, and claim the promise. How is this done? It is done through prayer and faith. Our faith must be based on a firsthand knowledge of God. No secondhand religion is good enough. We must be able to say, "I know in whom I believe." The Holy Spirit gives us personal experience of God's saving Grace. Christianity is no think-so-religion. It is based upon what you have seen and heard and felt. The only way to be a witness for the Lord is to be able to say, "I know that my Redeemer liveth." "I know that He has saved my soul." I know that His grace is sufficient." "I know that He answers prayers." "I know that He is a great physician." Are you a witness for the Lord? Do you have enough faith to share? How many souls have you brought to Christ? Jesus wants a witness in your household, on your job, in your church, and in your community.

I challenge you to be that witness.

CHAPTER XIV

The Wesleyan Concept of Spiritual Holiness

John Wesley is growing in stature both as a major Christian theologian and an exponent of the practice of the prophetic Christian message. While well-versed in philosophy and the metaphysical tenets of his day, he refused to capitulate to the Hellenistic philosophizing that has afflicted so many theologians of the western world.

Wesley maintains an unswerving loyalty to the Christian message as presented by the New Testament. He is a biblical theologian who insists that Jesus Christ is both the center and criterion of the Christian message.

John Wesley insisted that Christianity must be lived if it is to be properly understood. Only as one lives the Christian faith can one fully understand its meaning. Wesley advocated a practical religion that unfolds as it grows. A perfect understanding of Christian doctrine can only be attained as we strive to live the perfect Christian life. Therefore, Christian perfection is the centerpiece of the Wesleyan theological motif. It is here that he seeks to express in dynamic terms the fulness of life in the spirit. For Wesley, holy living is the key to holy thinking and holy dying.

THE HOLY SPIRIT IN THE WESLEYAN TRADITION

As Methodist Christians, we consider ourselves Protestant-Evangelicals. Along with other Protestants we believe in justification by faith alone.

As Methodists, we insist that once we have been saved or "born again," we must move on toward perfection. This implies holy living and holy dying. Methodists believe that it is the Holy Spirit that makes possible the new birth as well as the desire to grow toward perfection.

As to the nature and work of the Holy Spirit, Methodists do not agree.

The Wesleyan Concept of Spiritual Holiness

On the subject of the nature and work of the Holy Spirit, Methodists fall into three main categories, namely:

1. *The Conservative Wing*

    They are often called Calvinists, Methodists, or Kewickians of the victorious life movement. They believe in the "Second Blessing" or the "Second Crisis experience," in which the believer, in response to confession of need, consecration, and faith, receives a "Baptism in the Holy Spirit" which gives more power to witness for Christ. They also believe that they are free from indwelling sin, as long as they abide in Christ.

2. *The Pentecostal Methodists*

    To the radical left are the Pentecostal Methodists, who stress the receiving of special spiritual gifts, especially the speaking in tongues.

3. *The Center Position*

    In the center or main stream, several biblical terms are used, such as the second work of grace, which takes place after regeneration or the "rest of faith": "For we which have believed do enter into rest," as he said, ". . . as I have sworn in my wrath, if they shall enter into my rest. Although the works were finished from the foundation of the world."[1]

    "*Entire sanctification*" "And the very God of peace sanctify you wholly: and I pray God your whole spirit and soul and body be presented blameless unto the coming of our Lord Jesus Christ."[2]

    "*Perfect Love*" "Herein is our love made perfect, that we may have boldness in the day of judgement: because he is, so are we in this world. There is no fear in love: but perfect love casts out fear: because fear hath torment. He that feareth is not made perfect in love."[3]

    "*The Second Blessing*" "And in this confidence I was minded to come unto you before, that ye might have a second benefit."[4]

    "*Baptism in the Holy Spirit*" "For John truly baptized with water; but ye shall be baptized with the Holy Ghost not many days hence. . . . But ye shall receive power, after that the Holy Ghost is come upon you: and ye shall be witnesses unto me both in Jerusalem, and in all Judea, and in Samaria and unto the uttermost parts of the earth."[5]

Wesley discovered that it is not easy to logically interpret and systematically present all of the truths that the Bible teaches (all of the biblical teachings) on the Holy Spirit. This makes it one of the most difficult biblical doctrines. It defies systematic explanation or interpretation.

Therefore, John Wesley did not present a systematic and consistent view of the Holy Spirit. This is one of the reasons why we find such divergent views among Methodists.

In the four great ecumenical church councils, the Holy Spirit received minor consideration. It was not until 1054, that it commanded the center of the theological stage. This controversy caused a rupture in Christendom that has not healed to this day.

Methodists believe that all Christians need subsequently to be filled with the Holy Spirit,

> and be not drunk with wine wherein is excess: but be filled with the Spirit.[6]

Wesley also believed that sanctification begins at conversion, simultaneously with justification.

Concerning Baptism in the Holy Spirit, Methodists have held two different positions. Some have held that no Christian should seek the baptism of the Holy Spirit since in the light of 1 Cor. 12:13, each believer is baptized with the Holy Spirit when he becomes a Christian. This was expressed concisely by Merril Unger:

> The regenerating work of the Holy Spirit never occurs apart from his simultaneous baptizing, indwelling and sealing . . . wrought instantly, simultaneously and eternally in the believer, the moment he believes.[7]

Others hold that the baptism in the Holy Spirit is not always linked with conversion-initiation; but rather, in Luke-Acts, the baptism in the Holy Spirit is seen as subsequent to regeneration. Hence this usage is both scriptural and Wesleyan. George Allen Turner summarizes and concludes this matter when he writes:

> When all evidence is given, it seems fair to conclude that for Luke-Acts, water baptism is linked with repentence, regeneration, initiation and rebirth in the Holy Spirit. The "Promise of the Father and the Son, to believers." (Acts 1:5; 8:12, 19:2) is linked with the baptism in the Holy Spirit, not primarily as done initially for conversion initiation, but rather for purity (Acts 15:19), and power in order that they might be effective as witnesses of Jesus and the resurrection. . . . "In the Holy Spirit: . . . come to those with no prior acquaintance with the gospel. Even in Acts 2:38-41, there is no evidence that the gift was bestowed immediately at conversion.[8]

It is reasonably safe to say that Wesley held to the view that one is baptized with the Holy Spirit when one is justified, thus connecting it with water baptism and initiation. Wesley was a part of a tradition that linked water baptism with the Holy Spirit-"Baptismal regeneration." The burden of proof is upon those who insist that he thought otherwise.

THE WESLEYAN CONCEPT OF DIVINE REVELATION

Before we pursue Wesley's concept of the Holy Spirit further, we should say a word about his concept of Divine Revelation.

For Wesley, Divine Revelation is made possible by the acts of God as well as the words of God. God not only speaks through history, He also acts within history. What God does is as important as what God says. Wesley believes that in both the Old Testament and the New Testament, doctrine is established not only upon words attributed to God, but also upon acts performed by God. Therefore, Divine Revelation is mediated through both words and deeds.

We know God to be a deliverer, because he delivers those who trust in Him. The Negro Spiritual expresses it, "Didn't my Lord Deliver Daniel? Then why not any man?"

John Wesley believes that just as Divine Revelation is made possible through Scripture it is also clarified by Scripture. No one passage of Scripture can reveal the fulness of Divine Revelation. One passage is clarified by another passage and amplified by still another and so on. Therefore, the Scripture is all that is necessary unto salvation.

There is no complete agreement among Methodist theologians regarding Wesley's view of the Holy Spirit. To most Methodists, this is not a crucial matter. The chief question asked by most Methodists is, can John Wesley's theology speak to our day? Most will reply in the affirmative. We believe that Wesley's teaching concerning the Holy Spirit is both relevant and authentic, because it is grounded in sound Christian doctrine. It transcends any particular period in history. It also unites Christian theology and Christian practice.

John and Charles Wesley had a great influence far beyond Methodist circles. Wesleyan theology became the magnetic force within the entire Holiness movement. Wesley never intended to create a theological scholasticism with a monolithic ecclesiastical institution.

The formulation of Christian Doctrine must be founded upon knowledge and a clear understanding of the Scripture. It must be based upon the fulness of the truth of Divine Revelation as found in the Bible. While Wesley believes in the sufficiency of the Bible for Divine Revelation and human salvation, he also believes in the usefulness of tradition and inspiration. This is why, in his works, one will find references to Christian and secular history as well as to sacred Scripture.

Any careful study of Wesley's view must recognize the comprehensiveness of the Wesleyan approach. Any presentation of Wesley's conception of the Holy Spirit must be seen against this theological methodology.

METHODISM AND THE PENTECOSTAL-CHARISMATIC MOVEMENT

We Methodists are facing today a powerful Pentecostal-Charismatic movement that has shaken the entire Christian world. Even the mighty Roman

Catholic Church has been forced to come to grips with this religious phenomenon.

Methodism has always been very close to this movement, both in its historical beginnings, and also in the popular mind. It has always had a doctrinal affinity with this movement. It was the Methodist movement that inspired modern Christianity to take a whole new approach to Christian pneumatology.

Methodism has always been careful to avoid many of the excesses and frivolities of this movement. Some Methodists have gone to great length to disassociate Methodism from the more radical and extreme expressions of Pentecostalism; not without justification and some success. Despite these efforts there remains a close identity of Methodism with the broader Holiness Movement.

This is emphasized by many Methodist historians and theologians. Dr. Albert Outler says:

> I believe that Wesley's unique contribution to all of Christian tradition was his insistence that there is no biblical tension between salvation by faith alone and Holy living which issues in love. It is that which makes him more than the house Theologian of Methodism.[9]

There is no doubt that the Methodist "middle way" can have a moderating and balancing influence upon the new thrust of Pentecostalism in this era. Therefore, Methodism has much to contribute.

John Wesley is not always consistent in his interpretation of Christian doctrine. However, Wesley's conception of the Holy Spirit is consistent with his general theological position.

Within the present Charismatic movement there are three main streams of religious interpretation:

1. The central: The return to Wesley, that seeks to hold together both the interest in the "warm heart," and the political and social emphasis.
2. On the right is a Puritanical, legalistic, moralistic interpretation that is grounded in an individualistic pietism that often leads to antinomianism.
3. On the left is a strong, mystical, and emotional emphasis.

Wesleyan theology is by no means the only theological influence that helped to shape the charismatic movement. Much charismatic understanding has found philosophical validity in other theological interpretations.

Therefore, a return to "The Whole Wesley" is of vital importance to any Methodist who embraces the modern, Charismatic movement. It must avoid becoming a parochial, fundamentalist, reactionary response to the work of the Holy Spirit. This requires a thorough grounding in Methodist history

The Wesleyan Concept of Spiritual Holiness

and polity. The restudy of Wesleyan views of the Holy Spirit is more than an interesting and informational undertaking; it is pragmatic necessity.

Wesley saw correctly that:

> Perfection of love must be the goal of grace, not in mere terminology, but in life, and that love had in it the absolute mandate to be the church, the body of Christ, God's temple in which his Spirit dwells.[10]

The Holy Spirit is involved with all of life; therefore, all of life must become changed by the Holy Spirit. Any other form of Holiness is foreign to New Testament teaching.

THE WESLEYAN SYNTHESIS: THE HOLY SPIRIT AND HOLY LIVING

John Wesley did not hesitate to use terminology commonly used in the Holiness movement. His use of "Spirit-baptism" is different from that of many Pentecostal groups. This difference remained in many ways very similar.

It has often encouraged our reexamination of the Biblical, historical, and theological rationale for our use of the language, especially in its relation to the working of the Holy Spirit.

We Methodists have never insisted upon "speaking in tongues" and other superficial expressions of the Spirit as the criterion by which we judge the validity of "The life in the Spirit."

Wesley always insisted upon New Testament "Agape" love as the true test of Spiritual Holiness. For Wesley, the fulness of life in the Spirit is validated by Holy Living and Holy Dying. He believed that salvation by faith alone is validated by a Holy life of love that strives toward Christian Perfection.

Wesley saw no inherent conflict between salvation by faith alone and good works. To him, Salvation was not the fruits born of good work, thereby hoping to earn salvation, but rather the fruits of good work born because the believer has already been saved by faith alone.

Melvin E. Dieter says:

> It was Wesley who brought this unity to the fore. He saw it in the covenant promises of the Bible. It represented a via media, the understanding of which he flushed partially out of the "via media" of his Anglicanism through Cramer and the Mystics of the 19th Century. He also built into it the strong balance which the study of the early church brought to his understanding of the nature of Christian truth and life. Along with these studies in the Eastern Tradition it freed him from slavishly interpreting the nature of God's redemptive dealings with men in the strongly forensic tones of those who adhered mainly to Western Theological tradition rooted more exclusively in such theologians as Augustine and Tertullian. The strong creational--incarnational motifs of the equally ancient Eastern tradition, that of the

Gregories and Basil balanced him at this point. All these put him at some variance with the Augustinian Luther and the mentors of his early evangelical faith-the Moravians.[11]

Even in Wesley's lifetime, his view of entire sanctification was not shared by all of his adherents. In one of his letters, Wesley alludes to the conflict between Fletcher and himself. This conflict has not been entirely resolved even today. Burt Pope clarifies this argument when he writes:

> There has been a tendency among some teachers of religion in modern times so to speak of Christian perfection as to seem to make it the entrance into a new order of life, one namely of higher consecration under the influence of the Holy Ghost. That this higher life is the secret of entire consecration there can be no doubt. But there is no warrant in Scripture for making it a new dispensation of the Spirit or a Pentecostal visitation superadded to conversion. "Have ye received the Holy Spirit since ye believed?" means, "Did ye receive the Holy Spirit when ye believed?" In other words entire consecration is the stronger energy of a spirit already in the regenerate, not a spirit to be sent down from on high. This kingdom of God is already within if we would let it come in its perfection neither "since" in this passage or the "after" in "after that ye believe" (Eph. 1:13) has anything corresponding in the original Greek.[12]

Entire sanctification or Christian perfection begins at conversion when the Holy Spirit baptizes us into the one body which is Christ. Entire sanctification is the realization of the meaning of this new life in Christ, and the fulfillment of the hope of salvation. This does not often occur instantaneously. It is a gradual process, a growing in grace. A development of the divine within the human, until one arrives at the full stature of Divine Grace through faith in Jesus Christ.

Entire sanctification is the ever-widening dimension of Christian ethics and the ever deepening dimension of spirituality.

Daniel Steel expresses it more clearly and profoundly when he writes:

> The convert to faith in Christ receives the indwelling presence of the Holy Spirit by virtue of his participation (through faith responding to the grace of God in Christ), in the status of sonship to God. . . . This union with Christ is symbolized and sacramentally effected by baptism. . . . The resurrection life which is entered upon at baptism is life in the spirit and the indwelling presence of the spirit, is simply one aspect of the sharing of the resurrection, as well as the decisive act of justification is foreshadowed and proleptically summed up, so that the effects of the sacrament are partly active and partly potential, the indwelling presence of the Spirit, a Person, and not a *Domim Gratiae*, is mediated to the believer through baptism as a sacrament of conversion, but that personal presence comes to be apprehended more fully and more deeply as the Christian proceeds on the course of his life in the spirit.[13]

Entire sanctification is the spiritual man bringing forth spiritual fruit. An apple tree does not produce apples in order to become an apple tree. It produces apples because it is already an apple tree. So it is with a Christian. We do not do good works hoping by so doing to be saved; we do good works because we are saved. Good works is not the means of salvation but the fruits of salvation.

In his letter to Joseph Benson in 1770, Wesley wrote:

> You allow the whole thing that I contend for; An entire deliverance from sin, a recovery of the whole image of God, the loving God, with all ones heart, soul and strength; And you believe God is able to give you this; Yea to give it to you in an instant . . . if they like to call this receiving the Holy Ghost, they may. Only the phrase in that sense is Scripturally not quite proper; For they all received the Holy Ghost when they were justified. God then sent forth the Spirit of His Son into hearts crying, "Aba, Father."[14]

In his theology of the Holy Spirit, Wesley once more unites what the Roman Catholic church and the Protestant Reformation, put asunder. He unites faith and works in a new synthesis of spiritual Holiness and Christian perfection. This new synthesis represents a middle way between Romanism and Calvinism. Wesley believed that good works is an essential experience of Christian salvation in the same way that bearing fruit is essential to the nature of a fruit tree. He also holds firmly to the belief in salvation by faith alone. Wesley's theology of the Holy Spirit is informed by a careful appraisal of the apostolic fathers, the early apologetic theologians, Eastern Orthodoxy, Roman Catholicism, Protestantism, and his own religious experience.

If we are to be true heirs of Wesley, we must be careful not to abandon his middle way between a theology of pure subjective experience and a rigid reformation scholasticism. We must continue to offer correction to the rampant religious subjectivism of our day, but we must be mindful also of the danger of falling into the pitfalls of a new scholasticism. The Wesleyan safeguard is his Biblically rooted theology of the Holy Spirit. It can show us the way to a living reality of the righteousness of God in Christ that will serve to undergird our new approach to the perplexing problems of our technological society. I am thoroughly convinced that the Wesleyan theology of via media (middle way) is the theology of the future.

It can lead both church and society into a dynamic life of righteousness and true holiness. The genius of Wesleyan theology is that it continually calls the church to the affirmation of its commitment to the supreme authority of the all-sufficient and eternally relevant Scripture. It encourages careful exegesis, prayerful analysis, and a practical application of the Word. All of this activity must be founded upon a personal encounter with the Christ as the new being, who is the author and finisher of our faith and the consummation of salvation history.

As sons and daughters of Wesley, we believe that the same Spirit who spoke the Word through inspired men, The same Spirit that overshadowed the Blessed Virgin, The same Spirit who became the Incarnate Word, The same Spirit that empowered the early church is working in the lives of individual persons and in the church to bring about the consummation of salvation history. We believe that this same Spirit is preparing the way for the glorious manifestation of divine grace through faith in Jesus Christ. It is this Holy Spirit who makes Christ real in the human heart, in the church, and in human society.

Any Christian Theology that ignores the experiential realm of true righteousness, human liberation, and social justice is obsolete before it is written. This is what Wesley means when he says:

> If experience refutes the doctrine, I should be clearly convinced that we had all mistaken the meaning of those Scriptures.[15]

The rise of the Black Church in America is the prime example of the truth of Wesley's statement. When an individualistic pietism blinded American Christianity to the Satanic nature of human slavery and white racism, it was this Wesleyan concept of individual and social righteousness that gave birth to the Black church in general, and Black Methodism in particular. Any theology that permits social inertia in the face of injustice and human oppression is unChristian on its face. It is a denial of the working of the Holy Spirit in the human heart, and a false representation of Christian ethics.

We must never engage in theologizing for its own sake. It must always have as its purpose the preparing of the human heart and human society to work with the Holy Spirit in bringing in the Kingdom.

This is what Dieter means when he writes:

> Any attempt to maintain Wesley's faith along Holy Life, understanding, must be careful not to divide that which Wesley believes that the Scripture clearly had made one. Wesley insisted that what God has joined together, let neither exegeters, nor historical theologians put asunder. You cannot use Scripture against Scripture itself. Any understanding of Scripture which in practice denies the possibility of the fulfillment of the promise of the gracious covenant of full salvation in Christ or which does not encourage and in some way produce a life of holiness by faith here and now is deficient and may even deny the gospel itself.[16]

Christian theology like Christian experience is not static. It is ever changing to meet the needs of the changing times. While it is always changing, it remains eternally the same in essence. Under the Holy Spirit and the Incarnate Word, it must continue to seek to correct whatever deficiencies our changing experiences may reveal.

The Black Methodist Church in America was born of such a commitment. Because of this commitment the Black church serves as the conscience

The Wesleyan Concept of Spiritual Holiness

of America in the field of human rights. This is indeed a noble undertaking. However, we must never become so determined to flee these evils of human oppression that we leave the previous cargo "Agape love" behind.

The Black church like the rest of Christendom must ever seek the guidance and empowerment of the Holy Spirit to enable it to keep its balance and stay its course.

We too must sing with that Methodist poet who prayed:

> An inward baptism of pure fire,
> Where with to be baptized, I have
> Tis all my longing souls desire.
> Tis, only this my soul can save.
>
> Transform my nature into thine:
> Let all my powers thine impress feel;
> Let all my soul become divine
> And stamp me with thy spirit's seal.[17]

THE HOLY SPIRIT BESTOWS UPON ONE THE ESSENCE OF FAITH

And they were filled with the Holy Ghost (Acts 4:31). The gift of tongues was not the only gift given in Acts 4:31. This is not the Chief reason that the disciples were filled with the Holy Ghost. Wesley states that:

> It was to give them the mind of Christ. Those Holy fruits of the spirit which whosoever hath not, is none of his; to fill them with love, joy, peace, longsuffering, gentleness, goodness; to endure them with faith, with meekness and temperance; to enable them to crucify the flesh, with its affections and lust, its passions and desires, and in consequence of that inward change, to fulfill all outward righteousness; to walk as Christ also walked in the work of faith, in the patience of hope, the labor of love.[18]

Thus John Wesley insists that the Holy Ghost is given to bestow upon the believer the essentials of the Christian religion. These are the fundamental gifts of the spirit. Wesley calls them the ordinary gifts of the spirit. They are the gifts that will last throughout the ages. It is plain practical Christianity, not a set of opinions, or a system of doctrines, but Christ in the hearts and lives of men. The plain, practical faith has its beginning in the human heart when the believer received the spirit of adoption whereby he can now cry "Abba Father." He now calls Christ Lord by the Holy Ghost, and the Spirit himself bears witness with his spirit that he is a child of God. It is this spirit that makes him dead to the world. He no longer lives, but Christ now through His Holy Ghost lives in him.

The essence of the Christian faith is the love of God being shed abroad in the heart through faith in Christ. The Holy Spirit is the power of God through Christ performing the work of the divine grace in the human heart. Not only does the Holy Spirit enable one to abstain from doing evil, but fills him with a burning desire to do good.

The Holy Spirit guarantees the success of one's labor in Christ. The early church grew mightily and prevailed because of this spiritual power with which the church was endowed. The Holy Spirit is given in order to inspire and empower us to do good works. Wesley says:

> And permit me to ask, do you put forth all your strength in the vast work you have undertaken? Do you labor herein with your might or exerting every faculty of your soul, using every talent which God hath lent you, and that to the uttermost of your power?[19]

Wesley believed that the Holy Spirit works in and through secular society as well as through ecclesiastical organization. This is another way of affirming the priesthood of all believers. It is the work of the Holy Spirit to create, restore, and sustain Scriptural Christianity.

"THE WESLEYAN CONCEPT OF THE FIRST FRUITS OF THE SPIRIT"

> There is therefore no condemnation to them which are in Christ Jesus who walk not after the flesh but after the spirit.[20]

One of the first fruits of the Holy Spirit is that of Christian assurance. He enables us to know in whom we believe (I Cor. 2:12), which spirit, "Beareth witness with their spirit, that they are the children of God." This spiritual knowledge cleanses the conscience. It enables the believer to possess a good conscience toward God. One is no longer haunted by past guilt. One is no longer overcome by fear and anxiety,

> That in simplicity of Godly sincerity, not with fleshly wisdom, but by grace of God they have had their conversation in the world.[21]

Wesley summarizes what he means by the work of the Holy Spirit within the human heart when he writes:

> They are not condemned . . . for inward sin, even though it does remain . . . even in those who are the children of God by faith . . . and yet, for all this they are not condemned. Although they feel the flesh, the evil nature in them; although they are more sensible, day by day that their heart is deceitful and desperately wicked; yet, no longer as they do not yield thereto; so long as they give no place to the devil . . . so that the flesh hath not dominion over them, but they still walk with the spirit, there is no condemnation to them which are in Christ Jesus.[22]

It is the Holy Spirit that makes the natural man sensitive to his sinful condition. The natural man is in a state of sinfulness. Before the coming

The Wesleyan Concept of Spiritual Holiness

of the Holy Spirit in him, the natural man is in a state of spiritual sleep. The Holy Spirit can arouse him out of his sleep and make him aware of his sin and of Christ's power to save. Wesley says:

> By some awful providence, or his work applied with the demonstration of his spirit, God touches the heart of him that lay asleep in darkness and in the shadow of death.[23]

When this occurs the heart becomes aware of its sinful condition. He sees himself as God knows him to be—a sinner standing in the need of God's forgiving love. For the first time he hears the good news of the gospel, and through the Holy Spirit he believes, and is saved or liberated from his sin.

Wesley describes the threefold nature of man as follows:

> The natural, the legal, and the evangelical . . . a man may be sincere in any of these states not only when he has the spirit of adoption, but while he has the spirit of bondage unto fear. Yea, while he has neither this fear, nor love, for undoubtedly, there may be sincere heathens as well as sincere Jews, or Christians.[24]

Only the Spirit of divine love can arouse one out of this state of sleep. Only the Holy Spirit can free one from the bondage of the law.

"THE WESLEYAN ANALYSIS OF THE WITNESS OF THE SPIRIT"

Wesley warns us that one can be deceived:

> How many have mistaken the voice of their imagination for this witness of the Spirit of God, while they were doing the works of the devil! These are truly and properly enthusiasts and indeed in the worst sense of the word. But with what difficulty are they convinced thereof, especially if they have drunk deep into that spirit of error![25]

Wesley reminds us of the awful blindness of this state and the near impossibility of rescuing such persons. Wesley also counsels that we should be careful to avoid all extremes as the works of the devil. We must be careful then to rightly understand the true nature of the witness of the spirit:

> What is this witness or testimony of our spirit: What is the testimony of God's Spirit; and how does he bear witness with our spirit that we are the children of God.[26]

Wesley insists that here we have a twofold witness; the human spirit and the divine Spirit.

1. The witness of the human spirit.

   a. "As many as are led by the Spirit of God, into all holy tempers and action." They are the sons of God (for which he has the infallible assurance of Holy writ). Secondly, I am thus led by the spirit of God: he will easily conclude "therefore, I am a son of God."[27]

   b. By Keeping the Commandments of God, "Hereby we know, that we know Him if we keep His Commandments (1 John 2:3)." Whoso keepeth His Word in him verily is the love of God perfected: Hereby, know we that are in Him that we are indeed the children of God. "If ye know that He is righteous, ye know that every one that doeth righteousness is born of Him." "We know that we have passed from death unto life because we love the brethren (I John 3:14)." "Hereby we know that we are of the truth and shall assure our hearts before Him (v. 19) namely, because we love one another, not in words neither in tongue but in deeds and in truth." Hereby know we that we dwell in Him, because He hath given us of His loving Spirit" (I John 4:3), and hereby we know that he abideth in us by the obedient Spirit which he hath given us (I John 3:24).[28]

As one reads the Word of God, he can know whether he has the marks of a child of God. We know that we are children of God, not by speaking in tongues or casting out devils or healing the sick or performing miracles. The Devil can imitate all of these, thereby deceiving the very elect. But the Devil cannot produce the essential gifts of the Spirit which are love, faith, peace, etcetera.

If you are truly a child of God, If you truly possess the mark of love to God and love to neighbor, you will be conscious of being right with God. This immediate consciousness of God's love in you is the self-evident assurance that you are a child of God.

> Your conscience informs you from day to day, if you do not take the Name of God within your lips, unless with seriousness and devotion, with reverence and Godly fear.[29]

2. What constitutes that testimony of God's Spirit witnessing to my spirit I am a child of God?

Wesley replied:

> The testimony of the Spirit is an inward impression on the soul, whereby the Spirit of God indirectly witnesses to my spirit that I am a child of God: That Jesus Christ hath loved me, and given himself for me and that all my sins are blotted out and I, even I, am reconciled to God.[30]

The Wesleyan Concept of Spiritual Holiness

It is the Spirit of God who takes the initiative. He invades my spirit. It is His Spirit who frees me from sin and makes me right with Him. It is His Spirit that makes me know that He loves me.

What does it mean to be filled with the Holy Spirit? It means that these disciples became aware of being endowed with a new quantity of spiritual power that enabled them to witness in effective ways never before known by them. John Wesley divides the gifts of the Spirit into two general categories: namely, the ordinary fruits of the Spirit, and the extraordinary gifts of the Spirit. Concerning the ordinary gifts Wesley says:

> Let us take a nearer view of these His ordinary fruits, which we are assured will remain throughout all ages; of that great work of God among the children of men, which we are used to express by one word Christianity, not as it implies a set of opinions, a system of doctrine, but as it refers to men's hearts and lives.[31]

Concerning the extraordinary gifts Wesley says:

> Whether these gifts of the Holy Ghost were designed to remain in the church throughout all ages, and whether or not they will be restored at the nearer approach of the restitution of all things are questions which it is not needful to decide. But it is needful to observe this, that even in the infancy of the church, God granted them with a sparing hand. Were all even prophets? Were all workers of miracles? Had the gift of healing? Did all speak with tongues? No, in no wise, perhaps not one in a thousand. Probably none, but the teacher in the church and only some of them.[32]

The early disciples were filled with the Holy Ghost for the purpose of bearing witness to the human spirit that the believer is a child of God. The Spirit of God bears witness to our spirit that we are the children of God. It is the Holy Ghost that enables the believer to cry "Abba, Father." It is through the Holy Ghost that we are able to know that:

> I live not, but Christ liveth in me, and the life which I now live in the flesh I live by faith in the Son of God, who loved me and gave Himself for me.[33]

Every believer is filled with the Holy Spirit at the time of conversion. It is this Holy Ghost that causes the love of God to be shed abroad in the human heart. God becomes the desire of his eyes and the joy of his heart; his portion in time and in eternity. It is the Holy Ghost that makes him realize that he who thus loves God cannot help but love his brother.

Wesley describes the working of the Holy Ghost in the Human heart as follows:

> By the same Spirit, he was enable to be temperate in all things, refraining his soul even as a weaned child He was crucified to the world and the world

to Him; superior to the desire of the flesh, the desire of the eye and the pride of life. By the same Almighty love was He saved, both from passion and pride; from lust and vanity; from ambition and covetousness; and from every temper which was not in Christ. . . . His soul was athirst to good. The Language of His heart continually was, My Father worketh hitherto and I work, My Lord went about doing good; and shall not I tread in His steps?[34]

It is the Holy Ghost that enables the believer to follow Christ and to strive toward Christian perfection.

It is the Holy Ghost that enables the Christian believer to spread the good news of Christian salvation throughout the world. It is the Holy Ghost who opens our eyes and enables us to see the world lying in wickedness. He makes us concerned about the sin and misery of the world. We cannot afford to stand idly by and see humanity drift to irretrievable destruction. It is the Holy Ghost who sustains our dedication to world missions. It is the work of the Holy Ghost that sustains the beatific vision of a redeemed world.

> The wolf shall then dwell with the lamb and the leopard shall lie down with the kid; And the calf and the young lion and the fatling together, and a little child shall lead them. They shall not hurt or destroy, saith the Lord, in all my holy mountain; For the earth shall be full of the knowledge of the Lord, as the waters cover the sea.[35]

The witness of the Spirit within the soul is seen by Wesley as the Chief Function of the Holy Spirit:

> This is the record, the testimony, the sum of what God testifies in all the inspired writings that God hath given unto us eternal life and this life is in His Son, the testimony now under consideration is given by the Spirit of God to and with our spirit: He is the person testifying. What He testifies to us is that we are the children of God. The immediate result of their testimony is the fruit of the Spirit. Namely, love, joy, long-suffering, gentleness, goodness; and without these the testimony itself cannot continue.[36]

Wesley justifies the testimony of the Spirit:

> I mean an inward impression of the soul whereby the Spirit of God immediately and directly witnesses to my spirit that I am a child of God: that Jesus Christ hath loved me, and given Himself for me; that all my sins are blotted out and I, even I, am reconciled to God.[37]

Wesley takes great pains to describe this condition of the soul when he says:

> Meantime, let it be observed. I do not mean that the Spirit of God testifies this by any outward voice. No, not always by an inward voice. Although

He may do this sometimes. Neither do I purpose, that He always applies to the heart (though He often may) one or more tests of Scripture. But, He so works upon the soul by His immediate influence and by a strong, though inexplicable operation that the stormy wind and troubled waves subside, and there is a sweet calm; the heart resting as in the arms of Jesus and the sinner being clearly satisfied that God is reconciled that all his iniquities are forgiven and his sins covered.[38]

John Wesley also affirms that God has also given us an indirect testimony of the Spirit. This he calls "a good conscience toward God." This comes as a result of our rational reflection upon our own Christian experience and upon our reflection upon Holy Scripture.

The Word of God says:

Everyone who has the fruit of the Spirit is a child of God: experience and inward consciousness tell me that I have the fruit of the Spirit and hence I rationally conclude, therefore, I am a child of God. This is likewise allowed on all hands, and so is no matter of controversy.[39]

According to Wesley, it is God who takes the initiative in Christian conversion. It is the Spirit of God that testifies to my spirit that I am a child of God. It is the testimony of the Divine Spirit that brings forth the fruit of the Spirit in the human soul. The testimony of the Spirit always records and brings forth the fruit. The fruit never gives rise to the testimony, but the testimony always gives rise to the accomplishment of the fruit of the Spirit. Therefore, they are inseparable.

We insist on the contrary that the fruit of the Spirit immediately springs from their testimony; not always indeed in the same degree, even when the testimony is first given; and much less afterward, neither joy nor peace is always at one stage; Knowledge nor love; as neither is the testimony itself always equally strong and clear.[40]

In this passage the test refers to two spirits: namely the Spirit of God and the spirit of man. Man's spirit and God's Spirit are two different entities.

Let us consider man's spirit as expressed in the human soul through human reason. When these faculties are brought to bear upon Christian conversion, the human spirit assures me that I am a child of God. They make me aware of the deep sincerity within my soul. When I observe my new state of being reconciled with God, my human insight tells me that I have undergone an inward change. My conscience tells me that I have undergone an inward change. My conscience tells me that the fruits of the Spirit are present within my soul. There is a new quality of joy, peace, etcetera, that I have not known before. Therefore, my spirit tells me that I am a child of God.

There is also another witness within my soul—the Spirit of God—the spirit of adoption, whereby we cry Abba, Father. It is the Spirit of the Son of God. This Spirit is something immediate and direct. It is a new power, a new reality, something beyond human intuition or human insight and reason. It is the power of the risen Christ—a new reality that supercedes reason. It is this new reality that makes me know that Christ loves me and that He gave Himself for me. This knowledge of divine love creates in us a new condition of reconciliation that enables us to love God and therefore love our fellow man in the Spirit of God. Now, we cannot love God till we know He loves us. We love Him, because He first loved us, and we cannot know His love to us till His Spirit witnesses it to our spirit. Till then we cannot believe it; we cannot say, "The life which I now live by faith in the Son of God, who loves me, and gave Himself for me."

> Then only when we feel
> Our interest in His blood,
> And cry with joy unspeakable,
> Thou art my Lord, my God![41]

The witness of the Divine Spirit is the work of God's free grace. It affirms that man is not justified before God because of his works. There is nothing man can do to deserve the witness of the Divine Spirit. It is bestowed upon him as the result of God's free grace through faith in His Son, Jesus Christ.

Jesus Christ paid our debt, thereby making possible our atonement—when by faith, we claim His righteousness, His Spirit enters our soul and assures us that we are children of God.

John Wesley stands upon the mountain peak of faith when he writes:

> To secure us from all delusion, God gives us two witnesses that we are His children. And this then testifies conjointly. Therefore, what God hath joined together let not man put asunder, and while they are joined, we cannot be deluded: Their testimony can be depended upon. They are to be trusted in the highest degree and need nothing else to prove what they assert.[42]

The assurance of the Divine Spirit that we are children of God is the bedrock of the Christian faith. Without it we build our spiritual house upon sinking sand.

Notes

Introduction

1. Acts 1:8, 2:1-2.
2. Report of the Joint Commission Between the Roman Catholic and World Methodist Council, p. 87.
3. *Ibid.*, p. 18.
4. Eph. 6:12.
5. Methodist Hymnal, No. 172.
6. Masterpieces of Religious Verse, ed. James Dalton, p. 187.

Chapter I

1. Acts 2:1-2.
2. Speaks, R.L., *The Church and Black Liberation*, p. 38.
3. Acts 1:13-16.
4. The Interpreter's Bible, Vol. 9, p. 36.
5. *Ibid.*, p. 41.
6. *Ibid.*, p. 37.
7. Rom. 8:1-10.
8. Rom. 8:11.
9. Tillich, Paul, *Systematic Theology*, Vol. 3, p. 26.
10. Rom. 7:26.
11. Report from Joint Commission's Bulletin World Methodist Council, p. 5.
12. *Ibid.*, p. 8.
13. Rom. 8:1-14.
14. Works of John Wesley, Vol. 6, New Creation, p. 21.
15. *Ibid.*, p. 6.
16. Rom. 8:12-17.
17. Rom. 14:17.
18. Matt. 5:8.
19. Wesley, John, Vol. 5, No. 15.
20. Suenenu, J., *A New Creation*, p. 57.
21. St. John 17:18.
22. Tillich, Paul, *Systematic Theology*, Vol. III, p. 19.
23. *Ibid.*, p. 183.
24. A.M.E. Zion Hymnal. No. 161.
25. *Ibid.*, No. 192.

26. Tillich, Paul, *Systematic Theology*, Vol. 3, p. 219.
27. Rom. 8:14.
28. Tillich, Paul, *Systematic Theology*, Vol. 3, p. 219.
29. *Ibid.*, p. 291.
30. *Ibid.*, p. 116.
31. *Ibid.*, p. 123.
32. *Ibid.*, p. 131.
33. *Ibid.*, p. 281.

CHAPTER II

1. Psalms 119:9-16.
2. Exod. 20:1-3.
3. Rom. 8:11.
4. Joel 12:28-29.
5. Gal. 4:4-7.
6. Heb. 1:1-6.
7. Deut. 18:15-22.
8. Matt. 5:38-39.
9. Rom. 8:1-11.
10. St. John 3:16.
11. St. John 1:32-33.

CHAPTER III

1. Acts 2:1-3.
2. Gal. 2:7.
3. Schweitzer, Albert, *Out of My Life and Work*, p. 17.
4. Ezek. 36:26.
5. Matt. 16:18.
6. Knight, W. B., *Master Book of New Illustrations*, p. 289.
7. Evans, L. H., *Life's Hidden Powers*, p. 17.
8. *Ibid.*, p. 18.
9. A.M.E. Zion Hymnal, No. 161.
10. Acts 2:14-21.
11. Acts 13:10-13.
12. Acts 1:6-8.
13. Acts 1:13-14.
14. Acts 2:1.
15. A.M.E. Zion Hymnal, No. 168.
16. Acts 1:14.
17. Acts 1:4.

CHAPTER IV

1. Interpreter's Dictionary of the Bible, p. 26.
2. Theological Dictionary of the New Testament, Vol. VI, pp. 334-335.
3. *Ibid.*, p. 335.

4. *Ibid.*, p. 335.
5. *Ibid.*, p. 337.
6. *Ibid.*, p. 338.
7. *Ibid.*, pp. 338-339.
8. *Ibid.*, p. 339.
9. *Ibid.*, p. 344.
10. *Ibid.*, p. 346.
11. *Ibid.*, p. 397.
12. *Ibid.*, p. 406.
13. *Ibid.*, p. 412.
14. *Ibid.*, p. 121.
15. *Ibid.*, p. 349.
16. *Ibid.*, p. 355.
17. Gen. 1:2.
18. Interpreter's Bible, p. 468.
19. *Ibid.*, pp. 359-365.
20. *Ibid.*, pp. 365-366.
21. Tillich, Paul, *Systematic Theology*, Vol. 3, p. 111.
22. Gen. 1:26.
23. *Ibid.*, p. 112.
24. *Ibid.*, p. 374.
25. *Ibid.*, p. 374.
26. *Ibid.*, p. 381.
27. *Ibid.*, p. 118.
28. *Ibid.*
29. Op. cit., Interpreter's Bible Dictionary, p. 622.
30.
31. Rom. 8:37-39.
32. Rom. 8:9.
33. Eph. 3:16-17.
34. *Ibid.*
35. *Ibid.*, pp. 630-639.
36. 2 Cor. 3:17.

CHAPTER V

1. African, *Idea of God* (London: Edinburgh House Press, 1950), pp. 1-19.
2. Frobenius, Leo, *The Voice of Africa* (London: The Oxford University Press, 1913), pp. 25-291.
3. *Ibid.*, p. 17.
4. Parrinder, E. G., *African Traditional Religion* (London: S.P.C.K., 1968).
5. Yates, Walter L., *The Quest for a Black Theology* (Philadelphia: Pilgrim Press, 1970).
6. The Ghana Bulletin of Theology, Vol. 3, No. 10, June, 1971.
7. Mbiti, John S., *African Religions and Philosophy* (New York: Doubleday and Co., Inc., 1970).
8. *The Akan Doctrine of God* (London: Frank Cass Co., 1968).
9. *Ibid.*, pp. 7-12.

Notes

10. *Ibid.*, p. 9.
11. Parrinder, E. G., *African Traditional Religion* (London: S.P.C.K., 1968).
12. Unknown.
13. Cone, James, *Black Theology*.
14. Unknown.
15. *Ibid.*

CHAPTER VI

1. Acts 2:2.
2. Gen. 2:7.
3. St. John 3:8.
4. St. John 1:4.
5. Isa. 6:1.
6. Acts 2:3.
7. Rev. 10:9.
8. Acts 2:4.
9. Tillich, Paul, *Systematic Theology*, Vol. 3, p. 266.
10. Interpreter's Bible, Vol. 7, p. 7.
11. 1 Cor. 14:1-5.
12. Matt. 7:16.
13. Gal. 5:22.
14. Tillich, Paul, *Systematic Theology*, Vol. 3, p. 97.
15. *Ibid.*, p. 102.
16. Blackwood, Andrew W., *The Holy Spirit in Your Life*, p. 82.
17. St. John 5:30.
18. Acts 2:17-18.
19. Acts 2:32-34.
20. Acts 2:36.
21. Tillich, Paul, *Systematic Theology*, Vol. 3, p. 176.
22. *Ibid.*, p. 318.
23. *Ibid.*, p. 389.
24. Rom. 8:1-3.
25. Rom. 8:4.
26. Tillich, Paul, *Systematic Theology*, Vol. 3, p. 273.
27. Prov. 23:7.
28. Rom. 8:11.
29. Rom. 15:16.
30. A.M.E. Zion Hymnal, No. 160.
31. Titus 3:5-7.
32. Rom. 8:26.
33. Kung, Hans, *On Being a Christian*, pp. 468-469.

CHAPTER VII

1. Theology Today, July, 1982, p. 148.
2. St. John 7:17.

3. Girder, J.K., "The Holy Trinity." Christianity Today.
4. Knight, W. B., *Master Book of New Illustrations,* p. 216.
5. Lockyer, H., *All the Doctrines of the Bible,* p. 122.
6. Theology Today, July, 1982, p. 148.
7. *Ibid.*, p. 147.
8. St. John 14:11-17.
9. Lockyer, H., *All the Doctrines of the Bible,* p. 122.
10. *Ibid.*, p. 123.
11. Theology Today, p. 153.
12. *Ibid.*, p. 162.
13. *Ibid.*, p. 172.
14. Gen. 1:26.
15. Heb. 1:1-2.
16. Lockyer, H., *All the Doctrines of the Bible,* p. 49.
17. Prov. 8:1.
18. Gen. 15:1.
19. Num. 12:8.
20. Exod. 25:22.
21. Exod. 25:8.
22. Exod. 28:3.
23. Guthrie, D., *New Testament Theology,* p. 510.
24. *Ibid.*, p. 512.
25. Interpreter's Bible, Vol. 11, p. 297.
26. Guthrie, D., *New Testament Theology,* p. 611.
27. McDonnell, H., *New Testament Studies,* p. 97.
28. *Ibid.*, p. 102.
29. A.M.E. Zion Hymnal.
30. St. John 10:18.
31. St. John 14:26.
32. A.M.E. Zion Hymnal, No. 57.
33. *Ibid.*, No. 72.
34. McDonnell, H. *New Testament Theology,* p. 172.
35. *Ibid.*, p. 172.
36. Luke 1:37.
37. See Work of St. Thomas Aquinas.
38. Tillich, Paul, *Systematic Theology,* Vol. 3.
39. Walker, Willison, *The History of the Christian Church.*
40. Tillich, Paul, *Systematic Theology,* Vol. 3.
41. *Ibid.*, Vol. 3.
42. *Ibid.*, Vol. 3, p. 218.
43. *Ibid.*, Vol. 3.
44. *Ibid.*, Vol. 3.
45. *Ibid.*, Vol. 3.
46. McDonnell, H., *New Testament Theology,* p. 97.
47. *Ibid.*, p. 107.
48. *Ibid.*, p. 117.
49. *Ibid.*, p. 108.

CHAPTER VIII

1. 2 Cor. 5:17-18.
2. Acts 19:1-6.
3. Acts 2:40-43.
4. Acts 5:1-3.
5. Acts 2:37-40.
6. Rom. 3:28.
7. John 16:1-13.
8. John 3:3-5.
9. DeWolf, Harold, *A Theology of the Living Church*, pp. 288-289.
10. Matt. 10:29-30.
11. Matt. 3:1-2.
12. Matt. 11:11.
13. Carlyle, Thomas, *Pilgrim's Progress*.
14. Luke 13:3.
15. Amos 2:15.
16. *Ibid.*, 3:5.
17. *Ibid.*, 2:1.
18. See American History.
19. Knight's Sermon Illustrations.
20. Locke, John.
21. Luke 15:7.
22. Khayyam, Omar.
23. Tillich, Paul, *Systematic Theology*, Vol. 3, p. 219.
24. Acts 2:38.
25. Knight's Sermon Illustrations.
26. Tillich, Paul, *Systematic Theology*, Vol. 3, p. 97.
27. Gen. 3:11-12.
28. Ezek. 1:31.
29. Psalms 51:1-7.
30. Acts 9:6.
31. Matt. 16:24-25.
32. Knight's Sermon Illustrations.
33. Matt. 16:24.
34. Matt. 6:10.
35. 2 Cor. 5:1.
36. Rev. 21:1.
37. Matt. 16:14.
38. Jones, E. Stanley, Christian Conversation.
39. Knight's Sermon Illustrations.
40. Prov. 3:5-6.
41. Job 22:21.
42. Psalms 111:10.
43. Rom. 7:18-21.
44. Acts 1:8.
45. Matt. 16:24.
46. Traditional.

47. John 4:9.
48. John 4:20.
49. John 4:12.
50. John 4:29.
51. Isa. 6:2.
52. Isa. 6:1-3.
53. A.M.E. Zion Hymnal.
54. Acts 22:6-11.
55. Methodist Hymnal, No. 229.
56. Psalms 19:1.
57. Isa. 6:1.
58. Rom. 2:20.
59. 2 Cor. 5:17.
60. Acts 9:6.
61. Acts 1:8.
62. Acts 4:5-12.
63. Knight's Sermon Illustrations.
64. A.M.E. Zion Hymnal.
65. *Ibid.*, No. 151.
66. *The Works of John Wesley*, Journal I, Sermon II, pp. 233-234.
67. *Ibid.*, Journal I, p. 424.
68. DeWolf, Harold, *A Theology of the Living Church*, pp. 288-289.

CHAPTER IX

1. Matt. 7:7.
2. Psalms 121:2.
3. Psalms 121:6.
4. A.M.E. Zion Hymnal.
5. Isa. 53:7.
6. Isa. 53:1.
7. Acts 2:1-5.
8. Bonhoffer, D., *The Cost of Discipleship*.
9. Traditional.
10. Phil. 2:5.
11. Luke 2:52.
12. A.M.E. Zion Hymnal.

CHAPTER X

1. Theology Today, July, 1982, p. 143.
2. 2 Cor. 5:1-2.
3. Tillich, Paul, *Systematic Theology*, Vol. 3, p. 11.
4. 2 Cor. 5:2-5.
5. Tillich, Paul, *Systematic Theology*, Vol. 3, p. 16.
6. Gen. 1:29.
7. Tillich, Paul, *Systematic Theology*, Vol. 3, p. 21.
8. Gen. 1:31.

Notes

9. St. John 1:1-5.
10. 2 Cor. 5:5.
11. Winkworth, Susanna, "Theologia Germanica," p. 67.
12. Tillich, Paul, *Systematic Theology*, Vol. 3, p. 24.
13. Gen. 2:7.
14. Gen. 23-24.
15. Wesley, John, *Concept of Perfection* (Kansas City: Beacon Hill Press, 1964), p. 122.
16. St. John 3:16.
17. Tillich, Paul, *Systematic Theology*, Vol. 3, p. 125.
18. *Ibid.*, p. 26.
19. *Ibid.*, p. 29.
20. Tillicke, H., "The Evangelical Faith," pp. 69-70.
21. John 14:27.
22. Winkworth, Susanna, "Theologia Germanica," p. 68.
23. A.M.E. Zion Hymnal.
24. Psalms 19:1-2.
25. Luke 1:35.
26. 1 Cor. 14:33.
27. Tillich, Paul, *Systematic Theology*, Vol. 2, p. 120.
28. *Ibid.*, p. 122.
29. *Ibid.*, p. 132.
30. *Ibid.*, p. 137.
31. Rom. 8:26-27.
32. Traditional.
33. St. John 14:13-19.
34. St. John 11:22.
35. 1 John 5:11.
36. St. John 17:25.
37. Clark, Glenn, "I Will Lift Up Mine Eyes," p. 44.
38. St. John 18:2.
39. Clark, Glenn, "I Will Lift Up Mine Eyes," p. 47.
40. James 2:15.
41. Matt. 17:20.
42. Mark 11:24.
43. 1 Cor. 2:9.
44. Isa. 53:4.

CHAPTER XI

1. St. John 16:13.
2. St. John 3:34.
3. St. John 3:35.
4. St. John 7:15-17.
5. Matt. 5:9.
6. Shakespeare, W., "The Merchant of Venice," Act V, Scene I.
7. Acts 2:1-2.
8. Tillich, Paul, *Systematic Theology*, Vol. 3, p. 265.

9. *Ibid.*, p. 157.
10. Rom. 5:3-5.
11. Psalms 133.
12. Josh. 1:9.
13. Prov. 3:5.
14. "Encyclopedia of Religious Quotations," p. 320.
15. *Ibid.*, p. 321.
16. A.M.E. Zion Hymnal.

CHAPTER XII

1. Jer. 10:17.
2. Mark 10:52.
3. 1 Cor. 6:19-20.
4. Clark, Glenn, "I Will Lift Up Mine Eyes," p. 144.
5. *Ibid.*, p. 144.
6. *Ibid.*, p. 145.
7. Matt. 20:26-27.
8. St. John 15:7.
9. Matt. 17:19-21.
10. Exod. 15:26.
11. Psalms 103:2-3.
12. Rom. 8:11.

CHAPTER XIII

1. Acts 1:6-8.
2. Knight's Sermon Illustrations, p. 182.

CHAPTER XIV

1. Heb. 4:3.
2. 1 Thess. 5:23.
3. 1 John 4:17.
4. 2 Cor. 1:15.
5. Acts 1:5.
6. Eph. 5:18.
7. Unger, Merril, "Wesley's Theology," p. 115.
8. *Wesleyan Theological Journal*, Vol. 14, No. I, p. 66.
9. *Ibid.*, p. 10.
10. *Ibid.*, p. 27.
11. *Ibid.*, p. 11.
12. *Ibid.*, p. 35.
13. *Ibid.*, p. 32.
14. *Ibid.*
15. *Ibid.*
16. *Ibid.*, p. 13.
17. *Ibid.*, p. 13.

Notes

18. *The Works of John Wesley*, Vol. 1, p. 328.
19. *Ibid.*, p. 418.
20. Wesley, John, "The Plain Account of Christian Perfection."
21. *Ibid.*, p. 71.
22. *Ibid.*, p. 23.
23. *The Works of John Wesley*, Vol. 6.
24. *Ibid.*, p. 7.
25. *Ibid.*, Vol. 5, p. 11.
26. *Ibid.*, Vol. 1, p. 124.
27. Rom. 8:16.
28. 1 John 3:24.
29. *The Works of John Wesley*, Vol. 1, p. 125.
30. *Ibid.*, Vol. 5, p. 125.
31. *Ibid.*, Vol. 5, p. 129.
32. *Ibid.*, Vol. 5, p. 131.
33. Gal. 2:20.
34. *The Works of John Wesley*, Vol. 1.
35. Isa. 11:6.
36. *The Works of John Wesley*, Vol. 5, p. 123.
37. *Ibid.*, p. 124.
38. *Ibid.*, p. 121.
39. *Ibid.*, Vol. 1, p. 117.
40. *Ibid.*, Vol. 5.
41. A.M.E. Zion Hymnal.
42. *The Works of John Wesley*, Vol. 1.

www.ingramcontent.com/pod-product-compliance
Lightning Source LLC
Chambersburg PA
CBHW062043220426
43662CB00010B/1637